CrOSSWOrDS WORD SearCHes
LOgIC PUZZLES & SURPRISES!

minD
STRETCHERS

CRANBERRY EDITION

EDITED BY STANLEY NEWMAN

The Reader's Digest Association, Inc.
New York, NY / Montreal

Project Staff

EDITORS
Sandy Fein, Robert Ronald

PUZZLE EDITOR
Stanley Newman

PRINCIPAL PUZZLE AUTHORS
George Bredehorn, Stanley
Newman, Dave Phillips,
Peter Ritmeester

SERIES ART DIRECTOR
Andrée Payette

DESIGNER
Tara Long

ILLUSTRATIONS
©Norm Bendel

COPY EDITOR
Diane Aronson

**MANAGER, ENGLISH
BOOK EDITORIAL**
Pamela Johnson

VICE PRESIDENT, BOOK EDITORIAL
Robert Goyette

The Reader's Digest Association, Inc.

**PRESIDENT AND
CHIEF EXECUTIVE OFFICER**
Mary G. Berner

**PRESIDENT, READER'S DIGEST
COMMUNITY**
Lisa Sharples

**NORTH AMERICAN CHIEF
MARKETING OFFICER**
Lisa Karpinski

ISBN 978-1-55475-072-6

Address any comments about *Mind Stretchers, Cranberry Edition* to:

Stanley Newman
Mind Stretchers Puzzle Editor
P.O. Box 69
Massapequa Park, NY 11762

To order copies of this or other editions of the *Mind Stretchers* book series,
call 1-800-846-2100 in the United States and 1-800-465-0780 in Canada.

Visit us on the Web, in the United States at **rd.com**
and in Canada at **readersdigest.ca**

Printed in the United States of America

1 3 5 7 9 10 8 6 4 2

US 4967/L-20

Contents

Dear Puzzler,

Based on the letters and e-mails I receive, I know that one of the Mind Stretchers puzzle types that readers are most likely to have trouble with is the ABC logic puzzles. So I thought I'd give you some extra help in getting started with those—tips that aren't mentioned in the Meet the Puzzles section that's a part of every edition.

There are three one-star ABC's in each Mind Stretchers volume, and these pointers should make those three as easy for you as … you know what! As you read, you might like to follow along with the first one-star ABC in this volume, which is on page 38.

■ Based on the placement of the letters and arrows outside the grid, write lightly in each box the letters that are logically possible to go there. Remember that "blank" is also a possibility, which you can indicate with a long dash.

■ There will always be just two possibilities for the initial square of a row or column that has a letter and arrow right beside it: that letter or a blank. And that letter must appear either in the outer-edge box, or one box in from the outer edge. If it's the latter, the box between that letter and the outer edge must be blank. You should blacken in any box you've identified as being blank.

■ Any box of the grid that has no arrows pointing to that box's row or column will always have four possibilities to start with: A, B, C, or blank.

■ In one- and two-star ABC puzzles, once you've correctly filled in the possibilities for each square, there will always be at least one square that can have only one possible letter—any letter that appears only once in a particular row or column.

■ As you write a letter into a particular square, be sure to erase it as a possibility for all the other squares in its row and column. Each letter you fill in should enable you to identify at least one more letter for another box.

Is there some other Mind Stretchers puzzle variety that you're finding especially puzzling? I hope you'll write to let me know. Your comments on any aspect of Mind Stretchers are most welcome. You can reach me by regular mail at the address below, or by e-mail at mindstretchers@gmail.com.

Best wishes for happy and satisfying solving!

Stanley Newman
Mind Stretchers Puzzle Editor
P.O. Box 69
Massapequa Park, NY 11762

(Please enclose a self-addressed stamped envelope if you'd like a reply.)

■ Foreword

Meet the Puzzles!

Mind Stretchers is filled with a delightful mix of classic and new puzzle types. To help you get started, here are instructions, tips, and examples for each.

WORD GAMES

Crossword Puzzles

Edited by Stanley Newman

Crosswords are arguably the world's most popular puzzles. As presented in this book, the one- and two-star puzzles test your ability to solve straightforward clues to everyday words. "More-star" puzzles have a somewhat broader vocabulary, but most of the added challenge in these comes from less obvious and trickier clues. These days, you'll be glad to know, uninteresting obscurities such as "Genus of fruit flies" and "Famed seventeenth-century soprano" don't appear in crosswords anymore.

Our 60 crosswords were authored by more than a dozen different puzzle makers, all nationally known for their skill and creativity.

Clueless Crosswords

by George Bredehorn

A unique crossword variation invented by George, these 7-by-7 grids primarily test your vocabulary and reasoning skills. There is one

simple task: Complete the crossword with common uncapitalized seven-letter words, based entirely on the letters already filled in for you.

EXAMPLE	SOLUTION

Hints: *Focusing on the last letter of a word, when given, often helps. For example, a last letter of G often suggests that IN are the previous two letters. When the solutions aren't coming quickly, focus on the shared spaces that are blank—you can often figure out whether it has to be a vowel or a consonant, helping you solve both words that cross it.*

Split Decisions

by George Bredehorn

Crossword puzzle lovers also enjoy this variation. Once again, no clues are provided except within the diagram. Each answer consists of two words whose spellings are the same, except for two consecutive letters. For each pair of words, the two sets of different letters are already filled in for you. All answers are common words; no phrases or hyphenated or capitalized words are used. Certain missing words may have more than one possible solution, but there is only one solution for each word that will correctly link up with all the other words.

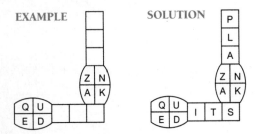

EXAMPLE   SOLUTION

Hints: Start with the shorter (three- and four-letter) words, because there will be fewer possibilities that spell words. In each puzzle, there will always be a few such word pairs that have only one solution. You may have to search a little to find them, since they may be anywhere in the grid, but it's always a good idea to fill in the answers to these first.

Triad Split Decisions
by George Bredehorn
This puzzle is solved the same way as Split Decisions, except you are given three letters for each word instead of two.

EXAMPLE   SOLUTION

Word Searches

Kids love 'em, and so do grownups, making word searches perhaps the most widely appealing puzzle type. In a word search, the challenge is to find hidden words within a grid of letters. In the typical puzzle, words can be found in vertical columns, horizontal rows, or along diagonals, with the letters of the words running either forward or backward. Usually, a list of words to search for is given to you. But to make word searches harder, puzzle writers

ANSWERS!

Answers to all the puzzles are found beginning on page 233, and are organized by the page number on which the puzzle appears.

sometimes just point you in the right direction, such as telling you to find 25 foods. Other twists include allowing words to take right turns, or leaving letters out of the grid.

Hints: One of the most reliable and efficient searching methods is to scan each row from top to bottom for the first letter of the word. So if you are looking for "violin" you would look for the letter "v." When you find one, look at all the letters that surround it for the second letter of the word (in this case, "i"). Each time you find a correct two-letter combination (in this case, "vi"), you then scan either for the correct three-letter combination ("vio") or the whole word.

NUMBER GAMES

Sudoku
by Conceptis Ltd.
Sudoku puzzles have become massively popular in the past few years, thanks to their simplicity and test of pure reasoning. The basic Sudoku puzzle is a 9-by-9 square grid, split into 9 square regions, each containing 9 cells. Each puzzle starts off with roughly 20 to 35 of the squares filled in with the numbers 1 to 9. There is just one rule: Fill in the rest of the squares with the numbers 1 to 9 so that no number appears twice in any row, column, or region.

EXAMPLE

8	4					7	1	
3			7	1	8			9
		5	9		3	6		
	9	7	8		1	2	3	
	6						9	
	3	1	2		9	7	6	
		4	3		2	9		
1			5	9	4			6
9	8						5	3

SOLUTION

8	4	9	6	2	5	3	7	1
3	2	6	7	1	8	5	4	9
7	1	5	9	4	3	6	8	2
5	9	7	8	6	1	2	3	4
2	6	8	4	3	7	1	9	5
4	3	1	2	5	9	7	6	8
6	5	4	3	8	2	9	1	7
1	7	3	5	9	4	8	2	6
9	8	2	1	7	6	4	5	3

Hints: *Use the numbers provided to rule out where else the same number can appear. For example, if there is a 1 in a cell, a 1 cannot appear in the same row, column, or region. By scanning all the cells that the various 1 values rule out, you often can find where the remaining 1 values must go.*

Hyper-Sudoku

by Peter Ritmeester

Peter is the inventor of this unique Sudoku variation. In addition to the numbers 1 to 9 appearing in each row and column, Hyper-Sudoku also has four 3-by-3 regions to work with, indicated by gray shading.

EXAMPLE

SOLUTION

Square Routes

by Conceptis Ltd.

In this innovative cousin of Sudoku, each puzzle consists of a group of circles arranged in a square grid. Numbers are filled in some of the circles, and circles are connected to other circles with straight lines, forming paths within the grid. The object is to fill in the empty circles so that all of the numbers 1 to 5 (or 1 to 6, or 1 to 7 in larger puzzles) appear exactly once in each row, column, and path.

EXAMPLE

SOLUTION

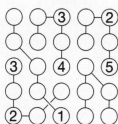

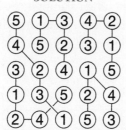

Hints: *The "weaving" of the paths through multiple rows and columns makes for an extra level of challenge as compared to Sudoku, but the logical solving process is similar. As in Sudoku, the best way to get started is to use the numbers provided to rule out where certain numbers cannot go.*

LOGIC PUZZLES

Find the Ships

by Conceptis Ltd.

If you love playing the board game Battleship, you'll enjoy this pencil-and-paper variation! In each puzzle, a group of ships of varying sizes is provided on the right. Your job: Properly place the ships in the grid. A handful of ship "parts" are put on the board to get you started. The placement rules:

1. Ships must be oriented horizontally or vertically. No diagonals!

2. A ship can't go in a square with wavy lines; that indicates water.

3. The numbers on the left and bottom of the grid tell you how many squares in that row or column contain part of ships.

4. No two ships can touch each other, even diagonally.

EXAMPLE

SOLUTION

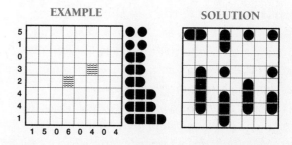

Hints: *The solving process involves both finding those squares where a ship must go and eliminating those squares where a ship cannot go. The numbers provided should give you a head start with the latter; the number 0 clearly implying that every*

square in that row or column can be eliminated. If you know that a square will be occupied by a ship, but don't yet know what kind of ship, mark that square, then cross out all the squares that are diagonal to it—all of these must contain water.

ABC

by Peter Ritmeester

This innovative new puzzle challenges your logic much in the way a Sudoku puzzle does. Each row and column in an ABC puzzle contains exactly one A, one B, and one C, plus one blank (or two, in harder puzzles). Your task is to figure out where the three letters go in each row. The clues outside the puzzle frame tell you the first letter encountered when moving in the direction of an arrow.

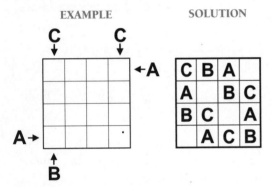

EXAMPLE   SOLUTION

Hints: *If a clue says a letter is first in a row or column, don't assume that it must go in the first square. It could go in either of the first two squares (or first three, in the harder puzzles). A good way to start is to look for where column and row clues intersect (for example, when two clues look like they are pointing at the same square). These intersecting clues often give you the most information about where the first letter of a row or column must go. At times, it's also possible to figure out where a certain letter goes by eliminating every other square as a possibility for that letter in a particular row or column.*

Number-Out

by Conceptis Ltd.

This innovative new puzzle challenges your logic in much the same way a Sudoku puzzle does. Your task is to shade squares so that no number appears in any row or column more than once. Shaded squares may not touch each other horizontally or vertically, and all unshaded squares must form a single continuous area.

EXAMPLE

5	3	1	4	3
4	5	3	4	2
2	1	2	3	4
1	3	2	1	4
3	4	2	5	4

SOLUTION

5	3	1	4	3
4	5	3	4	2
2	1	2	3	4
1	3	2	1	4
3	4	2	5	4

Hints: *First look for all the numbers that are unduplicated in their row and column. Those squares will never be shaded, so we suggest that you circle them as a reminder to yourself. When there are three of the same number consecutively in a row or column, the one in the middle must always be unshaded, so you can shade the other two. Also, any square that is between a pair of the same numbers must always be unshaded. Once a square is shaded, you know that the squares adjacent to it, both horizontally and vertically, must be unshaded.*

Star Search

by Peter Ritmeester

Another fun game in the same style of Minesweeper. Your task: find the stars that are hidden among the blank squares. The numbered squares indicate how many stars are hidden in squares adjacent to them (including diagonally). There is never more than one star in any square.

EXAMPLE   SOLUTION

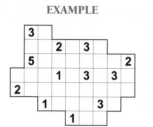
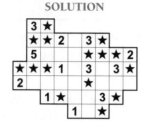

Hint: *If, for example, a 3 is surrounded by four empty squares, but two of those squares are adjacent to the same square with a 1, the other two empty squares around the 3 must contain stars.*

123

by Peter Ritmeester

Each grid in this puzzle has pieces that look like dominoes. You must fill in the blank squares so that each "domino" contains one each of the numbers 1, 2, and 3, according to these two rules:

EXAMPLE

				1	
		3			
3				2	
	2				
		1		1	

SOLUTION

2	1	2	3	1	3
3	2	3	1	2	1
1	3	1	2	3	2
3	1	2	3	2	1
1	2	3	1	3	2
2	3	1	2	1	3

1. No two adjacent squares, horizontally or vertically, can have the same number.

2. Each completed row and column of the diagram will have an equal number of 1's, 2's, and 3's.

Hints: *Look first for any blank square that is adjacent to two different numbers. By rule 1 above, the "missing" number of 1-2-3 must go in that blank square. Rule 2 becomes important to use later in the solving process. For example, knowing that a 9-by-9 diagram must have three 1's, three 2's, and three 3's in each row and column allows you to use the process of elimination to deduce what blank squares in nearly filled rows and columns must be.*

VISUAL PUZZLES

Throughout *Mind Stretchers* you will find unique mazes, visual conundrums, and other colorful challenges, each developed by maze master Dave Phillips. Each comes under a new name and has unique instructions. Our best advice? Patience and perseverance. Your eyes will need time to unravel the visual secrets.

In addition, you will also discover these visual puzzles:

Line Drawings

by George Bredehorn

George loves to create never-before-seen puzzle types, and here is another unique Bredehorn game. Each Line Drawing puzzle is different in its design, but the task is the same: Figure out where to place the prescribed number of lines to partition the space in the instructed way.

Hint: *Use a pencil and a straightedge as you work. Some lines come very close to the items within the region, so being straight and accurate with your line-drawing is crucial.*

One-Way Streets

by Peter Ritmeester

Another fun variation on the maze. The diagram represents a pattern of streets. A and B are parking spaces, and the black squares are stores. Find a route that starts at A, passes through all the stores exactly once, and ends at B. (Harder puzzles use P's to indicate parking spaces instead of A's and B's, and don't tell you the starting and ending places.) Arrows indicate one-way traffic for that block only.

EXAMPLE   SOLUTION

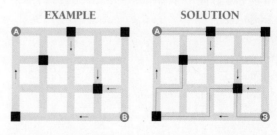

No block or intersection may be entered more than once.

Hints: *The particular arrangement of stores and arrows will always limit the possibilities for the first store passed through from the starting point A and the last store passed through before reaching ending point B. So try to work both from the start and the end of the route. Also, the placement of an arrow on a block doesn't necessarily mean that your route will pass through that block. You can also use arrows to eliminate blocks where your path will not go.*

BRAIN TEASERS

To round out the more involved puzzles are more than 150 short brain teasers, most written by our puzzle editor, Stanley Newman. Stan is famous in the puzzle world for his inventive brain games. An example of how to solve each puzzle appears in the puzzle's first occurrence (the page number is noted below). You'll find the following types scattered throughout the pages.

* *Invented by and cowritten with George Bredehorn*

** *By George Bredehorn*

But wait...there's more!

At the top of many of the pages in this book are additional brain teasers, organized into three categories:

• **QUICK!:** These tests challenge your ability to instantly calculate numbers or recall well-known facts.

• **DO YOU KNOW ...:** These more demanding questions probe the depth of your knowledge of facts and trivia. ·

• **HAVE YOU ...** and **DO YOU ...:** These reminders reveal the many things you can do each day to benefit your brain.

For the record, we have deliberately left out answers to the **QUICK!** and **DO YOU KNOW ...** features. Our hope is that if you don't know an answer, you'll be intrigued enough to open a book or search the Internet for it!

■ Meet the Authors

STANLEY NEWMAN (puzzle editor and author) is crossword editor for *Newsday*, the major newspaper of Long Island, New York. He is the author/editor of over 150 books, including the autobiography and instructional manual *Cruciverbalism* and the best-selling *Million Word Crossword Dictionary*. Winner of the First U.S. Open Crossword Championship in 1982, he holds the world's record for the fastest completion of a *New York Times* crossword—2 minutes, 14 seconds. Stan operates the website www.StanXwords.com and also conducts an annual Crossword University skill-building program on a luxury-liner cruise.

GEORGE BREDEHORN is a retired elementary school teacher from Wantagh, New York. His variety word games have appeared in the *New York Times* and many puzzle magazines. Every week for the past 20 years, he and his wife, Dorothy, have hosted a group of Long Island puzzlers who play some of the 80-plus games that George has invented.

CONCEPTIS (www.conceptispuzzles.com) is a leading supplier of logic puzzles to printed, electronic, and other gaming media all over the world. On average, ten million Conceptis puzzles are printed in newspapers, magazines and books each day, while millions more are played online and on mobile phones each month.

DAVE PHILLIPS has designed puzzles for books, magazines, newspapers, PC games, and advertising for more than 30 years. In addition, Dave is a renowned creator of walk-through mazes. Each year his corn-maze designs challenge visitors with miles of paths woven into works of art. Dave is also codeveloper of eBrainyGames.com, a website that features puzzles and games for sale.

PETER RITMEESTER is chief executive officer of PZZL.com, which produces many varieties of puzzles for newspapers and websites worldwide. Peter is also general secretary of the World Puzzle Federation. The federation organizes the annual World Puzzle Championship, which includes difficult versions of many of the types of logic puzzles that Peter has created for *Mind Stretchers*.

■ Master Class: **Games on the Go!**

The Six Best Car Games for Puzzle Fans

Whether it's for a vacation, a family celebration, or just a car pool, most of us find ourselves on a lengthy auto trip at least once in a while. Parents have long kept their restless children amused on the highway with car games, but as far as I know, not much has been written on the subject for grownups. If you've got the puzzling mind I know you have, then I'll bet you'd be interested in some ways to help pass the time in an entertaining, mentally challenging manner while on the road with your passenger-partners.

That's why I've assembled the following collection of car games for this Master Class. Unlike the puzzles in *Mind Stretchers*, none of them require pencils, paper, a game board, or a table, so they're ideal for playing while traveling. As you'll see, some will work just as well on an airplane or a train as they do in a car. And all you need to bring along to play any of these games is your brain!

Last to First

This is a broader version of the kids' game Geography that you probably played as a child. In Geography, each player must think of a city (or perhaps any geographical location) that starts with the same letter as the last letter of the previous location given. Players have a fixed time limit to think of an answer (say 5 to 15 seconds), and the round ends when a player can't come up with an answer. The last person to give a valid answer gets a point and starts the next round. Answers may not be repeated in a round. The first person to score a predetermined number of points (perhaps 5 or 10) wins the game.

Here is what a "city" round might look like:

Los Angeles, Seattle, Evanston, Nome, Edmonton, Nashua, Albuquerque, East Lansing, Goose Bay (player can't think of a "Y" city, round ends).

In the more general Last to First, the categories need not be geographical. Good categories to use include last names of famous authors, foods, movie titles, makes or models of automobiles, beverages (generic and brand names), and sports/games. The basic rules are the same as Geography above, except that the player who starts any round gets to select the category.

Like It or Not

In this word game, one player, the "starter," thinks of a particular word characteristic, then creates a sentence of the form "I like __, but not __," where the two words are in the same category, but the first word fits the characteristic, and the second one does not. For example, if the characteristic chosen were "words that have an R," the first sentence might be "I like macaroni but not spaghetti," then "I like wrestling but not boxing," and so on.

What I like best about this game is the thinking required for formulating good sentences—where the two words are logically related, but only one of them fits the characteristic.

Unlike most guessing games, the other players don't say the answer when they think they've got it figured out. Instead, they ask the starter a question to confirm that they are right. Such a question might be, "So you like Scarlatti and not Beethoven?" When the starter confirms that the guesser's question is correct, the two players who know the answer alternate in forming sentences for the remaining players to guess. The round continues until the last person correctly identifies the word characteristic.

See the sidebar for some Like It or Not games for you to try.

Like It or Not

See if you can identify the word category in each of these four-sentence groups, which are listed in increasing order of difficulty. For an extra challenge, try to guess the answer by looking at only one sentence at a time. You'll find the answers upside-down at the bottom of this section.

1.

I like apples but not oranges.

I like radios but not televisions.

I like horses but not cows.

I like Renoir but not Picasso.

2.

I like Panama but not Nicaragua.

I like aluminum but not silver.

I like potato salad but not cole slaw.

I like music but not violins.

3.

I like desserts but not pies.

I like sports but not baseball.

I like paws but not feet.

I like spoons but not knives.

4.

I like pasta but not rice.

I like referees but not umpires.

I like trophies but not medals.

I like rivers but not creeks.

ANSWERS: 1. Six-letter words 2. Words with alternating vowels and consonants 3. Words that form a different word when spelled backwards 4. Words with two consecutive letters of the alphabet in succession.

A to Z

This is part word game, part observation game. In its simplest version, players must spot all the letters of the alphabet, from A to Z, on billboards, buildings, or other stationary objects while the car is in motion on the highway. Players indicate they have found a particular letter by calling it out and saying the word in which they found it, such as "K in PARK." Players must find their letters in order; for example, they are not permitted to announce a "G word" until they have located all the letters from A to F.

Only one player may use a particular letter found in a particular place. To prevent the game from becoming too easy, finding letters on moving vehicles isn't permitted, which eliminates the use of the letters on license plates. But we'll put license plates to good use in just a moment.

A tougher version of the game, which I've played with puzzle colleagues on car trips, requires the players to locate either words beginning with each letter of the alphabet in order, or things whose names start with each letter (generally not both in the same game). As they play either of these two versions, participants may have quite a bit of trouble finding certain letters of the alphabet (Q and X, for instance). To get players past obstacles like these, we've added this "wild card" rule: Spotting a misspelled word or grammatical error allows a player to skip past a letter of his or her choosing. Once found, such an error may be "banked" by the player until needed. If obtaining wild cards proves to be difficult, we allow players to find misspelled words or grammatical errors while on a driving break, since we've found restaurant menus to be particularly good sources of mistakes.

License Plates

In the children's version of License Plates, kids have to spot tags from as many different states and provinces as possible. There's also a word game variation, where kids form sentences using words that begin with the same letters as the three-letter sequence found on many license plates.

> **BTF 728** might result in "Broccoli tastes funny," for example.

The grownup License Plate game that I play with puzzler friends utilizes those same three-letter sequences, but we form single words rather than sentences. The object is to form the shortest possible word using the three letters, in the same order as they appear on the plate. Players take turns as the "caller," announcing the three letters from a plate when a "good" one is spotted. Too-easy ones, like HAT or NSE, should be avoided. In case of ties, the word closest to the beginning of the alphabet wins. If no one can think of a word for a particular sequence, then the letters may be used in any order. The shortest common BTF words include BEATIFY, BEAUTIFY, BLASTOFF, BOASTFUL and DOUBTFUL, plus there's the somewhat uncommon BOTFLY.

By the way, this game was the inspiration for the Sound Thinking puzzles that I create for each *Mind Stretchers* issue.

Twenty Questions

Because of its versatility and universal appeal, Twenty Questions is my personal favorite car game. You're probably familiar with how to play. One person thinks of an answer, and the other players take turns asking questions that can be answered by either "yes" or "no."

Traditionally, the answer must fall into one of three categories: Animal, Vegetable, or Mineral. (Have you ever wondered why those categories? They're derived from the lyric of the "Major-General's Song" from Gilbert and Sullivan's operetta *The Pirates of Penzance*: "I've information vegetable, animal, and mineral.")

The round ends either after 20 questions have been asked, or when someone correctly guesses the answer. The correct guesser earns the right to select the next answer.

The version of Twenty Questions that I most often play has these modifications from the above:

■ The number of questions allowed isn't limited to 20 or any other preset number, but the answerer is encouraged to provide small-but-relevant hints if the questioners aren't making sufficient progress.

n A qualified yes or no answer should be given for "maybe" or "not exactly" situations. For example, in a recent game where my answer was Colonel Harland Sanders of fried-chicken fame, someone asked if he was an inventor. Always wanting to give the maximum assistance possible but not wanting to mislead, I answered that he wasn't known primarily as an inventor, but might well have held some patents (thinking about his secret ingredients and food-preparation process). [See sidebar for more on this.]

■ Additional categories are added to Animal, Vegetable, and Mineral. They are Place (such as Paris or a kitchen); Event (such as birthday party or the creation of the universe), Creative Work (such as a book, song, or painting), and Concept (such as jealousy). To move the game along, the answerer gives the category before the first question is asked.

■ As you might imagine, adding these extra categories might result in all manner of unusual or outlandish answers. That's why we require any answer to be something that all the players can be reasonably expected to have heard of, and must be fully described in five words or less. This will nip in the bud such monstrosities as "The concept of justice in the mind of Oliver Wendell Holmes when he wrote his 'fire in a crowded theater' Supreme Court decision."

By my very nature as a puzzle author and

More on Colonel Sanders

My curiosity was piqued while playing Twenty Questions with the subject of Colonel Harland Sanders, and I wanted to find out if the fried-chicken mogul held any patents. Thanks to the World Wide Web (starting out with a Google search on "Harland Sanders patent"), it took me only a few minutes to unearth the two 1960s U.S. patents granted to him: one for his "food preheating, cooking and warming device," the other for his "process of producing fried chicken under pressure." A copy of the original drawings submitted with the patent applications, plus highly detailed descriptions, can be viewed online at www.freepatentsonline.com/3156177.pdf. and www.freepatentsonline.com/3245800.pdf.

The same search results also turned up a 2006 article from the trivia magazine *mental_floss*, which explained why Sanders would never have patented his secret recipe of "11 herbs and spices." In short, a patent application would have required him to reveal the recipe, which would have become public record once the patent was granted.

Of course, this digression doesn't have a lot to do with car games. But I've included it here so you can see how easy it can be to follow through on whatever your intellectual curiosity might bring to mind. Whether you're playing car games, solving crosswords, or watching a TV game show, you should always be on the lookout for things to find out more about. The unending desire to "learn more" is an important ingredient in keeping your mind active and alert.

editor, I would always steer clear of "ungettables" of that latter sort anyway, even if they were allowed by the rules. I find it much more satisfying, as do my fellow players, to think of people and things that everyone knows, but which might be hard to guess. In this way, the people I play the game with, who are at least as clever as I'd like to think I am, will enjoy figuring out the answer as much as I did coming up with it.

For example, in the "People" subcategory of Animal, I try to use well-known people in unusual occupations, such as Colonel Sanders (see above), Mathew Brady (Civil War photographer), or Fred Flintstone (Stone Age cartoon character, who worked in a gravel pit). This is to make the answer as "impervious" as possible to standard occupational categories such as film star, politician, scientist, etc.

Silly Sentences

This game doesn't involve a puzzle to be solved. It's a test of your memory, creativity, and word power. The rules are very simple: The person chosen to start a game says any word. The next person adds a word, and then the next player adds another word, and so on, with the goal of creating a grammatically correct (though often nonsensical) sentence. But here's the key rule: every word must start with the same letter. At the beginning of his or her turn, each player must restate the entire sentence from memory, before adding a new word. For example, if the first person says "Pirates," and there are four players, a game might start like this:

Player 1: Pirates
  Pl. 2: Pretty pirates
  Pl. 3: Pretty pirates play
  Pl. 4: Pretty peculiar pirates play
  Pl. 1: Pretty peculiar pirates play pranks
  Pl. 2: Pretty peculiar pirates play puny pranks
  Pl. 3: Pretty peculiar pirates play puny parrot pranks
  Pl. 4: Pretty peculiar pirates play puny parrot pranks, parrying

And so on. You'll be surprised at how long and creative these sentences can get!

One important note: Before you start, establish whether players are allowed to add words like "the," "a," or "and" or prepositions like "on" or "in" when they add their words. Allowing these makes it much easier to add words, but that actually makes the game *harder*, as sentences get even longer.

Players are disqualified when they incorrectly restate the sentence. The winner is the last active player to recite the entire sentence without a mistake.

Final Words

It's been said that the greatest enemy of an active mind is boredom. So I hope I've given you some ideas that you'll be able to put to good use the next time you're on the road, to successfully battle the "beast of boredom."

—Stanley Newman

★ Duplications by Gail Grabowski

ACROSS

1 Helps with the dishes
6 Golf-course vehicle
10 Mix together
14 __ donna (temperamental person)
15 Diva's solo
16 Out of kilter
17 Firewood igniter
19 Two-wheeler
20 Water vapor
21 Becomes more profound
23 Historical times
25 Pulled apart
26 Furthermore
29 Gallery exhibition
32 Leno's network
35 Swimming spot
37 Yew or eucalyptus
38 Enthusiastic
40 Orb beyond Neptune
42 Boise's state: Abbr.
43 Pay hike
44 Fall zodiac sign
45 Segment
47 Aardvark's meals
48 Snakelike swimmer
49 Having an aroma
52 Ohio clock setting: Abbr.
53 Wicked
55 Rabbit relative
57 Soap-opera segment
60 Highway haulers
63 Cry of sorrow
64 Publishing employee
67 Be concerned
68 Leg joint
69 Laundry dirt
70 Fraternal organization
71 Proofreading notation
72 Curvy letters

DOWN

1 Typist's stat.
2 Tax-deferred accts.
3 Brad of *Ocean's Eleven*
4 Game-show host
5 North African desert
6 Purring pet
7 Desertlike
8 Chinese side dish
9 Begin to like
10 Cavalry sword
11 Type of small plane
12 Annoys
13 Deli loaf
18 Intelligent
22 Political strength
24 Zebra feature
26 Orchard fruit
27 "That's the truth!"
28 Leave one's car unlawfully
30 Four-door vehicle
31 Fireplace floor
33 Outperforms
34 Wave's high point
36 Envelope enclosure: Abbr.
39 Motor-club letters
41 Desert haven
46 Kid around with
50 Time keepers
51 Earth-moving machine
54 Carpenter's grippers
56 Mideast leaders
57 Airline to Israel
58 Word of warning
59 Fencing weapon
61 "How sweet __!"
62 Indefinite amount
63 Top poker card
65 So far
66 Second notes of the scale

★ Starbursts

Which starburst is in the middle of the pile, having the same number of starbursts below it as above it?

CENTURY MARKS

Select one number in each of the four columns so that the total adds up to exactly 100.

Example: $\dfrac{6}{\boxed{8}} + \dfrac{\boxed{15}}{73} + \dfrac{\boxed{40}}{61} + \dfrac{29}{\boxed{37}} = 100$

$$\boxed{\dfrac{40}{23}} + \boxed{\dfrac{56}{26}} + \boxed{\dfrac{41}{18}} + \boxed{\dfrac{16}{19}} = 100$$

★ Power Play

Find these items that can be powered by electricity, hidden in the diagram either across, down, or diagonally.

```
G E L T T E K M O H L M
I R O O J C F A N D A I
K E I J O U D R I F W C
E T E L E V I S I O N R
F N C O H T H C V R M O
L I O O I W O P E I O W
L R A H A D O A R R W A
I P O S P T A O S E E V
R R H H P E N R R T R E
G E I A M P L I F I E R
R C L O C U F E C I F R
E L B A T N R U T H O Z
```

AMPLIFIER
CLOCK
DISHWASHER
FAN
FIRE
GRILL
IRON
JUICER
KETTLE
LAPTOP
LAWNMOWER
MICROWAVE
PRINTER
RADIO
TELEPHONE
TELEVISION
TOASTER
TURNTABLE

INITIAL REACTION

Identify the well-known proverb from the first letters in each of its words.
Example: L. B. Y. L. Answer: Look Before You Leap

M. T. _____

★ Sudoku

Fill in the blank boxes so that every row, column, and 3x3 box contains all of the numbers 1 to 9.

	5					2	8	
	7		8	5				9
9				6		3		1
					1			2
7		6				9		5
1		9						
5		8		2				4
6				8	9		7	
2	9				5			

MIXAGRAMS

Each line contains a five-letter word and a four-letter word that have been mixed together (the order of the letters in each word has not been changed). Unmix the two words on each line and write them in the spaces provided. When you're done, find a two-part answer to the clue by reading down the letter columns in the answers. Example: D A R I U N V E T = DRIVE + AUNT

CLUE: Golf group

O P A L U S O F T = _ _ _ _ _ + _ _ _ _

S I N G O L O O T = _ _ _ _ _ + _ _ _ _

F E X I E A R M Y = _ _ _ _ _ + _ _ _ _

W A C H E R E E L = _ _ _ _ _ + _ _ _ _

★ Look Sharp by Sally R. Stein

ACROSS

1 Norway's largest city
5 Practice boxing
9 Water-balloon sound
14 Walk heavily
15 __ and hearty
16 Diamond-studded headpiece
17 How takeout is ordered
18 Nest eggs, for short
19 Blacksmith's heavy device
20 Seafood selection
22 Sir __ Newton
23 "__ about time!"
24 Mom or dad's sister
26 Take a small taste of
30 Mar. follower
31 Same old grinds
35 Far __ (off the mark)
36 Guys
37 Skeptic's remark
38 Sounding poor, as a piano
39 Cape __, MA
40 Tiny piece of pollen
41 Norse explorer __ the Red
42 Negative debate side
43 "Relax, soldier!"
44 Arnaz of I Love Lucy
45 Bother persistently
46 Outfoxed
47 Pre-Easter period
49 Citrus drink
50 Casts a ballot
53 Like the narrowest of victories
59 Digital music players
60 Grad
61 Traveled by bus
62 Spooky
63 Apple center
64 Bullfight cheers
65 Small songbirds
66 Sharp, as an appetite
67 British hot drinks

DOWN

1 Makes a decision
2 Snail-like
3 Letterhead illustration
4 Aroma
5 Changed auto gears
6 Eiffel Tower locale
7 Word of regret
8 Made into a new form
9 Dry cleaner's challenge
10 Thin-lines jacket pattern
11 Volcanic flow
12 Operatic solo
13 Bath-powder ingredient
21 Lulu
25 Caterer's coffeemaker
26 Filled fully
27 Blazing
28 Short skirts
29 Wrote down, as an appointment
30 A member of
32 WWII sub
33 Using few words
34 War horse
39 Place to hang a jacket
40 Control the wheel
42 MSNBC alternative
43 Belly, more formally
48 Letters before tees
49 Sky blue
50 Range of sight
51 Phone-co. employee
52 Ripped
54 Shampoo additive
55 Not-so-fast running gait
56 Excavation
57 Notion
58 Loch __ monster

★ Square Routes

Fill in the blank circles so that every row, column, and path contains all of the numbers from 1 to 5.

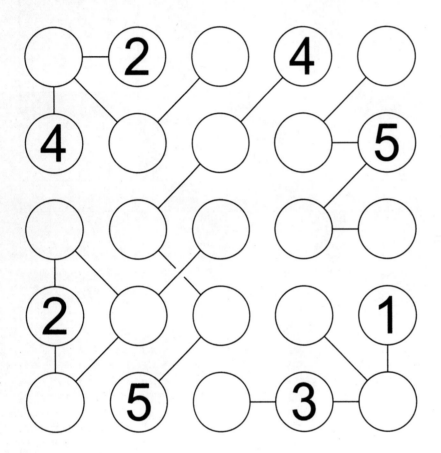

WRONG IS RIGHT

Which of these four words is misspelled?

A) affront   B) frontier

C) frontispiece   D) effrontory

★★ Line Drawing

Draw three straight lines, each from one edge of the square to another edge, so that the letters in each of the five regions form a word, four of which are the same length.

THREE OF A KIND

Find the three hidden words in the sentence that go together in some way.
Example: Chefs were <u>bus</u>ily slicing <u>car</u>rots and <u>cab</u>bage. Answer: bus, car, cab.

Now, let's have none of your eternal malarkey.

★ Veggie Surprise

Find these vitamin-rich foods that are hidden in the diagram, either across, down, or diagonally. (BRUSSELS and SPROUTS are hidden separately.) There's one additional 11-letter answer in the category, not listed below, that's also hidden in the diagram. What's that food?

```
S  P  I  N  A  C  H  X  K  A  L  F
R  N  R  E  L  D  C  O  L  E  E  P
P  E  O  I  R  N  E  O  B  Y  G  E
L  A  W  A  S  P  A  R  A  G  U  S
K  E  H  O  N  B  U  T  S  O  M  W
A  C  G  R  L  S  A  E  S  N  S  I
S  R  U  U  S  F  C  E  E  I  L  S
P  T  T  E  M  U  I  B  R  O  E  L
R  L  L  I  T  E  C  L  C  N  T  I
O  S  E  T  C  R  V  C  U  S  T  T
U  K  E  K  E  H  O  I  I  A  U  N
T  L  K  S  A  R  O  E  D  R  C  E
S  E  E  P  B  L  P  K  N  N  M  L
C  A  B  B  A  G  E  I  E  G  E  D
Y  R  E  L  E  C  P  E  A  S  H  K
```

ARTICHOKE
ASPARAGUS
BEET
BROCCOLI
BRUSSELS SPROUTS
CABBAGE
CELERY
CHARD
CRESS
ENDIVE
KALE
LEEK
LEGUME
LENTILS
LETTUCE
ONIONS
PEAS
SPINACH
TURNIP

WHO'S WHAT WHERE?

The correct term for a resident of the Caribbean nation of Barbados is:

    A) Barbadino   B) Barbader

    C) Barbadite   D) Barbadian

★ All Wet by Sally R. Stein

ACROSS

1 Burns slightly
6 Sports cable network
10 Right away, in memos
14 Charged towards
15 Nile queen, for short
16 Nothing, in Mexico
17 Scarlett of *Gone With the Wind*
18 Inning enders
19 "__ well that ends well"
20 Home gardener's device
23 Use a couch
24 Zodiac lion
25 Forty Thieves' adversary
27 WWII turning point
30 "Please send a letter"
33 Large coffee brewer
34 __ in the neck (pest)
35 Lightweight wood
39 Miss America contestants, for instance
43 Be a burglar
44 Historical times
45 Hawaiian neckwear
46 Pleasingly thin
49 Workout centers
50 Street driving hazard
53 Tic-tac-toe win
55 Anger
56 Water-softener chemical
62 Well-ventilated
64 Public-sch. auxiliaries
65 Cowboy, often
66 Sneeze site
67 Blood components
68 Vote into office
69 Change for $5
70 Whirlpool

71 They're worn under shoes

DOWN

1 Black bird
2 "That's funny!"
3 Med.-school course
4 Very seldom
5 Take a long look
6 Supply-and-demand sci.
7 Fake coin
8 Tabby or Siamese
9 Cash-register key
10 Santa __, CA
11 Nacho-chip dip

12 Speak without a script
13 Ziti or spaghetti
21 Person from Des Moines
22 Rain cloud
26 Play, as a drum
27 Gives a name to
28 "Darn it!"
29 Penny-__ poker
31 Prearrange, as an outcome
32 Retired for the night
34 Sofa cushion
36 Easter flower
37 Appear to be
38 Sale condition

40 Corned-beef creation
41 Poetic "before"
42 Brother of Moses
47 Tick by
48 Got snug
49 Fly alone
50 Spinet or baby grand
51 Hunter constellation
52 To the point
54 Mean people
57 Difficult
58 British exclamation
59 Oil cartel
60 Playing-card pack
61 Creative pursuits
63 "I'd be happy to!"

★ Number-Out

Shade squares so that no number appears in any row or column more than once. Shaded squares may not touch each other horizontally or vertically, and all unshaded squares must form a single continuous area.

3	5	3	1	3
1	4	1	5	3
2	4	4	4	1
5	3	1	2	5
5	1	3	3	3

THINK ALIKE

Unscramble the letters in the phrase PUT GULL to form two words with the same or similar meanings. Example: The letters in BEST RATING can be rearranged to spell START and BEGIN.

_____   _____

★ Seven Circles

Start in the center circle, pass through the other six circles exactly once, then return to the center. You may not retrace your path.

SMALL CHANGE

Change one letter in each of these two words, to form a common two-word phrase.
Example: PANTRY CHEW Answer: PASTRY CHEF

TOY DIG

_____

★ Able-Bodied by Gail Grabowski

ACROSS

1 Clothes-dryer buildup
5 Kid around
9 Farm units
14 Once more
15 Woodwind instrument
16 Heavy knock
17 Container for valuables
19 Raring to go
20 Lawn material
21 Insurance broker
22 Furious
23 Not winning or losing
24 Moisten, as a turkey
26 Youngster
28 Secret writing
29 Morning moisture
32 Purple fruits
33 Garden tool
34 Practice boxing
35 Thorny flower
36 Difficult journeys
38 Cover with tar
39 Acorn producers
40 Fish eggs
41 All gone, as food
42 Cloud's place
43 Pull apart
44 Dashboard devices
45 Made a solemn promise
47 Disastrous
48 Male bee
50 Paid out
52 School transport
55 Salary increase
56 "That's a shame!"
58 Followed a curved path
59 Suffix for differ
60 Land surrounded by water
61 Borscht vegetables

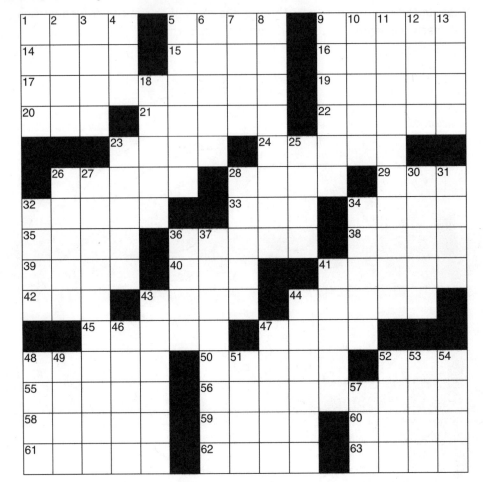

62 Sandwich breads
63 Melt

DOWN

1 Scottish girl
2 Long-division word
3 Geek
4 A pair of
5 Ran at a slow pace
6 Receded
7 In the near future
8 Student's reading
9 "Relax, soldier!"
10 Monotonous song
11 Rough hiking trail
12 Part of EMT: Abbr.
13 Agile
18 Hammers' targets
23 Uses a stopwatch
25 Citrus drinks
26 Loose outer garment
27 Hoarse speaker's sound
28 "Bravo!" or "Hurrah!"
30 Roof overhangs
31 Small songbird
32 Paid athletes
34 Elbow room
36 Dogwood, for example

37 Car with a rumble seat
41 The third planet
43 Coarse wool fabrics
44 Traces of color
46 Beginning stage
47 Low poker card
48 Dull-colored
49 Steak preference
51 Small horse
52 Cluster of shrubs
53 West Coast school: Abbr.
54 Veer off course
57 Ignited

★ One-Way Streets

The diagram represents a pattern of streets. A and B are parking spaces, and the black squares are stores. Find the route that starts at A, passes through all stores exactly once, and ends at B. Arrows indicate one-way traffic for that block only. No block or intersection may be entered more than once.

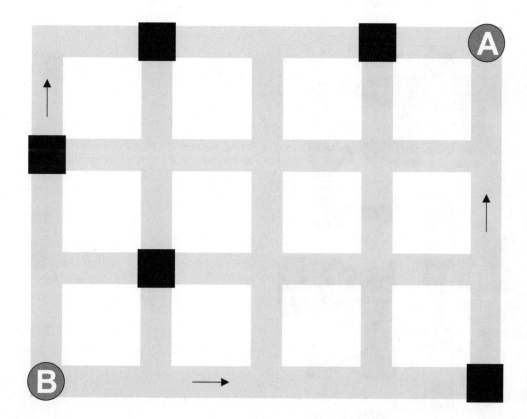

SOUND THINKING

There is only one common uncapitalized word whose consonant sounds are Y, N, S, and N, in that order. What is it?

_____

★★ Split Decisions

In this clueless crossword puzzle, each answer consists of two words whose spellings are the same, except for the consecutive letters given. All answers are common words; no phrases or hyphenated or capitalized words are used. Some of the clues may have more than one solution, but there is only one word pair that will correctly link up with all the other word pairs.

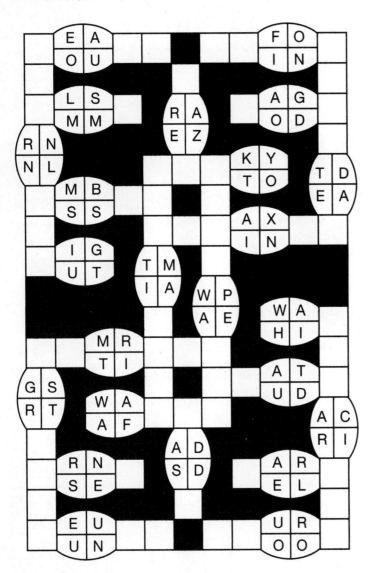

TRANSDELETION

Delete one letter from the word FOCAL and rearrange the rest, to get a baby animal. Then delete a different letter from FOCAL and rearrange the rest, to get a different baby animal.

_____   _____

★ Star Search

Find the stars that are hidden in some of the blank squares. The numbered squares indicate how many stars are hidden in the squares adjacent to them (including diagonally). There is never more than one star in any square.

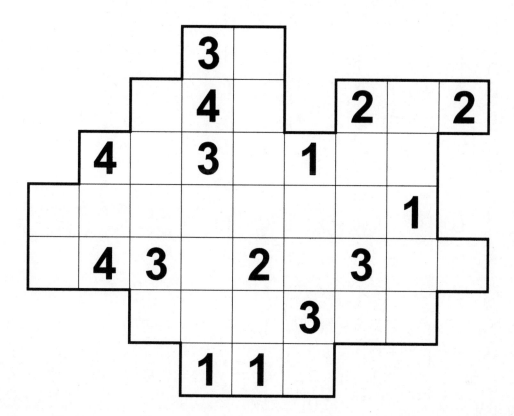

CHOICE WORDS

Form three six-letter words from the same category, by selecting one letter from each column three times. Each letter will be used exactly once.

Example: B A B C O T　　Answer: BOBCAT, JAGUAR, OCELOT
　　　　　J O E U A R
　　　　　O C G L A T

R　E　L　V　E　R　　_ _ _ _ _ _

S　A　R　K　E　Y　　_ _ _ _ _ _

V　O　C　L　E　T　　_ _ _ _ _ _

★ Make Some Noise

Find these "audible" words that are hidden in the diagram, either across, down, or diagonally.

```
S  I  N  S  C  W  D  K  W  N  G  R
T  R  I  L  L  H  D  R  N  N  E  N
G  A  E  G  A  I  Y  A  O  L  L  I
W  Z  N  E  S  N  B  G  L  N  X  D
E  I  U  C  H  E  D  O  P  L  E  Y
S  G  L  B  L  C  H  B  R  O  A  R
J  A  N  L  B  B  L  W  O  R  G  T
P  L  O  A  R  U  E  H  H  O  U  P
M  W  I  G  B  B  H  I  O  O  M  S
B  L  A  R  E  B  O  A  H  W  H  I
C  I  T  O  T  U  O  S  I  O  L  W
L  A  Y  W  S  H  T  H  U  D  H  B
A  W  B  E  A  W  E  D  C  O  I  U
S  S  I  H  L  N  I  C  O  E  S  Z
V  S  A  L  B  Q  G  P  B  U  F  Z
```

BANG
BELLOW
BLARE
BLAST
BOOM
BUZZ
CHEERS
CLAP
CLASH
DIN
DRONE
ECHO
GONG
GROWL
HISS
HOLLER
HOWL
HUBBUB
ROAR
SHOUT
SING
THUD
TRILL
TWANG
WAIL
WHINE
WHOOP
YELP

IN OTHER WORDS

There is only one common uncapitalized word that contains the consecutive letters AKR. What is it?

_____

★ Fond Four by Gail Grabowski

ACROSS

1 Network that covers the NYSE
5 Take a bite of
10 Health resorts
14 Solemn vow
15 "... happily ever __"
16 Part of the foot
17 Creative thought
18 Not a soul
19 Caveman's discovery
20 Elegant prom dress
22 Knocked for a loop
23 Ceases
24 Bicycle part
25 Remove, as paint
28 Frugality
30 Rocks that are mined
31 Mattress covering
33 Debtor's letters
35 Penna. neighbor
36 "Nonsense!"
38 Doberman's warning
39 French friend
40 Actor's representative
41 Thick carpet
42 Caught sight of
44 Acquire molars
46 Makeshift dwellings
47 Coward's lack
49 Light-bulb units
51 Tomato
55 Money in Italy
56 Place of safety
57 Diva's solo
58 Getz or Kenton of jazz
59 Modify, as a law
60 Mannerly man
61 Playthings
62 Thaws
63 Potato buds

DOWN

1 Hairdo
2 Nothing, in Mexico
3 Bingo call
4 Latin dances
5 Hair knot
6 Under way, to Sherlock Holmes
7 Loads, as cargo
8 Where Nashville is: Abbr.
9 Before, in poems
10 African expedition
11 Pro boxing match
12 Ranchland unit
13 Storage building
21 Shrill bark
22 Needing washing
24 You, in the Bible
25 Fizzy drink
26 __ de menthe
27 Party veggie platter
28 Camp shelter
29 Synagogue scroll
31 Winter coaster
32 Term of endearment
34 Strongly recommend
36 Prepares, as a fishhook
37 Matures
41 Slow leak
43 Hoaxes
44 Current fashions
45 Actress Longoria
47 Book of fiction
48 Major happening
49 Wagon-train direction
50 Sedan or coupe
51 Weak, as an excuse
52 Hunter's quarry
53 Toe the __ (obey)
54 Has a snack
56 Sandwich meat

★ Hyper-Sudoku

Fill in the blank boxes so that every row, column, 3x3 box, *and* each of the four 3x3 gray regions contains all of the numbers 1 to 9.

	4			9		2		8
2			4		7		1	9
1								4
				8	4			
4	7	9	2		6	3		5
	3		9			1	2	
		2		4	9		6	1
9				6		8	5	
		8	1					

MIXAGRAMS

Each line contains a five-letter word and a four-letter word that have been mixed together (the order of the letters in each word has not been changed). Unmix the two words on each line and write them in the spaces provided. When you're done, find a two-part answer to the clue by reading down the letter columns in the answers.

CLUE: Music or marble

W O G H E R A T E = _ _ _ _ _ + _ _ _ _

N O C A M E O L K = _ _ _ _ _ + _ _ _ _

P A R A M O R C E = _ _ _ _ _ + _ _ _ _

T E A D I C K E T = _ _ _ _ _ + _ _ _ _

★★ Looking Back

Which of the rear-view mirrors shows the true reflection of the scene?

BETWEENER

What three-letter word belongs between the word at left and the word at right, so that the first and second word, and the second and third word, each form a common compound word?

BELL __ __ __ SCOTCH

★ 123

Fill in the diagram so that each rectangular piece has one each of the numbers 1, 2, and 3, under these rules: 1) No two adjacent squares, horizontally or vertically, can have the same number. 2) Each completed row and column of the diagram will have an equal number of 1's, 2's, and 3's.

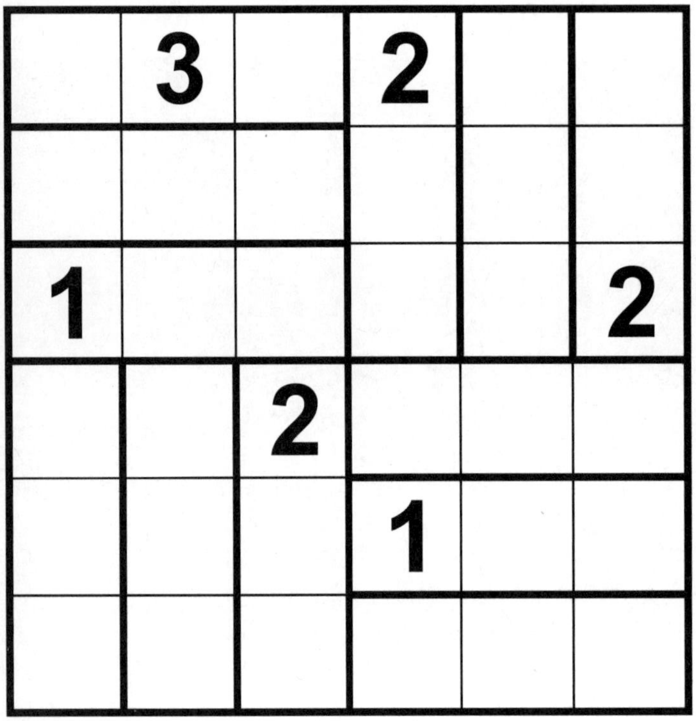

	3		2		
1					2
		2			
			1		

SUDOKU SUM

Fill in the missing numbers from 1 to 9, so that the sum of each row and column is as indicated.

EXAMPLE

	12	14	19
6			3
17	6		
22		8	

ANSWER

	12	14	19
6	1	2	3
17	6	4	7
22	5	8	9

	18	14	13
18		4	
9	6		
18			7

★ Physics 101 by Sally R. Stein

ACROSS

1 Neck-warming cloth
6 Spruce up a manuscript
10 Give off
14 Less ruddy
15 Prepare, as potatoes
16 Sentence in a film script
17 Sports stadium
18 Norway's capital
19 Poker-game precursor
20 Keep a Senate proposal moving
23 Mediocre grade
24 Chimp or gorilla
25 Like desert terrain
29 Hushed "Hey you!"
31 Pod veggie
34 Jai __
35 Farm storage building
37 Notions
39 Human dynamos
42 Accumulate
43 Footnote abbr.
44 Runner's distance
45 Trio following Q
46 Ripens
48 Purple flower
50 Pigpen
51 Coop dweller
52 Reluctance to purchase
61 Barbell metal
62 Very dry, as a climate
63 Hawaiian greeting
64 Hot beverages
65 Ceramic floor piece
66 Funnel-shaped
67 Out of danger
68 Snakelike swimmers
69 Parts of a saw

DOWN

1 Fitness centers
2 Be concerned
3 Actor Guinness
4 Nevada city
5 Neighbor of Spain
6 Overact
7 Run quickly
8 Water-surrounded land
9 Inventor Edison
10 Gladden
11 Short skirt
12 A fan of
13 High-schooler, usually

21 Thickly packed
22 Choose to participate
25 Kid-lit elephant
26 Grads
27 Charged towards
28 Disposes (of)
29 Schemes
30 Piece of den furniture
31 Danger
32 National bird
33 So far
36 "That's clear"
38 Floor model
40 Exams for attys.-to-be

41 Santa's helpers
47 Dance excitedly
49 Without damage
50 Sight or taste
51 Keeps a low profile
52 Uses a 30 Down
53 Region
54 Package of bread
55 A Great Lake
56 Window ledge
57 Lotion additive
58 __ of the above
59 IOU
60 Apiece

★ ABC

Enter the letters A, B, and C into the diagram so that each row and column has exactly one A, one B, and one C. The letters outside the diagram indicate the first letter encountered, moving in the direction of the arrow. Keep in mind that after all the letters have been filled in, there will be one blank box in each row and column.

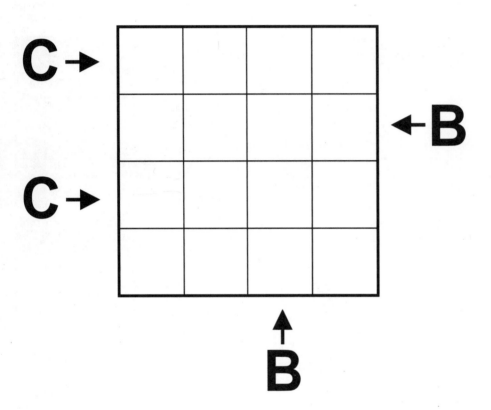

CLUELESS CROSSWORD

Complete the crossword with common uncapitalized seven-letter words, based entirely on the letters already filled in for you.

★ Find the Ships

Determine the position of the 10 ships listed to the right of the diagram.
The ships may be oriented either horizontally or vertically. A square with wavy
lines indicates water and will not contain a ship. The numbers at the edge of the
diagram indicate how many squares in that row or column contain parts of ships.
When all 10 ships are correctly placed in the diagram, no two of them will touch
each other, not even diagonally.

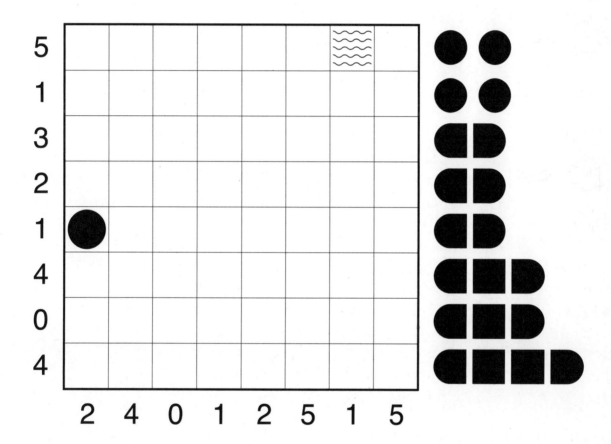

TWO-BY-FOUR

The eight letters in the word CHILDREN can be rearranged to form a pair of common four-letter
words in only one way. Can you find the two words?

— — — —   — — — —

★ "C" in the Kitchen

Try to find these "C" kitchen words that are hidden in the diagram either across, down, or diagonally, and you'll discover that one of them isn't there. What's the missing answer? (CRANBERRY and SAUCE are hidden separately.)

```
S  E  Y  S  P  O  H  C  S  C  C  U  S  T  A  R  C  D  C  C
A  G  V  N  Z  O  C  R  H  R  S  O  H  E  R  S  R  R  U  R
U  C  O  R  P  C  E  E  O  A  T  T  C  P  S  A  A  B  N  A
X  E  A  O  E  T  E  U  T  N  N  K  O  O  T  Q  I  U  O  N
E  M  R  C  S  S  T  F  U  B  A  A  U  S  N  C  D  O  C  B
K  A  C  I  C  O  N  W  O  E  R  C  U  R  C  U  C  B  O  E
O  R  N  O  N  R  C  O  R  R  R  C  A  R  C  B  T  A  C  R
O  A  O  S  R  S  E  A  C  R  U  C  O  R  O  E  X  M  R  R
C  C  E  C  U  B  A  P  U  Y  C  I  C  E  P  A  N  A  C  Q
C  H  E  R  R  I  E  S  D  L  S  T  N  E  M  I  D  N  O  C
C  A  N  A  P  E  S  C  C  S  I  S  T  O  R  R  A  C  H  C
O  R  K  C  O  C  A  H  A  T  C  F  C  R  A  C  R  I  O  C
N  C  E  C  R  B  E  N  C  N  A  U  L  B  H  E  P  N  A  S
D  A  U  V  B  R  T  T  A  A  R  S  U  O  K  S  S  R  C  A
I  R  C  A  R  C  N  K  B  S  A  U  P  O  W  E  V  A  D  U
M  V  G  I  C  A  K  E  B  S  M  R  O  C  R  E  P  E  S  C
E  E  E  H  R  K  C  A  A  I  E  C  U  V  L  H  R  L  U  O
N  F  I  R  U  I  R  J  G  O  L  V  P  I  H  C  K  P  A  T
T  P  U  Y  S  C  W  S  U  R  C  W  O  L  F  I  L  U  A  C
V  C  R  E  T  S  I  N  A  C  A  R  R  O  T  C  H  O  P  N
```

CABBAGE
CAKE
~~CANAPÉS~~
CANISTERS
CARAMEL
CARP
CARROTS
CARVER
CAULIFLOWER
CHEESE
~~CHERRIES~~
CHIPS
CHOPS
COCONUT
COD
CONDIMENTS
CONSERVE
COOKER
CORK
~~CORN~~
COUNTER
CRAB
CRANBERRY SAUCE
CREPES
CROISSANTS
CROUTONS
CRUST
CUBE
CUP
CURRANTS
CUSTARD

INITIAL REACTION

Identify the well-known proverb from the first letters in each of its words.

F. B. C. _____

★ Flabbergasted by Gail Grabowski

ACROSS

1 IRS-form experts
5 Uproars
9 Prepares to be photographed
14 Be durable
15 Robin's residence
16 Major happening
17 Opera solo
18 Filled tortilla
19 Like marsh plants
20 Walk unsteadily
23 Sight or smell
24 Stop-sign color
25 Dairy animal
28 Golf-course distances: Abbr.
29 Spinning toy
32 Where a ship docks
35 Tartan pattern
37 Female horses
38 Carpet or linoleum
42 Plays a trick on
43 Reef material
44 Kitchen nook
47 Fistful of dollars
48 Businesses: Abbr.
51 Pub beverage
52 Wild equine
54 Defeatist's words
56 Ride-smoothing auto part
61 Up and about
63 Nastase of tennis
64 Lessen
65 Extra tire
66 Shopping center
67 Once more
68 Uses a vegetable peeler
69 Racetrack postings
70 Apple computers, for short

DOWN

1 Stylish
2 Said good-bye
3 Cambodians and Iranis
4 Men-only parties
5 Poker-hand starter
6 First word of a letter
7 Hollywood award
8 Mall tenants
9 Lima's country
10 Baking appliance
11 Farmer's kernels for planting
12 Conclusion
13 Pig's digs
21 "Scram!"
22 Poem of praise
26 Calif. neighbor
27 Lb. and kg.
30 Rower's need
31 Snapshot, for short
33 '60s "transistor" appliance
34 Bucket
35 Flag holder
36 Physician, informally
38 Aluminum wrap
39 Texas flag symbol
40 Solemn pledge
41 Historical period
42 Prescription regulator: Abbr.
45 Tic-__-toe
46 Igloo dweller
48 Beach shelter
49 "Just a moment!"
50 Scatters
53 Course with lettuce
55 Coffee lightener
57 Add to the payroll
58 Metallic rocks
59 Eagle or egret
60 Tennis-match units
61 Poisonous snake
62 Resort with hot springs

★ Missing Links

Find the three rings that are linked together, but linked to no others on the page.

SMALL CHANGE

Change one letter in each of these two words, to form a common two-word phrase.

BEER JUG

★ Square Routes

Fill in the blank circles so that every row, column, and path contains all of the numbers from 1 to 5.

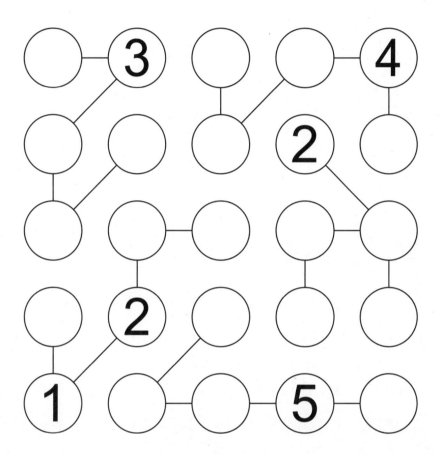

WRONG IS RIGHT

Which of these four words is misspelled?

A) burgher   B) burglar

C) homburg   D) burgandy

★ Still in the Box

Find these words that are hidden in various box shapes in the diagram. One answer is shown to get you started.

J	G	I	G	V	U	N	W	P	M	O	D	D	B	R
H	T	F	D	U	S	U	Y	E	N	R	E	V	N	A
C	A	O	X	U	E	D	W	E	G	H	H	D	D	N
T	U	N	T	U	I	O	P	Q	P	N	B	Z	W	E
N	C	U	O	H	D	N	E	O	E	U	N	W	A	F
T	H	E	D	Q	R	O	L	J	T	D	E	T	N	C
L	H	F	D	Z	B	P	Q	M	I	I	G	A	X	Z
C	B	L	A	T	H	U	P	T	N	G	D	R	Y	T
D	F	T	S	E	S	O	T	H	Y	T	U	N	H	S
F	D	P	Q	K	L	D	A	B	C	X	D	N	A	L
O	R	J	H	K	H	E	T	W	S	S	L	E	D	L
G	I	D	K	U	N	S	M	N	R	E	V	C	Z	N
I	N	O	E	I	O	P	L	J	H	D	Z	J	U	S
L	A	R	Q	L	E	D	S	L	O	T	L	N	I	T
G	E	K	H	F	A	E	Y	B	C	B	N	U	R	F

BRAND-NEW
GIFT
JUST IN
LATEST
MINT
MODERN
OPEN
ORIGINAL
RED-HOT
UNHANDLED
UNSPOILED
UNTOUCHED
~~UNUSED~~
UNWANTED
UP-TO-DATE

WHO'S WHAT WHERE?

The correct term for a resident of Maine is:

A) Mainite   B) Mainer

C) Mainian   D) Nor'easter

★ Fruit Openers by Sally R. Stein

ACROSS

1 Curbside pickup
6 Reduces, as expenses
10 Travel rtes.
13 Fraction of a pound
14 High-school dance
15 Horse's meal
17 Newspapers and TV stations
18 Remedies for poisons
20 Winter malady
22 Oxygen or aluminum
23 Is appropriate for
26 Last word in prayer
27 ___ Angeles
28 61, in Roman numerals
29 Install, as draperies
31 Emphatic Spanish agreement
33 *Othello* villain
35 Leaves the premises
37 Is not, slangily
39 Drain-clearing plungers
43 Cafeteria plate holder
44 Postal delivery
45 Scissors sound
46 Concerning, in memos
48 Pesky insect
50 Air-conditioning unit: Abbr.
51 Transgression
53 Not fooled by
55 Found the source of, as a phone call
57 Etch deeply
59 Portion of corn
60 Most overcast
63 Horse's sound
67 Having no slack
68 Money in France
69 Provide food for a party
70 Pounds and kilograms: Abbr.
71 Minor dispute
72 Double-curve letters

DOWN

1 Actor Cruise or Hanks
2 Regret
3 In addition
4 Flying-saucer story genre
5 Physical well-being
6 Tax expert: Abbr.
7 Large coffeemaker
8 Indian carving
9 Happy expressions
10 Den or kitchen
11 TV magazine show
12 Shorthand expert
16 Retired jets: Abbr.
19 "Not me," for one
21 Customary practice
23 Radar image
24 Praise highly
25 Solving
26 Way back when
30 Standard level
32 Tastes, as of tea
34 Mideast sultanate
36 Knee-to-ankle area
38 Overused, as a phrase
40 Secondary thoroughfare
41 Make happy
42 Tater
47 Is jealous of
49 Hypnotic state
51 Religious group
52 Spouse's relative
54 Prepare to play golf
56 Regions
58 Repetitive routines
61 Mrs., in Mexico
62 Two-year-old
64 Part of TGIF
65 "Wow!"
66 Divs. of a day

★ Sudoku

Fill in the blank boxes so that every row, column, and 3x3 box contains all of the numbers 1 to 9.

6	2	3	4	7	9	8	5	1
1	9	4	6	5	8	7	3	2
7	8	5	3	2	1	9	6	4
2	7	9	8	4	5	3	1	6
8	5	1	9	6	3	4	2	7
4	3	6	7	1	2	5	9	8
3	1	7	5	8	6	2	4	9
9	6	8	2	3	4	1	7	5
5	4	2	1	9	7	6	8	3

MIXAGRAMS

Each line contains a five-letter word and a four-letter word that have been mixed together (the order of the letters in each word has not been changed). Unmix the two words on each line and write them in the spaces provided. When you're done, find a two-part answer to the clue by reading down the letter columns in the answers.

CLUE: Cooper classic

W H E R E N O N T = _ _ _ _ _ + _ _ _ _

I N T O N E O R T = _ _ _ _ _ + _ _ _ _

G U R U P E L O N = _ _ _ _ _ + _ _ _ _

H E G I S T O N E = _ _ _ _ _ + _ _ _ _

★ 123

Fill in the diagram so that each rectangular piece has one each of the numbers 1, 2, and 3, under these rules: 1) No two adjacent squares, horizontally or vertically, can have the same number. 2) Each completed row and column of the diagram will have an equal number of 1's, 2's, and 3's.

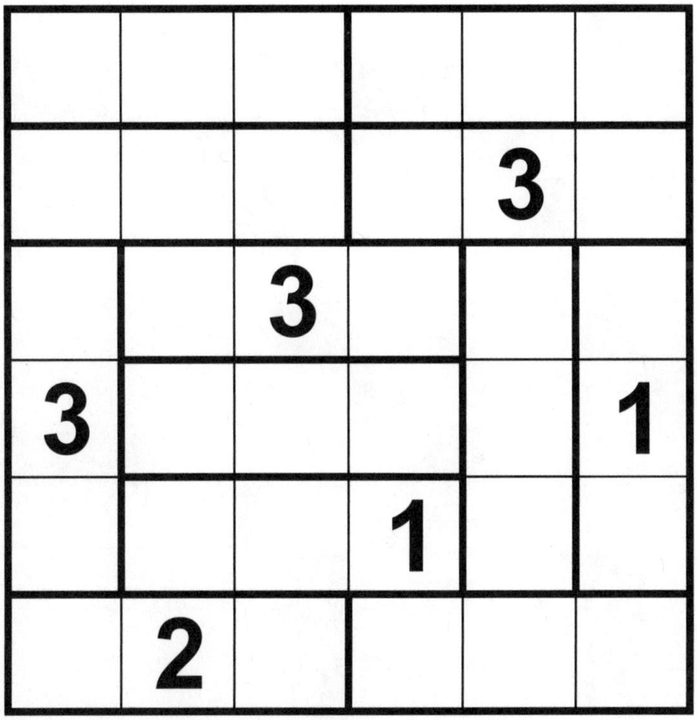

				3	
		3			
3					**1**
			1		
	2				

ADDITION SWITCH

Switch the positions of two of the digits in the incorrect sum at right, to get a correct sum.
Example: 955+264 = 411. Switch the second 1 in 411 with the 9 in 955 to get: 155+264 = 419

$$\begin{array}{r} 228 \\ +301 \\ \hline 520 \end{array}$$

★ Rhyme Time by Sally R. Stein

ACROSS

1 Fights with
6 Astronauts' org.
10 Air pollution
14 Make happy
15 Airline of Israel
16 Angel's topper
17 Talked too much
18 Traveled
19 Assistant
20 "YIELD RIGHT OF WAY," for one
21 Nursery-rhyme plum finder
23 Give off
25 Praiseful verses
26 Attend without a date
29 Praise highly
31 Scottish cap
34 Steer clear of
35 Feeling of hunger
36 Singer Guthrie
37 Nursery-rhyme guy who "takes a wife"
40 Leave in a hurry
41 Concludes
42 In the lead
43 New immigrant's class: Abbr.
44 Lodge brothers
45 Attractive
46 Like auto crankcases
48 Skillets
49 Nursery-rhyme spider fearer
53 Digital music player
57 Citrus drinks
58 Banana cream and coconut custard
59 Escape from
60 Nation north of Chile
61 Sandwich cookie
62 Honeydew, for one
63 Manuscript enclosure: Abbr.
64 Butterfly catchers
65 Software purchasers

DOWN

1 That woman's
2 Jai __
3 Crooned
4 Formerly
5 Slightly less than a dozen
6 Inexperienced in
7 Actor Baldwin
8 Plummeted
9 Despite the fact that
10 Piece of the action
11 Business-district thoroughfare, often
12 Ye __ Shoppe
13 Attendee
21 Irish dance
22 Peculiar
24 Assembled from a kit
26 Embarrassing mistake
27 Roundish shapes
28 Ungracious players
29 Touches down
30 Hill-building bugs
32 __ once (suddenly)
33 Like old bread
35 Flamingo's color
36 Glue and rubber cement
38 Have trust in
39 Make, as a salary
44 Shade tree
45 Portion of butter
47 Copy of a magazine
48 Mexican coins
49 Navigation references
50 Creative thought
51 Blaze
52 Mile fractions
54 White as a sheet
55 Aroma
56 Family rooms
59 Australian bird

★ One-Way Streets

The diagram represents a pattern of streets. A and B are parking spaces, and the black squares are stores. Find the route that starts at A, passes through all stores exactly once, and ends at B. Arrows indicate one-way traffic for that block only. No block or intersection may be entered more than once.

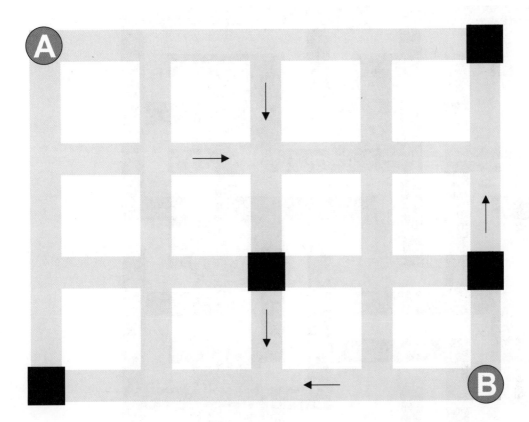

SOUND THINKING

Common words whose consonant sounds are Z and N include ZANY and OZONE. What six-letter word is pronounced with the same consonant sounds in the same order?

_____

★ No Three in a Row

Enter the maze at left, pass through all the squares exactly once, then exit, all without retracing your path. You may not pass through three squares of the same color consecutively.

SAY IT AGAIN

What three-letter word can be either a body of water or a verb meaning "howl?

— — —

★ Star Search

Find the stars that are hidden in some of the blank squares. The numbered squares indicate how many stars are hidden in the squares adjacent to them (including diagonally). There is never more than one star in any square.

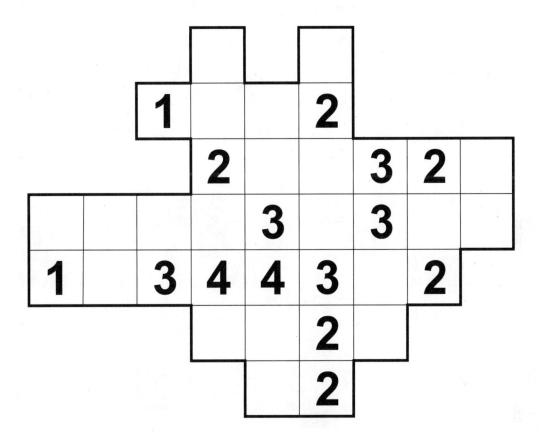

CHOICE WORDS

Form three six-letter words from the same category, by selecting one letter from each column three times. Each letter will be used exactly once.

A	H	A	U	G	F
C	A	R	I	N	T
T	M	O	R	F	E

_ _ _ _ _ _

_ _ _ _ _ _

_ _ _ _ _ _

★ Put It Together by Gail Grabowski

ACROSS

1 Not many
5 Castle protection
9 Business bigwig
14 Italian capital
15 Part of the foot
16 Like Humpty Dumpty
17 Duration
19 Hotel prices
20 Sneaky
21 Soda-bottle size
22 Not quite right
23 Walking stick
24 Italian city
26 In the know
28 Home plate, for one
29 That woman
32 A couple of times
33 Bullring "Bravo!"
34 Theater production
35 Solemn vow
36 Of few words
38 Not wild
39 Chinese-food staple
40 Sailor's "yes"
41 Loose-leaf filler
42 To the __ degree
43 Snow glider
44 Fraternity members
45 Church doctrine
47 Bicyclist's challenge
48 Cook's cover-up
50 Pay hike
52 By way of
55 Brutish sort
56 Catalog page to fill in
58 Allude (to)
59 Docking spot
60 Molecule part
61 Unable to sit still
62 Talk back to

63 Nevada city

DOWN

1 __ and crafts
2 Aluminum wrap
3 Television award
4 Very small
5 Member of the Corps
6 Make a speech
7 High point
8 Winter undergarments
9 Team spirit
10 Bush's successor
11 Become more fit
12 Takes advantage of
13 Minus
18 Distress signal
23 Hidden supply
25 Words of understanding
26 Look forward to
27 Sorcery
28 Not at all interested
30 Residences
31 Wide-spouted pitcher
32 Ripped apart
34 Stable compartment
36 Folk story
37 Pupil-dilating liquids
41 More ashen
43 Military guard
44 Penny pinchers
46 Valentine flowers
47 Stays out of sight
48 Magic-spell opener
49 Hammer part
51 Opera solo
52 Cast a ballot
53 Household appliance
54 Bullets, briefly
57 Miles away

★ Keyword

Find these 22 words and phrases that are hidden in the diagram, either across, down, or diagonally. At first glance, they may appear to be from several different categories, but in fact they are all related—to the multiple meanings of one of the words on the list. What's that keyword? (TIGHT and SPOT are hidden separately.)

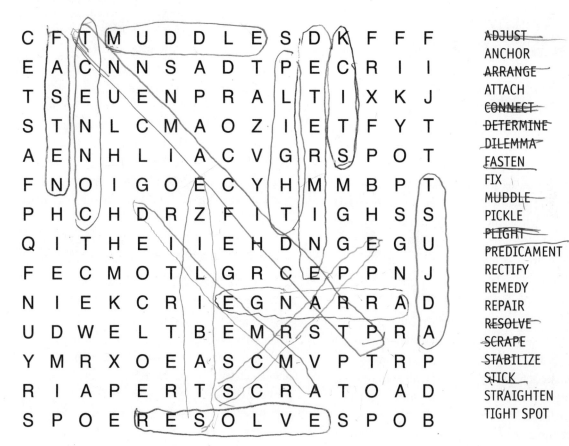

ADJUST
ANCHOR
ARRANGE
ATTACH
CONNECT
DETERMINE
DILEMMA
FASTEN
FIX
MUDDLE
PICKLE
PLIGHT
PREDICAMENT
RECTIFY
REMEDY
REPAIR
RESOLVE
SCRAPE
STABILIZE
STICK
STRAIGHTEN
TIGHT SPOT

IN OTHER WORDS

There is only one common uncapitalized word that contains the consecutive letters BYG. What is it?

_____

bRain BREAtHER
MINDING YOUR MEMORY

In the interest of full disclosure, we admit it: Our favorite method for maintaining, and even boosting, your memory is to indulge in the brain games and exercises found in *Mind Stretchers*. But, as it happens, there's also a wide variety of additional ways in which to work on this important aspect of your brain health. Here are just a few suggestions:

Catch a whiff At your local health food store, purchase a bottle of either rosemary or basil essential oil. Tests of brain waves show that inhaling either of these scents increases the production of beta waves, which indicate heightened awareness. Just put a dab of the oil on your hair, wrists, or clothing—as you would with perfume or cologne.

Sound out the problem Listen to music often and sample various types. Researchers have found that listening to music can improve your ability to concentrate and help you remember what you've learned. Some types of music actually cause brain neurons to fire more quickly; the faster the beat, the more the brain responds.

Count on caffeine If you drink caffeinated beverages, you'll get a short-term boost in your ability to concentrate, and possibly longer-lasting benefits as well. In addition, these benefits appear to increase as you get older. A research study in Portugal concluded that elderly people who drink three or four cups of coffee a day were less likely to experience memory loss than people who drank a cup a day or less.

Give it oxygen #1 Take 120 milligrams of ginkgo biloba a day. This herb appears to improve blood flow to the brain, which helps brain cells get the oxygen they need to perform at their peak. This regimen is particularly helpful if you have diminished blood flow to the brain. If taking anticoagulants, do not use ginkgo biloba before checking with your doctor.

Give it oxygen #2 Another way to increase the flow of blood to the brain is with exercise. Any type of exercise, but especially aerobic exercise like walking or biking, seems to increase the number of nerve cells in the brain. It also helps prevent diabetes, stroke, and high blood pressure, all of which can contribute to memory lapses.

De-stress Find ways to reduce stress. Tension increases the level of stress hormones in the body and, over time, these hormones can affect the hippocampus—the part of the brain that controls memory. Yoga, meditation, and similar activities are proven to reduce the level of stress hormones, but any activity that's simple and fun is beneficial—from swinging in a hammock to playing with your children or grandchildren.

★★ Line Drawing

Draw two straight lines, each from one edge of the square to another edge, so that the sum of the numbers in each of the three regions is the same.

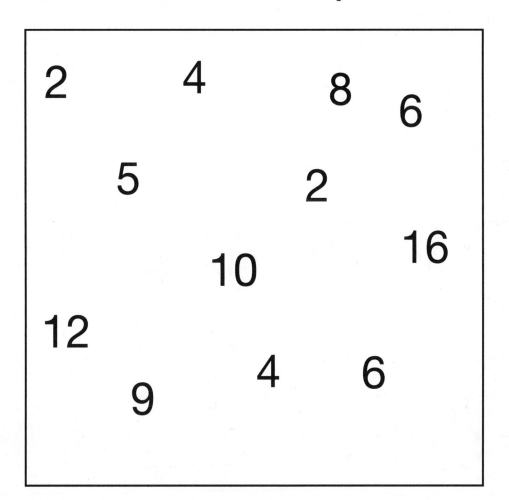

THREE OF A KIND

Find the three hidden words in the sentence that go together in some way.

The midnight train to Thailand leaves now.

★ ABC

Enter the letters A, B, and C into the diagram so that each row and column has exactly one A, one B, and one C. The letters outside the diagram indicate the first letter encountered, moving in the direction of the arrow. Keep in mind that after all the letters have been filled in, there will be one blank box in each row and column.

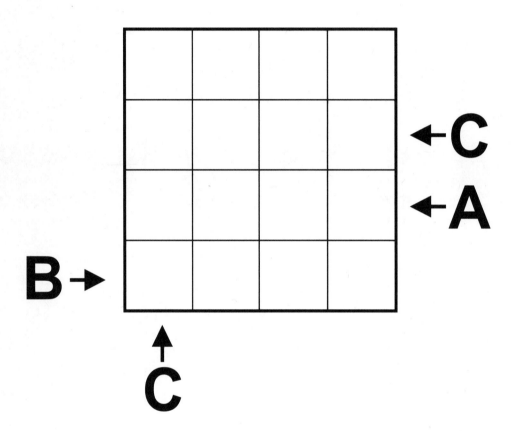

NATIONAL TREASURE

Find the one common four-letter word starting with Y that can be formed from the letters in KENYAN.

— — — —

★ That's the Price by Gail Grabowski

ACROSS

1 Big pig
4 British fellow
8 Camel's South American cousin
13 Magic-spell opener
15 Regulation
16 Wild West movie
17 Wander
18 China's continent
19 Hindu guru
20 Underwater explosive
23 Silent assent
24 Trembled
25 Like half-melted snow
27 Shouts for the matador
29 Female relatives
32 Banned insecticide, for short
35 Reason to close a window
38 Folklore bridge guard
39 Honolulu's island
41 Distant
42 Capital of Norway
43 Like potato chips
45 Pass, as legislation
48 Recipe abbreviation
49 Creek
51 Verse writer
53 Laundry appliances
56 Cooked in oil
59 Your and my
61 Simple drawing of a person
64 Pier
66 Sound quality
67 Important times
68 State-run game
69 One of the Great Lakes
70 Frolic
71 See-through
72 Stage-show backgrounds
73 Speak

DOWN

1 Like a rock
2 Woodwind instruments
3 Pictorial diagram
4 Saltine
5 "Keep quiet!"
6 False name
7 Oyster product
8 Goes ballistic
9 Attorney's expertise
10 No matter what
11 Interoffice note
12 Desertlike
14 Playground retort
21 Phone button
22 Rev, as an engine
26 War honoree
28 Strongbox relative
30 Right-angle shapes
31 Sow's supper
32 Physicians, informally
33 Pub missile
34 Decidedly inferior
36 Ceiling fixture
37 Golf hazard
40 Computer operator
44 Buys, as merchandise
46 Beverages from beans
47 Actress Hatcher
50 Got together
52 Striped feline
54 Ceremonies
55 Win a point
57 Italian coins
58 Serious play
59 Barn birds
60 "Now we're in trouble!"
62 Create with yarn
63 Catch sight of
65 Hwy.

★★ Five by Five

Group the 25 numbers in the grid into five sets of five, with each set having all of the numbers 1 through 5. The numbers in each set must all be connected to each other by a common horizontal or vertical side.

BETWEENER

What three-letter word belongs between the word at left and the word at right, so that the first and second word, and the second and third word, each form a common compound word?

CORN __ __ __ WEB

★ Shopping Center Whodunit

Solve this mystery by discovering which one of these six suspects, six weapons, and six locations is missing from the diagram. The others are all hidden either across, down, or diagonally. The individual words of all multiple-word answers are hidden separately. Ignore words contained within parentheses.

ARCHIE (the) ASSISTANT
BARBIE (the) BARGAIN BUYER
CATHY (the) CASHIER
COSIMA (at the) COSMETICS
 COUNTER
MANUEL (the) MANAGER
PERDITA (the) PERSONAL SHOPPER

BELT
COAT HANGER
ELBOW
HEAVY HANDBAG
SHARP NAILS
SHOPPING BASKET

BASEMENT
BOUTIQUE
CAFÉ
DEPARTMENT STORE
ESCALATOR
FITTING ROOM

```
B A S E M E E T Z E B G V B D N A H C E E
L E U N A M N L R S G N N V A B I O O I L
D S T O A E W O M C A S H I E R S U U H B
T E K E M I T A O A B G L L P M B O N C O
Y P P E K S K S O L D U B J E P I I T R W
E H S A S S I S T A N T Y T H R O S F A C
L A T B R M A E B T A B I E A E E H R O T
B D F A C T F B E O H C A H L G P E S S L
O N M R C A M Q B R S V S R A A T I G T E
X E A B C A R E R E Y U B N G N M C I O B
E U Q I T U O B N S H T A C U A S H A R P
H R B E L C U C I T E M S O C M I J N F C
H E A V H S Y O T A L A C S E M A N U E F
```

INITIAL REACTION

Identify the well-known proverb from the first letters in each of its words.

D. C. H. I. M. _____

★ Find the Ships

Determine the position of the 10 ships listed to the right of the diagram. The ships may be oriented either horizontally or vertically. A square with wavy lines indicates water and will not contain a ship. The numbers at the edge of the diagram indicate how many squares in that row or column contain parts of ships. When all 10 ships are correctly placed in the diagram, no two of them will touch each other, not even diagonally.

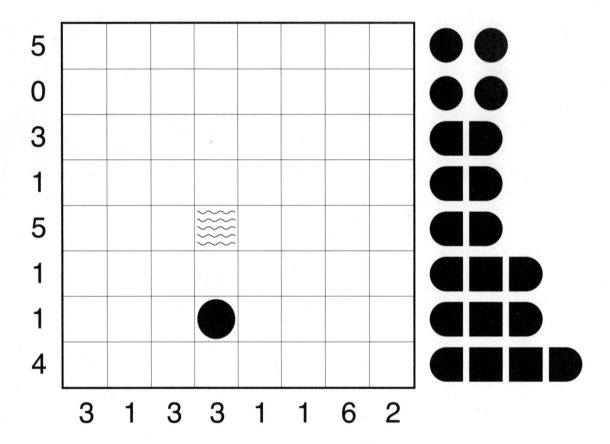

TWO-BY-FOUR

The eight letters in the word MENTALLY can be rearranged to form a pair of common four-letter words in only one way, if no four-letter word is repeated. Can you find the two words?

— — — —   — — — —

★★ Sudoku

Fill in the blank boxes so that every row, column, and 3x3 box contains all of the numbers 1 to 9.

3	4	9	1	8	7	6	5	2
2	7	5	4	3	6	1	9	8
6	1	8	5	9	2	7	3	4
1	8	6	9	7	5	4	2	3
7	3	2	6	4	8	9	1	5
5	9	4	3	2	1	8	6	7
9	2	3	8	1	4	5	7	6
4	6	1	7	5	3	2	8	9
8	5	7	2	6	9	3	4	1

MIXAGRAMS

Each line contains a five-letter word and a four-letter word that have been mixed together (the order of the letters in each word has not been changed). Unmix the two words on each line and write them in the spaces provided. When you're done, find a two-part answer to the clue by reading down the letter columns in the answers.

CLUE: Presidential home

S H O P A F T E N = _ _ _ _ _ + _ _ _ _

S P Y L A P P A H = _ _ _ _ _ + _ _ _ _

F A D R O P E T E = _ _ _ _ _ + _ _ _ _

D E S K M I M U R = _ _ _ _ _ + _ _ _ _

★ Down the Tubes by Sally R. Stein

ACROSS

1 Swampy areas
5 Removes, as one's hat
10 Polite term of address
14 Tulsa's loc.
15 Actress Roberts
16 Female voice range
17 Fearsome dinosaur, for short
18 Attacked by a bee
19 Horse-hoof sound
20 Vietnamese capital
22 Fawns' mothers
23 Donut feature
24 At an earlier time
26 Menial
27 Redeem one's chips
30 Table border
33 Confront boldly
34 Nosy ones
39 Comedian Laurel
40 News summary
42 Days before holidays
43 Not at all interesting
45 Run in
47 Special-interest grp.
48 Tours of duty
49 Gallon fraction
53 Carryall bags
55 Counteract
56 Circle of light
58 "Get out!"
62 On the summit of
63 Surprise greatly
65 Honolulu's island
66 On __ (burning)
67 Green citrus fruits
68 Pizza orders
69 Service charges
70 Run out, as a subscription
71 Shade trees

DOWN

1 This one and that one
2 Gumbo ingredient
3 Secluded valley
4 Tubular musical instrument
5 FM station employees
6 Perform better than
7 Tubular light source
8 Monetary penalty
9 Droops
10 Like he-men
11 Give the OK for
12 South Seas spot
13 Feeling blue
21 Part of the eye
25 Opening remarks
26 Zodiac lion
27 Performing group
28 Overture follower
29 Leave a mark on
31 High-tech "fingerprint"
32 Overshoot
35 Tubular submarine device
36 Tied in score
37 Take a breather
38 Retired jets: Abbr.
41 Letter pair in "pummel"
44 Took a breather
46 Numbered rds.
49 Hearty drink
50 Open, as shoelaces
51 Really like
52 Lassos
54 Flows slowly
56 Foyer
57 "What __ mind reader?"
59 Train line
60 "Excuse me!"
61 Tousle, as hair
64 Language suffix

★ Square Routes

Fill in the blank circles so that every row, column, and path contains all of the numbers from 1 to 5.

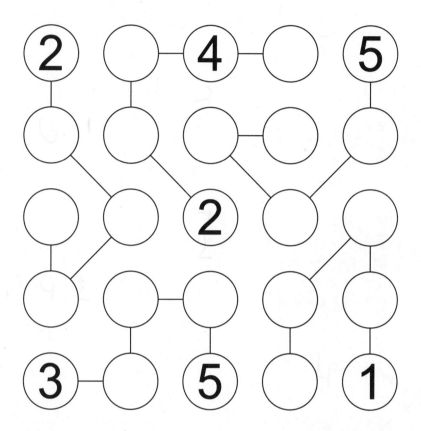

WRONG IS RIGHT

Which of these four words is misspelled?

A) somnolent   B) sojourn

C) sourkraut   D) soiree

★★ Triad Split Decisions

In this clueless crossword puzzle, each answer consists of two words whose spellings are the same, except for the consecutive letters given. All answers are common words; no phrases or hyphenated or capitalized words are used. Some of the clues may have more than one solution, but there is only one word pair that will correctly link up with all the other word pairs.

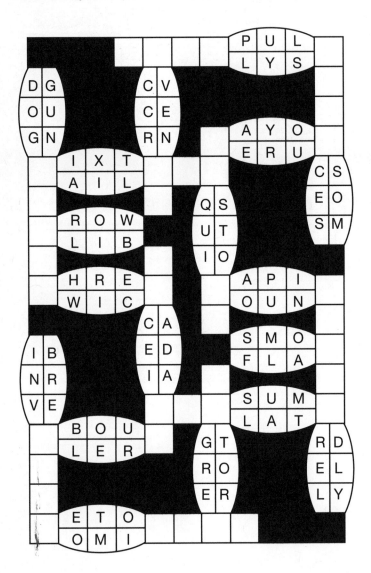

TRANSDELETION

Delete one letter from the word LAPSED and rearrange the rest, to get a courtroom term.

_____

★ 123

Fill in the diagram so that each rectangular piece has one each of the numbers 1, 2, and 3, under these rules: 1) No two adjacent squares, horizontally or vertically, can have the same number. 2) Each completed row and column of the diagram will have an equal number of 1's, 2's, and 3's.

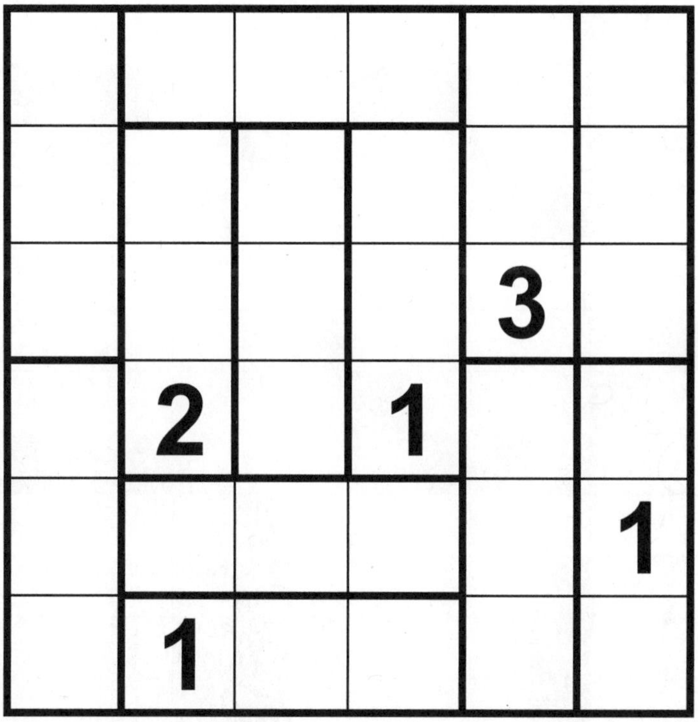

SUDOKU SUM

Fill in the missing numbers from 1 to 9, so that the sum of each row and column is as indicated.

	16	14	15
16		2	
18			4
11	1		

★ Jury Duty by Sally R. Stein

ACROSS

1 Golfer's shout
5 Slender
9 Postage purchase
14 Tel __, Israel
15 Change the decor of
16 Spooky
17 Painter Salvador
18 Very much
19 Place for a cummerbund
20 Winter vehicle
21 Prepare to reach a verdict
23 Adam and Eve's home
25 College website suffix
26 Like most store-bought soups
29 Paramedic's technique: Abbr.
31 "Hey you!"
35 Author Jong
36 No longer shackled
38 Your and my
39 Courtroom questioner
42 Insect in a colony
43 Alphabetizes
44 Is in first place
45 Sunbeams
47 Compass point opposite SSW
48 Confidential
49 French "yes"
51 On the __ (separately)
52 Trial's written record
57 Ocean liner, for one
61 Singer Lena
62 Poems of praise
63 Not in danger
64 Make a change to
65 Boyfriend
66 "Anything __?"
67 Eagles' homes
68 Wyatt of the Old West
69 Entryway

DOWN

1 Brief crazes
2 Flattened circle
3 Make angry
4 Data seen by a jury
5 Swapped
6 __ of Troy (mythical abductee)
7 Admired one
8 Phrase of denial
9 Stitched
10 Rip to shreds
11 Operatic solo
12 Fine rain
13 Tennis pro Sampras
22 Parisian cap
24 College officials
26 Aromatic wood
27 Sports venue
28 "Swell!"
29 Box for oranges
30 Poodles and parakeets
32 Sub tracking device
33 Shoe material
34 On-the-sly meeting
36 Office plant
37 Parceled (out)
40 __ boom (jet sound)
41 Took a break from court
46 Shakespearean poetic form
48 Starts to get out of bed
50 Computer owners
51 Harpoon
52 As compared to
53 Part to play
54 __ and crafts
55 After-bath wrap
56 Creative thought
58 Symbol of saintliness
59 In that case
60 Jury member

★ Number-Out

Shade squares so that no number appears in any row or column more than once. Shaded squares may not touch each other horizontally or vertically, and all unshaded squares must form a single continuous area.

1	3	4	3	2
5	1	5	4	3
2	3	5	2	2
2	4	5	5	1
2	5	3	2	5

THINK ALIKE

Unscramble the letters in the phrase POURS LYE to form two words with the same or similar meanings.

_____ _____

★ Looped Path

Draw a continuous, unbroken loop that passes through each orange and yellow square exactly once. Move from square to square in a straight line or by turning left or right, but never diagonally.

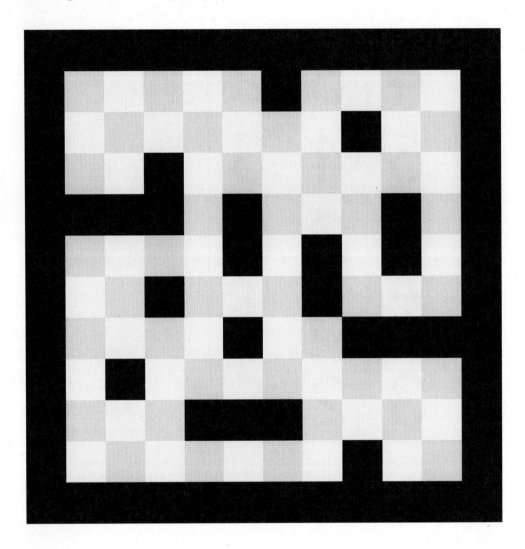

SAY IT AGAIN

What three-letter word can be either a type of tool or a past-tense verb?

— — —

★ Get-Together

Find these "assembled" words that are hidden in the diagram, either across, down, or diagonally.

```
C  N  F  E  C  O  M  P  O  U  N  D  S  H  J
O  O  F  R  T  E  Z  I  N  R  E  T  A  R  F
A  I  M  U  A  A  A  M  I  P  I  H  S  M  U
L  S  E  B  S  T  R  L  Y  T  A  B  S  E  S
I  U  L  M  I  D  E  E  L  R  O  L  O  R  A
T  F  G  M  T  N  L  R  M  O  M  E  R  G  E
I  E  N  S  I  D  A  O  N  O  Y  N  T  Y  L
O  N  I  B  E  X  N  T  K  I  L  D  M  S  D
B  U  M  M  F  I  S  T  I  R  S  G  E  U  E
W  O  R  E  Z  K  A  L  L  O  A  V  N  F  M
C  P  E  E  T  S  U  N  I  L  N  I  T  O  E
M  M  T  N  O  I  T  I  L  A  O  C  R  S  C
I  O  N  I  C  H  N  O  Q  N  U  F  U  S  G
U  C  I  X  L  W  Z  U  M  I  S  F  U  S  M
```

ALLOY
ASSORTMENT
BLEND
COALITION
COMBINATION
COMBINE
COMPOUND
CONGLOMERATE
FRATERNIZE
FUSE
FUSION
HARMONIZE
INTERMINGLE
MEDLEY
MERGE
MIX
STIR
UNION
UNITE
WHISK

WHO'S WHAT WHERE?

The correct term for a resident of Canton, Ohio, is:

A) Cantonese   B) Cantonite
C) Cantonian   D) Cantoner

★ Portions by Gail Grabowski

ACROSS

1 Piece of dining-room furniture
6 Alphabet intro
10 Corn holders
14 Same-old
15 Window section
16 Biblical paradise
17 Obstructing progress, informally
19 Ship of 1492
20 Toward the stern
21 Electrical unit
22 For all audiences, as a movie
24 Violin holder
25 "Wish you __ here"
26 Author Louisa May
29 Rooted for
32 Worth
33 Parts of socks
34 Get ready, casually
36 Computer image
37 Misfortune
38 Tiny quantity
39 Fender-bender result
40 Invoice
41 Passover feast
42 Excavates further
44 Kitchen gadgets
45 "American Beauty" flower
46 Stubborn animal
47 Floor covering
50 Look for
51 Sighs of relief
54 Region
55 Qualify for a team
58 Docking site
59 Just __ (slightly)
60 Sports complex
61 Pretzel topper
62 Butterfly catchers
63 Delicious

DOWN

1 Sandwich fish
2 Starting from
3 Intrude, with "in"
4 __-di-dah
5 Lift up
6 Orchard fruit
7 Fishhook attachment
8 Larry King's channel
9 Thermometer markings
10 Object displayed on a 1 Across
11 *Garfield* dog
12 Road curve
13 Unforeseen problem
18 In need of directions
23 "__ we there yet?"
24 Analogous thing
25 Roulette device
26 Eager
27 Secured, as a skate
28 Exact copy
29 Chills down
30 Wear down
31 Discourage
33 String for packing
35 Golfers' goals
40 Bridegroom's attendant
41 Formal head covering
43 "The Raven" author
44 Song for two
46 Track events
47 Toothpaste-tube tops
48 Opera solo
49 Fishing-line holder
50 Variety-show segment
51 High cards
52 Pursue
53 Remain
56 "Honest" president
57 Historic time

★★ One-Way Streets

The diagram represents a pattern of streets. A and B are parking spaces, and the black squares are stores. Find a route that starts at A, passes through all stores exactly once, and ends at B. Arrows indicate one-way traffic for that block only. No block or intersection may be entered more than once.

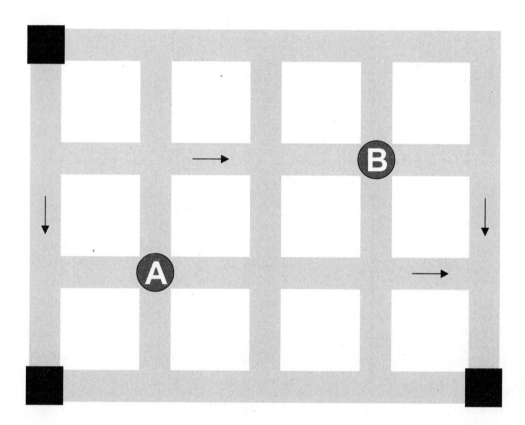

SOUND THINKING

There is only one common uncapitalized word whose consonant sounds are B, D, N, and T, in that order. What is it?

_____

★ Hyper-Sudoku

Fill in the blank boxes so that every row, column, 3x3 box, *and* each of the four 3x3 gray regions contains all of the numbers 1 to 9.

	2	5	9	6			8	
8	9		7			5	6	2
	3			8		4		
	4		5					6
5		7	1					
		8					5	3
6		3						
9			6	1			3	
1	8						7	9

CENTURY MARKS

Select one number in each of the four columns so that the total adds up to exactly 100.

$$\boxed{\begin{matrix} 31 \\ 20 \end{matrix}} + \boxed{\begin{matrix} 21 \\ 11 \end{matrix}} + \boxed{\begin{matrix} 50 \\ 25 \end{matrix}} + \boxed{\begin{matrix} 22 \\ 23 \end{matrix}} = 100$$

★ Star Search

Find the stars that are hidden in some of the blank squares. The numbered squares indicate how many stars are hidden in the squares adjacent to them (including diagonally). There is never more than one star in any square.

			1						
		2			4	3	3		
		3					2		
	1				3				
		3							2
	2					2	3		
		1			1				

CHOICE WORDS

Form three six-letter words from the same category, by selecting one letter from each column three times. Each letter will be used exactly once.

B	E	R	G	L	S	__ __ __ __ __ __
H	A	D	A	S	E	__ __ __ __ __ __
N	A	T	T	E	R	__ __ __ __ __ __

★ Punctuation Piece by Gail Grabowski

ACROSS

1 Arrest, slangily
5 Breakfast bread
10 Petty quarrel
14 Prefix for freeze
15 Think alike
16 Boxcar rider
17 Light-rail car
18 Move on hands and knees
19 Approximately
20 Endure a bad situation
23 Musical drama
24 Wooden pin
25 Sharp knock
28 "Absolutely!"
29 Cow sounds
33 Fix, as an appliance
35 Enthusiasm
37 Chauffeured vehicle
38 Shelving supports
42 Elaborate party
43 Fraction of a minute
44 Debris
47 Words of denial
48 Early afternoon hour
51 Spanish river
52 Teacup handle
54 Uproar
56 Interval of delay
61 Units of current
63 Lesser of two ___
64 Competent
65 Faucet problem
66 Track events
67 Impolite glance
68 Brings to a halt
69 Icy precipitation
70 Tax-form IDs

DOWN

1 Baseball aide
2 Not ready for picking
3 Ohio and Oregon
4 Stopwatch, for example
5 Dashboard device, for short
6 Fairy-tale monster
7 Mideast native
8 Clinch, as a deal
9 Bank employee
10 Loafer or moccasin
11 Painting of a person
12 Belly muscles
13 Also
21 West Florida city
22 Sweater size: Abbr.
26 Goals
27 Country-club instructor
30 Salad-dressing ingredient
31 Spheres
32 Ambulance sound
34 Implored
35 Wild guess
36 Folded tortilla
38 Hawaiian island
39 Skateboarder's arm protection
40 Portable bed
41 Steak-cutting utensil
42 Doberman's warning
45 Hawaiian neckwear
46 Restaurant patrons
48 Native American groups
49 Made from sheep hair
50 Selects from the menu
53 Competitor
55 Russian mountains
57 Poses a question
58 Good-natured
59 Happy feeling
60 Hushed "Hey!"
61 Pub beverage
62 Guys

★ ABC

Enter the letters A, B, and C into the diagram so that each row and column has exactly one A, one B, and one C. The letters outside the diagram indicate the first letter encountered, moving in the direction of the arrow. Keep in mind that after all the letters have been filled in, there will be one blank box in each row and column.

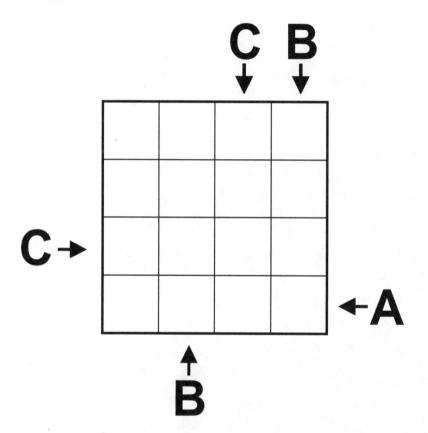

CLUELESS CROSSWORD

Complete the crossword with common uncapitalized seven-letter words, based entirely on the letters already filled in for you.

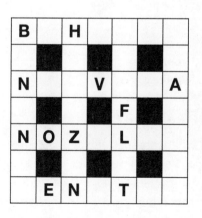

★★ Sequence Maze

Enter the maze, pass through all the color squares exactly once, then exit, all without retracing your path. You may not pass through two squares of the same color consecutively.

BETWEENER

What three-letter word belongs between the word at left and the word at right, so that the first and second word, and the second and third word, each form a common compound word?

LUNCH __ __ __ CAR

★★ Sudoku

Fill in the blank boxes so that every row, column, and 3x3 box contains all of the numbers 1 to 9.

		4	2					
	8		7	3			2	
		5	8			1		9
						9	7	5
	1						4	
8	5	6						
2		9			8	3		
	7			5	2		9	
					6	7		

MIXAGRAMS

Each line contains a five-letter word and a four-letter word that have been mixed together (the order of the letters in each word has not been changed). Unmix the two words on each line and write them in the spaces provided. When you're done, find a two-part answer to the clue by reading down the letter columns in the answers.

CLUE: Arguer's desire

L A W D A R L E D = _ _ _ _ _ + _ _ _ _

O A S U S C H E T = _ _ _ _ _ + _ _ _ _

S R C E N T E S T = _ _ _ _ _ + _ _ _ _

D U T I E D A L T = _ _ _ _ _ + _ _ _ _

★ In Place by Shirley Soloway

ACROSS

1 Oil cartel
5 Choral voices
10 Retired fast planes: Abbr.
14 Nothing, in Spain
15 Doozy
16 Milky gem
17 Exact duplicate
18 Two-stripe soldier, for short
19 Store event
20 Extremely happy
23 Electrified fish
24 Prefix meaning "three"
25 __ Moines, IA
28 German auto
31 Act testy with
36 "... __ saw Elba"
38 Fork prong
40 Road bend
41 Neither left nor right, politically
44 Florida city
45 __ of the above
46 In the center of
47 Most sensible
49 Sunbeams
51 Like a fox
52 Occupied a chair
54 Pull with force
56 Lowest-priority "location"
65 Vicinity
66 Be very fond of
67 "__ want for Christmas is ..."
68 Cultured fellow
69 One who doesn't mingle
70 Smith or Jones
71 Carbonated drink
72 Lauder of cosmetics
73 "That's too bad!"

DOWN

1 Not fooled by
2 Lowly chess piece
3 Prepare for publication
4 Lake boat
5 Unrestricted
6 Table extension
7 Sour-tasting
8 __ to (should)
9 Controls the wheel
10 Mediocre
11 Practice boxing
12 Statuesque
13 Snow vehicle
21 Pod veggie
22 Flinch
25 Floor models
26 Author Jong
27 Four-door car
29 Singer Celine
30 Due to get
32 Mystic glow
33 Gym dances
34 To no __ (useless)
35 Stuffed bear
37 Not doing anything
39 Sicilian volcano
42 Lariat
43 Informal greeting
48 "Hot" Mexican food
50 Take to court
53 Ruckuses
55 West African nation
56 Vacuum-cleaner supplies
57 Black-and-white cookie
58 Be disposed (to)
59 Informal farewell
60 Typeface
61 Family diagram
62 Mideast airline
63 __ mater
64 Fruity desserts

★★ Line Drawing

Draw three straight lines, each from one edge of the square to another edge, so that the letters in each of the six regions form a word.

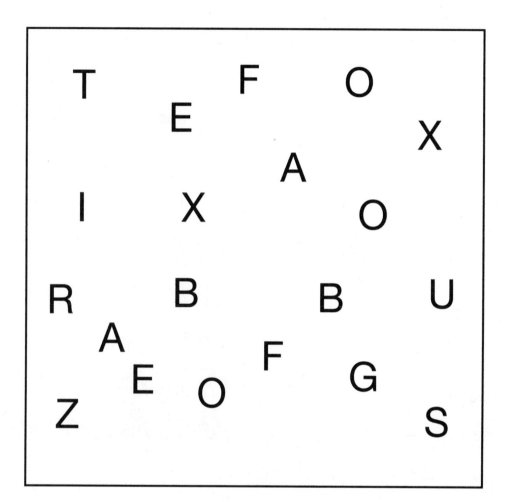

THREE OF A KIND

Find the three hidden words in the sentence that go together in some way.

To our dismay, bedlam ensued when our eyes opened.

★★ Find the Ships

Determine the position of the 10 ships listed to the right of the diagram. The ships may be oriented either horizontally or vertically. A square with wavy lines indicates water and will not contain a ship. The numbers at the edge of the diagram indicate how many squares in that row or column contain parts of ships. When all 10 ships are correctly placed in the diagram, no two of them will touch each other, not even diagonally.

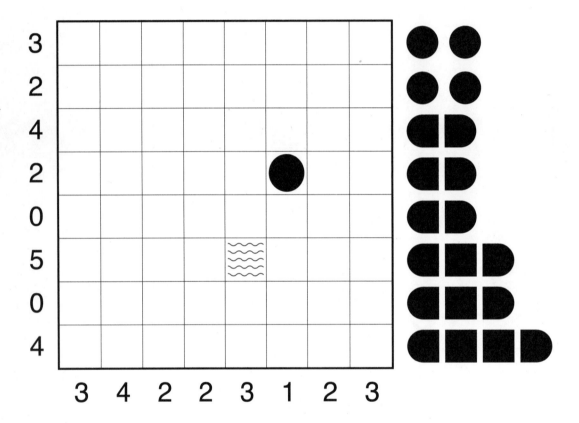

TWO-BY-FOUR

The eight letters in the word NOBILITY can be rearranged to form a pair of common four-letter words in only one way. Can you find the two words?

— — — —   — — — —

★ Square Routes

Fill in the blank circles so that every row, column, and path contains all of the numbers from 1 to 5.

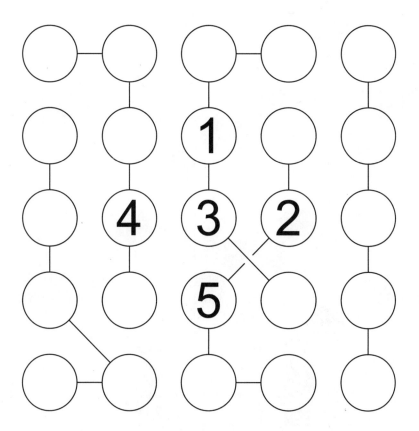

ADDITION SWITCH

Switch the positions of two of the digits in the incorrect sum at right, to get a correct sum.	4 6 2 + 3 1 5 ———— 6 7 8

★ Noisemakers by Sally R. Stein

ACROSS

1 Obtains
5 Wine barrel
9 Club regulation
14 Hard to find
15 Sandwich-cookie name
16 Rental document
17 Tucson's loc.
18 The Dalai __
19 Bulletin-board fasteners
20 Noisy winter vehicle
23 Take a break
24 That lady
25 Seasons, as popcorn
27 Household cleaning chemical
31 Noisy fight
35 Caviar source
36 Sgts., for example
39 "Sorry, __ at the office"
40 Noisy kitchen appliance
44 Collective-bargaining group
45 Chair or bench
46 Office neckwear
47 Ritzy residence
49 Seafood servings with shells
52 Dentist's concerns
55 Work-wk. start, usually
56 Software purchaser
59 Noisy gardening machine
64 End of a fable
66 Adam's second son
67 Great review
68 Item's cost
69 Location
70 Adam's home
71 War horse
72 Incoming-plane stats.

73 Mailed away

DOWN

1 Mardi __
2 Have coming
3 Threesome
4 "Oh, yeah?"
5 Dye, for instance
6 Jordanian or Saudi
7 Tourney rounds
8 Bearlike Australian beast
9 Crunchy sandwich, for short
10 Way back when
11 Doily material
12 Inquires

13 Toward sunset
21 Guys
22 Santa's helper
26 Excursion
27 Engage in debate
28 Complains
29 Have coming
30 Experts
32 Social stratum
33 To no __ (ineffective)
34 Monica of tennis
37 Type of poem
38 Thailand's former name
41 Competition on the water

42 Penny-__ poker
43 Loses one's footing
48 "Electric" fish
50 Note after fa
51 Makes noise while sleeping
53 Make fun of
54 Customary practice
56 Baseball officials
57 Prepare, as laundry
58 A Great Lake
60 Greek cheese
61 Walk through water
62 __-steven (tied)
63 Apartment payment
65 Showed the way

★★ Mail Call

From the comments below, match each postman with the dog he meets on his route.

SMALL CHANGE

Change one letter in each of these two words, to form a common two-word phrase.

REST TUNE

_____

★★ 123

Fill in the diagram so that each rectangular piece has one each of the numbers 1, 2, and 3, under these rules: 1) No two adjacent squares, horizontally or vertically, can have the same number. 2) Each completed row and column of the diagram will have an equal number of 1's, 2's, and 3's.

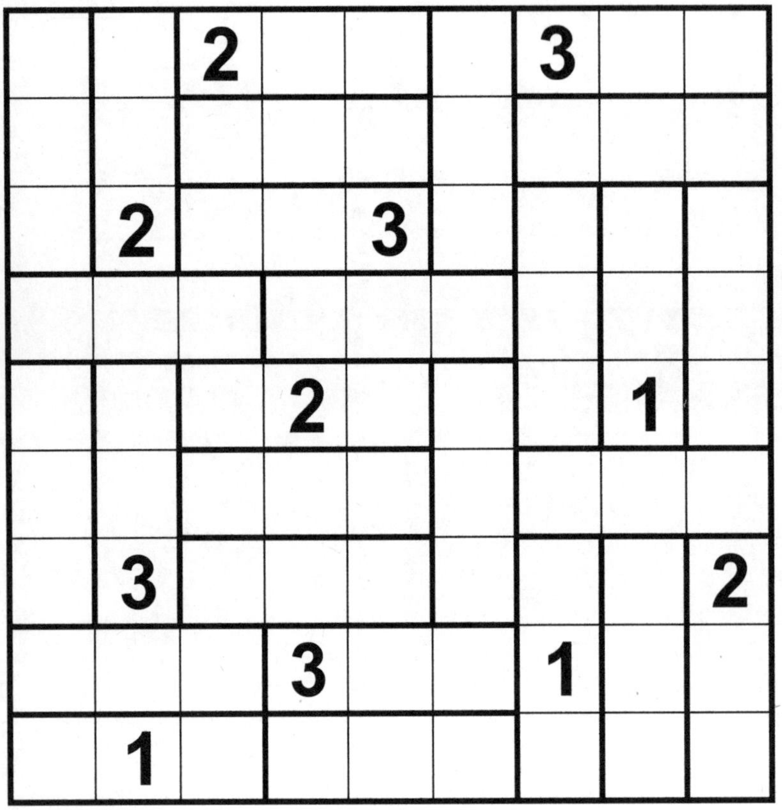

		2				3		
	2			3				
			2				1	
	3							2
			3			1		
	1							

WRONG IS RIGHT

Which of these four words is misspelled?

A) pursuade   B) pursue

C) purview   D) purloin

★ Number-Out

Shade squares so that no number appears in any row or column more than once. Shaded squares may not touch each other horizontally or vertically, and all unshaded squares must form a single continuous area.

2	2	5	1	4
1	2	3	1	5
5	2	4	3	3
5	5	5	2	3
3	4	2	5	3

THINK ALIKE

Unscramble the letters in the phrase SHUCK HAT to form two words with the same or similar meanings.

_____   _____

★ Piano Parts by Gail Grabowski

ACROSS

1 Circus routines
5 __ and proper
9 Washbowl
14 Barbecue rod
15 Artificial bait
16 Dwelling
17 Female singing voice
18 China's continent
19 Reschedule for later
20 Trick somebody
23 Little bit
24 Watermelon throwaways
25 Catch some Z's
27 V-shaped cut
30 Types of chickens
33 Not used
36 Catches, rodeo-style
38 Family auto
39 Chimps and orangutans
41 Painting or sculpture
42 Computer input
43 Harvests
45 Tureen fillers
48 Once around a track
49 Breakfast bowlful
51 Nosy one
53 Ranchland measures
55 Have confidence in
58 Trim the lawn
60 "Caps Lock" or "Print Screen"
64 Pop singer Baker
66 "So what __ is new?"
67 Cone-bearing tree
68 Bicycle wheels
69 Impolite glance
70 Explorer Ponce de __
71 Locomotive power
72 Scottish girl
73 Makes mistakes

DOWN

1 Pronto, in a memo
2 Slightly above-average grade
3 Book's name
4 Acquired illegally
5 Expects one will
6 Sneaky scheme
7 Spring flower
8 Lunch and dinner
9 Annoys persistently
10 Lincoln nickname
11 Tone down, as a statement
12 Creative thought
13 Dweeb
21 Scent
22 North Pole aide
26 Looked at
28 IRS-form experts
29 Long sandwiches
31 Pro __ (proportionally)
32 Break sharply
33 Drug-fighting cop
34 Sporting sword
35 Put on hidden recording gear
37 Astonish
40 Blueprint detail, briefly
44 Harsh commentary
46 Ceramic artisans
47 Angry
50 Summer zodiac sign
52 Lavender's color
54 Scent
56 Slalom contestant
57 Male singing voice
58 Wrestling surfaces
59 Step __ (hurry)
61 Not guilty, for one
62 Takes advantage of
63 Hankerings
65 Coffee alternative

★★ Tanks a Lot

Enter the maze somewhere at right, pass over all tanks from behind (thereby destroying them), then exit. You may not pass through any square more than once, and may not enter a square in the line of fire of a tank you have not yet destroyed.

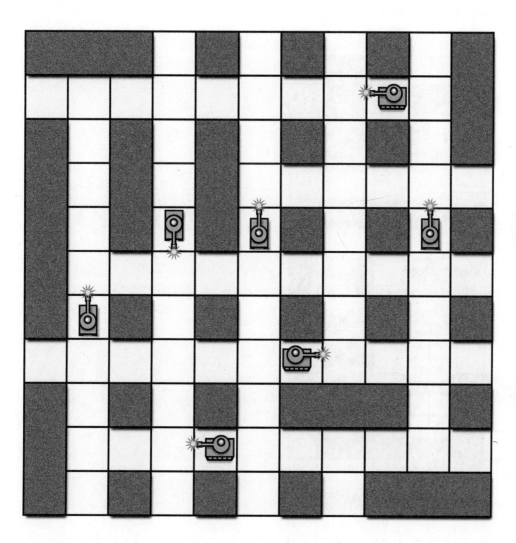

SAY IT AGAIN

What three-letter word can mean either "unfashionable" or "unconscious"?

— — —

★★ Split Decisions

In this clueless crossword puzzle, each answer consists of two words whose spellings are the same, except for the consecutive letters given. All answers are common words; no phrases or hyphenated or capitalized words are used. Some of the clues may have more than one solution, but there is only one word pair that will correctly link up with all the other word pairs.

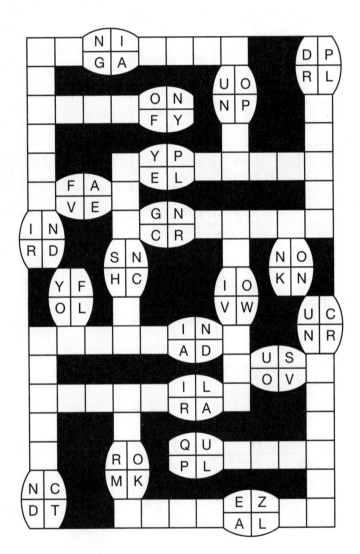

TRANSDELETION

Delete one letter from the word AVERRED and rearrange the rest, to get a type of book.

_____

★ Hyper-Sudoku

Fill in the blank boxes so that every row, column, 3x3 box, *and* each of the four 3x3 gray regions contains all of the numbers 1 to 9.

1	3	4		6		9	5	2
	5	9	4	2	1		6	
	8			9	5	3	4	
4					9			5
			5					9
9	1	5		7			8	
	9	3				5	9	
5			9	3	2	4		
						2		3

MIXAGRAMS

Each line contains a five-letter word and a four-letter word that have been mixed together (the order of the letters in each word has not been changed). Unmix the two words on each line and write them in the spaces provided. When you're done, find a two-part answer to the clue by reading down the letter columns in the answers.

CLUE: Feathery talker

S H O T B O R O M = _ _ _ _ _ + _ _ _ _

P E D A N N I S Y = _ _ _ _ _ + _ _ _ _

R A Z E V E R O N = _ _ _ _ _ + _ _ _ _

A L A M E B A D Y = _ _ _ _ _ + _ _ _ _

★ Let It Snow by Sally R. Stein

ACROSS

1 Large barrel
5 Stare, as at the sky
9 Ceramic floor pieces
14 Courtroom statement
15 Operatic solo
16 Battery terminal
17 Hymn ending
18 Swamplands
19 Colossal
20 Performed in a chorus
21 Type of cosmetic
23 Gorillas, for example
25 Point opposite WSW
26 Frightens
29 Makes illegal
31 Sound of an angry dog
34 __ Day (tree-planting celebration)
35 Bridle strap
36 At no cost
37 "Understand?"
40 Soft throw
41 Relatives of mice
42 Cowboy, often
43 Approves
44 "Filet" fish
45 Chardonnay factory
46 Woodcutter's tool
47 Army rank below maj.
48 Cereal selection
53 Short footrace
57 Open, as a knot
58 Soup-can damage
59 Cleveland's state
60 Signals via pager
61 Poker-hand starter
62 Seep
63 Desirable quality
64 Rolling stone's lack
65 Sandwich breads

DOWN

1 Tax experts: Abbr.
2 __ mater
3 Caught a look at
4 Aussie jumpers
5 Social blunders
6 Neighborhoods
7 Metal in brass
8 Make less difficult
9 Eagle claws
10 Very impressed
11 British noble
12 Rim
13 Crystal-ball user
22 Lincoln's coin
24 South American nation
26 __ say (unfortunately)
27 Criminal
28 Bottomless pit
29 Singer Midler
30 Ultimate objectives
31 Complaint
32 Allude (to)
33 Make another attempt
35 Authentic
36 Main entrance
38 Sound of an angry dog
39 Leaky-faucet sound
44 Most secure
45 Squanders
46 Take potshots
47 Lincoln's coins
48 Castro's land
49 Cash-register compartment
50 Highways: Abbr.
51 Abel's father
52 Casino game
54 Nautical greeting
55 Info on a shoebox
56 Farm implements

★ Put-Ons

Find these "wearable" words that are hidden in the diagram, either across, down, or diagonally. (Individual words of multiple-word answers are hidden separately.) There's one additional six-letter answer in the category, not listed below, that's also hidden in the diagram. What's that word?

```
R A C L E R A P P A L
A T L B E S J A E J I
I T O G S P I B N P V
M I T F T O O T F G E
E R H S A R U U F B R
F S E R D T M T S U Y
T B S R I S I N F L M
A N A X U W A G I I E
S W E N O E U V U R T
E U D M J A E T U E F
B A I L P R D T U R S
Y W G T O I U N O A K
R O B E S O U C U I H
T F R O C S K Q M S C
F R I P P E R Y E L K
E S I U G S I D O S I
K D T B R A G T Y G T
B R N N K E H E A A Y
O E O R E I G R T R K
R S I A N M H A E U I
D S H G E R R N L E W
R R S V L O I A B I C
A E A Q B F D O G O A
W G F P M I R U S F M
R A I M E N T T U I P
T L R Z S U U F I N U
K I L A N M K C E E T
D R A R E A T T I R E
E T U A H G E A J B G
```

APPAREL	GEAR
ATTIRE	GET-UP
CLOTHES	HAUTE COUTURE
CLOTHING	JEANS
COSTUME	KIT
DISGUISE	LIVERY
DRAPE	MUFTI
DRESS	RAGS
ENSEMBLE	RAIMENT
EQUIPMENT	REGALIA
FASHION	ROBES
FATIGUES	SPORTSWEAR
FINERY	SUIT
FRIPPERY	SUNDAY BEST
FROCK	TOGS
GARB	UNIFORM
GARMENT	WARDROBE

IN OTHER WORDS

There is only one common uncapitalized word that contains the consecutive letters CTW. What is it?

_____

IT'S NEWS TO ME: NEWSPAPER INSIGHTS

Before the traditional newspaper ceases to exist, we thought we'd share some thoughts about it. On the surface, many of these sound frivolous, but they actually contain some pretty astute observations.

I'm all in favor of keeping dangerous weapons out of the hands of fools. Let's start with typewriters.

—FRANK LLOYD WRIGHT

With the newspaper strike on, I wouldn't consider dying.

—BETTE DAVIS

USA Today has come out with a new survey. Apparently, three out of every four people make up 75 percent of the population.

—DAVID LETTERMAN

Never pick a fight with people who buy ink by the barrel.

—BILL CLINTON

Four hostile newspapers are more to be feared than a thousand bayonets.

—NAPOLEON BONAPARTE

If I want to knock a story off the front page, I just change my hairstyle.

—HILLARY CLINTON

Rage is the only quality which has kept me, or anybody I have ever studied, writing columns for newspapers.

—JIMMY BRESLIN

A free press can, of course, be good or bad, but, most certainly without freedom, the press will never be anything but bad.

—ALBERT CAMUS

A newspaper is lumber made malleable. It is ink made into words and pictures. It is conceived, born, grows up and dies of old age in a day.

—JIM BISHOP

A good newspaper, I suppose, is a nation talking to itself.

—ARTHUR MILLER

★★ One-Way Streets

The diagram represents a pattern of streets. P's are parking spaces, and the black squares are stores. Find the route that starts at a parking space, passes through all stores exactly once, and ends at the other parking space. Arrows indicate one-way traffic for that block only. No block or intersection may be entered more than once.

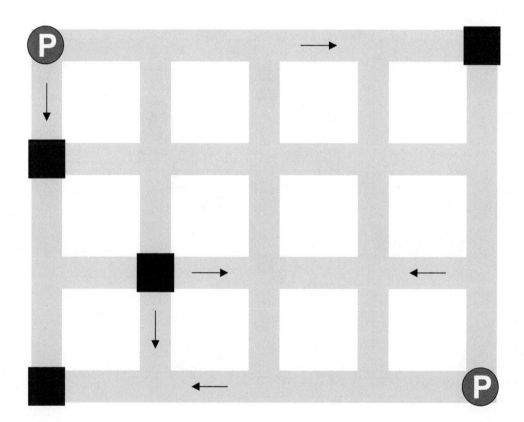

SOUND THINKING

Common words whose consonant sounds are D, F, N, and S include DEFENSE and DEFIANCE. What ten-letter adjective is pronounced with the same consonant sounds in the same order?

_____

★ Put Up with It by Gail Grabowski

ACROSS

1 Explosion
6 Move rapidly
10 Spinning toys
14 Sound from a broadcast
15 Woodwind instrument
16 Each, slangily
17 At a __ (completely stopped)
19 Cabbagelike plant
20 Garment border
21 Song for two
22 Prepared, as potatoes
24 Winter vehicle
25 Flat-topped elevation
26 Faced the pitcher
29 Gives orders
32 Proofreader's find
33 Room coolers
34 Santa syllables
36 Dutch cheese
37 In addition
38 General vicinity
39 Bottled soft drink
40 Grade-school basics
41 Go inside
42 Sort one's trash, perhaps
44 Aspects
45 Roll-call response
46 Apple discard
47 "Mashed" side order
50 Shopping center
51 Relaxing resort
54 Actor Baldwin
55 Approach rapidly
58 Slangy assent
59 Ranchland unit
60 Brutish sort
61 Indefinite amount
62 Tot's "little piggies"
63 Rims

DOWN

1 Big party
2 Minstrel's instrument
3 Eve's spouse
4 Transgression
5 Two-year-old
6 Fussed over, with "on"
7 Just __ (slightly)
8 Fa follower
9 Assistants
10 Buy raffle tickets, for example
11 Milky gem
12 Flag holder
13 Zoomed
18 Took to court
23 Opposite of WNW
24 Overeater's woe
25 Objects to
26 Stinging insects
27 Zeal
28 Make a swap
29 Twist or tango
30 Rich cake
31 Piece of paper
33 Story with a moral
35 Rowboat needs
40 Circus performer
41 Place for ring jewelry
43 So far
44 Make a crease in
46 Is concerned
47 Picks up the tab
48 Toast topping
49 Group of athletes
50 Female horse
51 Unforeseen problem
52 Sit for a portrait
53 Household pests
56 Prefix for system
57 Got married

★★ Sets of Three

Group all the symbols into sets of three, with each set having either all the same shape and three different colors, or all the same color and three different shapes. The symbols in each set must all be connected to each other by a common horizontal or vertical side.

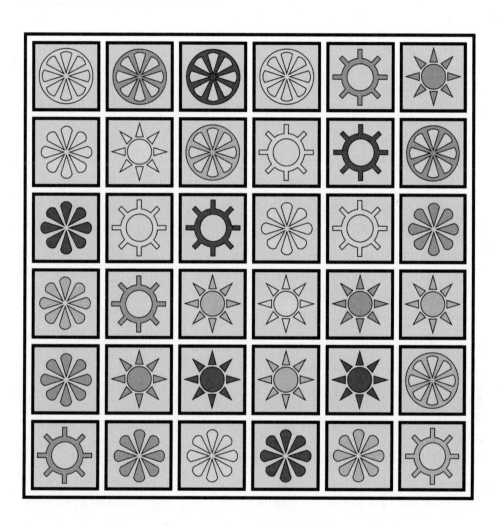

SMALL CHANGE

Change one letter in each of these two words, to form a common two-word phrase.

LOCK SHARK

★★ Star Search

Find the stars that are hidden in some of the blank squares. The numbered squares indicate how many stars are hidden in the squares adjacent to them (including diagonally). There is never more than one star in any square.

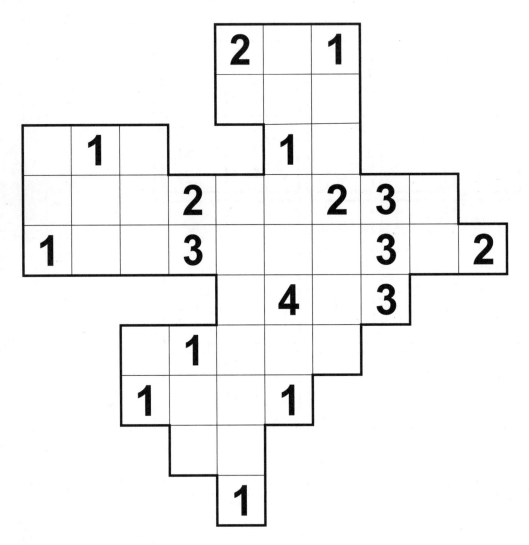

CHOICE WORDS

Form three six-letter words from the same category, by selecting one letter from each column three times. Each letter will be used exactly once.

M	O	N	A	T	E	_ _ _ _ _ _
P	O	L	A	R	E	_ _ _ _ _ _
T	A	L	G	U	S	_ _ _ _ _ _

★★ Triad Split Decisions

In this clueless crossword puzzle, each answer consists of two words whose spellings are the same, except for the consecutive letters given. All answers are common words; no phrases or hyphenated or capitalized words are used. Some of the clues may have more than one solution, but there is only one word pair that will correctly link up with all the other word pairs.

TRANSDELETION

Delete one letter from the word ANALOGY and rearrange the rest, to get a world nation.

_____

★★ Wee Ones by Shirley Soloway

ACROSS

1 Coll. marchers
5 Fragrant wood
10 Smooth-talking
14 Object of admiration
15 Sun-dried brick
16 Performing job
17 Dense-coated dog
20 Oozes
21 Most on one's guard
22 "... baked in __"
25 Comic's show
26 Char
29 1 a.m. to 3 a.m.
35 President before Wilson
36 Stitch's friend in a Disney film
37 Publish
38 Swelled head
39 Got nostalgic about
41 Top-rated record
42 Skip a big wedding
44 Wading bird
45 Fender imperfection
46 Embroidery stitch
48 Therefore
49 Mauna __
50 France, to Caesar
52 When
57 Mount climbed by Moses
61 East-coast seafood
64 Writer Wiesel
65 Moth-to-be
66 Business-letter letters
67 Telephone wire
68 Place a blot on
69 Caterer caller

DOWN

1 Tire holders
2 *Garfield* dog
3 Muscle quality
4 Electronic illustrations
5 Garfield, for one
6 www.tulane.__
7 Kid-vid explorer
8 First shepherd
9 Annul, as a law
10 Quaint caves
11 Mine find
12 Misfortunes
13 Health-food juice source
18 Egyptian snake
19 Exotic flower
23 Catalina or Cuba
24 Actor Estevez
26 Expensive
27 Top Boy Scout rank
28 In progress
30 Suspect's explanation
31 Affectionate
32 Wedding attendant
33 Regretting
34 Brief argument
39 Overhaul the machinery
40 Are: Sp.
43 Was in command in the cockpit
45 Samson's undoing
47 Wall sections
51 UCLA rival
52 Sir __ Guinness
53 Farm structure
54 Agitate
55 Dr. Gray's specialty
56 Lab fluids
58 US alliance
59 $ quantities
60 Does not exist
62 LIII doubled
63 It's north of Okla.

★★ ABC

Enter the letters A, B, and C into the diagram so that each row and column has exactly one A, one B, and one C. The letters outside the diagram indicate the first letter encountered, moving in the direction of the arrow. Keep in mind that after all the letters have been filled in, there will be two blank boxes in each row and column.

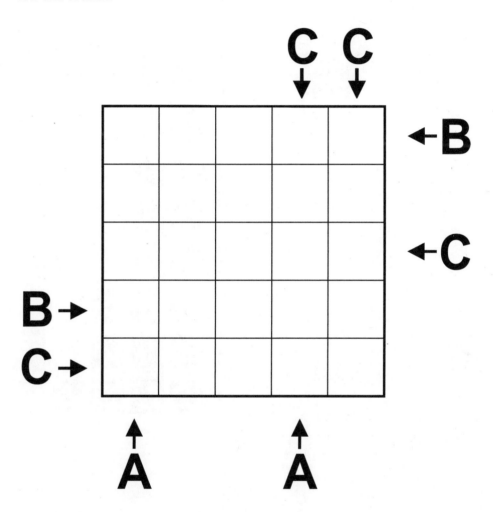

NATIONAL TREASURE

Find the one common four-letter word starting with A that can be formed from the letters in CANADIAN.

— — — —

★★ Find the Ships

Determine the position of the 10 ships listed to the right of the diagram. The ships may be oriented either horizontally or vertically. A square with wavy lines indicates water and will not contain a ship. The numbers at the edge of the diagram indicate how many squares in that row or column contain parts of ships. When all 10 ships are correctly placed in the diagram, no two of them will touch each other, not even diagonally.

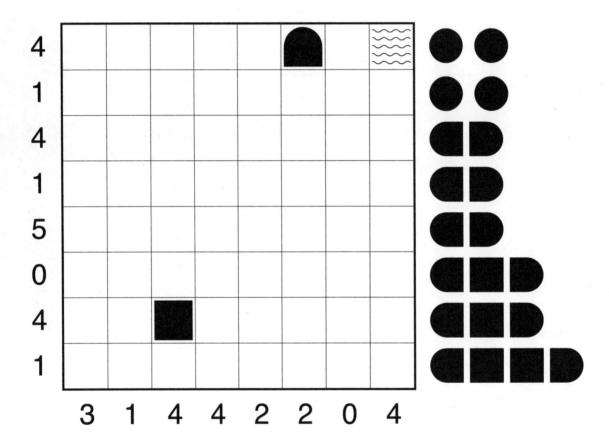

TWO-BY-FOUR

The eight letters in the word OFFENDER can be rearranged to form a pair of common four-letter words in two different ways, if no four-letter word is repeated. Can you find both pairs of words?

__ __ __ __   __ __ __ __

__ __ __ __   __ __ __ __

★★ Piecework by Fred Piscop

ACROSS

1 Radar reading
6 Razor sharpener
11 Salary max
14 Colonel insignia
15 Bearlike beast
16 Single
17 Physics-lab device
19 Criticize, slangily
20 Fancy footwear
21 Scarlett's husband
23 Blaster's need
26 Rink surface
27 Single-celled critters
29 Bother continually
31 Roofing pro
32 Draw forth
33 Board-game turn
34 Most August babies
37 Heed the alarm
38 Small canyon
39 Spanish snack
40 Actor Damon
41 Not "fer"
42 Soap units
43 No-goodnik
45 Proof of pedigree
46 With intensity
48 __-relief
49 Bit of sunshine
50 CD-player device
51 Execs, slangily
53 Make a choice
54 Butcher's gadget
60 Smelter input
61 Divas' deliveries
62 Spoiler
63 Popular Christmas tree
64 King of talk shows
65 Fell back

DOWN

1 Neptune's realm
2 Bit of butter
3 Swelled head
4 Shade providers
5 Can't stand
6 In-line item
7 Coin flip
8 Stadium cheer
9 Stadium cheer
10 Mimicking bird
11 Cryptographer, often
12 Singer Baker
13 Gnats and moles
18 Some Apples
22 Shoe lift
23 Heat unit
24 Gymnast Comaneci
25 Monopolist's foe
27 Set straight
28 Leonine locks
30 Overlay material
31 Bit of parsley
33 Waterlogged
35 La Scala offering
36 Fresh-mouthed
38 Highlander
42 Queen Isabella's realm
44 Skin-related
45 Socks set
46 Cool in manner
47 Blue Grotto isle
48 Warren Beatty film
51 Play the lead
52 Snooty sort
55 Notable time
56 Run on TV
57 Confer knighthood on
58 Language suffix
59 Deficit color

★★ Two Pairs

Among the 16 pictures below, find the two pairs of pictures that are identical to each other.

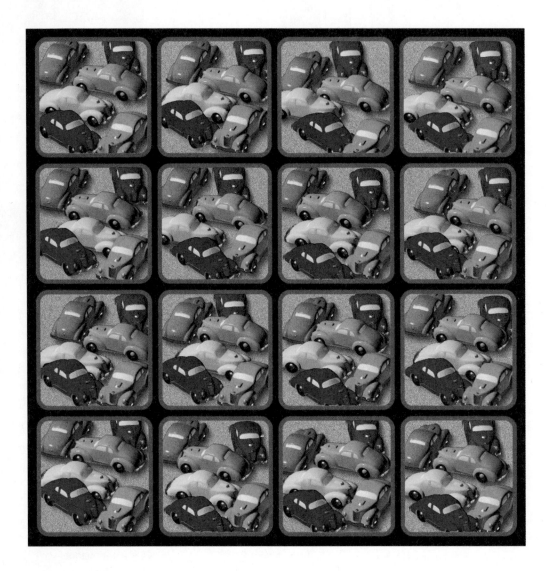

BETWEENER

What four-letter word belongs between the word at left and the word at right, so that the first and second word, and the second and third word, each form a common compound word?

PAN __ __ __ __ WALK

★★ Sudoku

Fill in the blank boxes so that every row, column, and 3x3 box contains all of the numbers 1 to 9.

			2	4	5			
	7	4				8	5	
	6		8				4	
2			4			7	3	8
			3	2	6			
4		3			8	2		5
	4			8	1		2	
	5	8			2	6	9	
			9		4		8	

MIXAGRAMS

Each line contains a five-letter word and a four-letter word that have been mixed together (the order of the letters in each word has not been changed). Unmix the two words on each line and write them in the spaces provided. When you're done, find a multipart answer to the clue by reading down the letter columns in the answers.

CLUE: Budget's business

V I S E V A L E R = _ _ _ _ _ + _ _ _ _

S A D R A C K E S = _ _ _ _ _ + _ _ _ _

A D U R S A L O N = _ _ _ _ _ + _ _ _ _

H E A D R U L O T = _ _ _ _ _ + _ _ _ _

★ Square Routes

Fill in the blank circles so that every row, column, and path contains all of the numbers from 1 to 5.

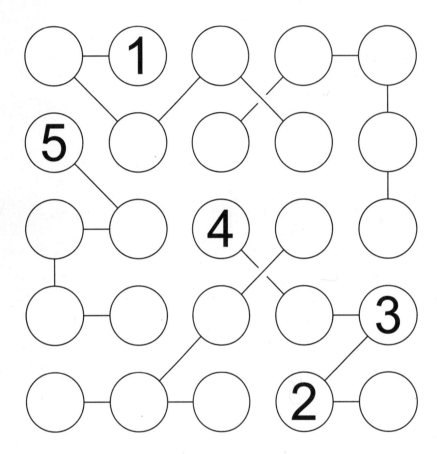

WRONG IS RIGHT

Which of these four words is misspelled?

A) innovate   B) innoculate

C) infuriate   D) inundate

★★ Sounds Correct by Frances Burton

ACROSS

1 Lucky break
5 Advantage
9 Helps in crime
14 Roof edge
15 Yuletide
16 Opera singer Callas
17 Stravinsky work
20 __ borealis
21 Size up
22 Nail polish
26 Wasn't colorfast
30 Compose for another
36 Traditional learning
37 Young fellows
38 Buenos __
39 Tree trimming, perhaps
41 Beginning
42 Set of computer instructions
43 Atlas entries
46 Feed the pot
47 Dramatist
49 Not as much
50 Old Testament book
52 Followed back
57 Hoo-ha
62 Accurate
66 Had leftovers, maybe
67 Be angry
68 Road sign
69 Course with carbs
70 Imitate
71 Musical sound

DOWN

1 Greek letter
2 Hawaiian island
3 From the top
4 Roman emperor
5 Twist together
6 Bambi's mother
7 "World" prefix
8 Pixie
9 Guitar boosters
10 Blocks off
11 Pennsylvania port
12 Food containers
13 Droops
18 Anger
19 Pepper's mate
23 Sound of surprise
24 All the rage
25 Curved letter
26 Aerial-photography medium
27 In the area
28 Author Jong
29 Express disapproval about
31 Gum amount
32 Keep up with
33 Cara of *Fame*
34 Campers' quarters
35 __ Park, CO
40 Needing refueling
41 In a shrewd manner
43 Recipe verb
44 In the past
45 Educator's deg.
48 Give a new look to
51 Substance partner
52 Catch
53 Author __ Mae Brown
54 Long time
55 Marker
56 Sicilian spewer
58 Extremely
59 Golden rule word
60 Boxer Spinks
61 Category
63 *SNL* network
64 As well
65 With it

★★ Number-Out

Shade squares so that no number appears in any row or column more than once. Shaded squares may not touch each other horizontally or vertically, and all unshaded squares must form a single continuous area.

1	3	5	5	5	4
1	2	4	6	5	3
5	1	6	3	2	1
6	1	4	3	4	2
4	1	3	3	1	2
2	6	2	1	3	2

THINK ALIKE

Unscramble the letters in the phrase BAIT SHOP to form two words with the same or similar meanings.

_____   _____

★★ Hyper-Sudoku

Fill in the blank boxes so that every row, column, 3x3 box, *and* each of the four 3x3 gray regions contains all of the numbers 1 to 9.

	4	7		6				
	8					6		7
							8	
			3			1	5	
7		2			4		3	
	1		2				7	
4		8	5		2		6	
		6					9	
	5			6				

CENTURY MARKS

Select one number in each of the four columns so that the total adds up to exactly 100.

$$\boxed{\genfrac{}{}{0pt}{}{20}{18}} + \boxed{\genfrac{}{}{0pt}{}{33}{29}} + \boxed{\genfrac{}{}{0pt}{}{42}{46}} + \boxed{\genfrac{}{}{0pt}{}{14}{11}} = 100$$

★★ Music Boxes by Fred Piscop

ACROSS

1 Oodles
6 Oodles
10 Séance sound
13 Golf pro Els
14 Mexican moolah
15 Identical
16 Clinton Presidential Center site
18 German river
19 Be a noodge to
20 Actor Mineo
21 Hockey venue
22 Auction signal
24 Muzzle loaders
26 *Howdy Doody* critter
31 Utter
32 *Damn Yankees* role
33 Notable times
35 Jrs.' exams
39 Simple rhyme scheme
40 Secluded valleys
42 Tater topper
43 Safari venue
45 "Get __!"
46 Tech's customer
47 Took the bait
49 Rocky Balboa portrayer
51 Denver neighbor
55 NASA spacewalk
56 Scopes trial org.
57 Wary of people
59 List of misprints
64 Apportion, with "out"
65 Candy on a stick
67 Candy shapes
68 Just beat
69 Monk's superior
70 __ nutshell
71 Drops from above
72 To-do list

DOWN

1 Facilitate
2 Cleveland's lake
3 Pantry invaders
4 Aniston's ex
5 Jennifer Lopez role of '97
6 Auto-loan ad letters
7 Tolstoy et al.
8 Writer Wilde
9 Gertrude Stein's colleague
10 High-tech "satellite" medium
11 Modify
12 Exec's extras
15 Wretched one
17 Worn down
23 German engraver
25 Global-positioning display
26 Harsh criticism
27 Brain area
28 __ Bator, Mongolia
29 Attractive eyes
30 Farm bundles
34 Election Day line
36 "Not to mention ..."
37 New driver, often
38 Ticked off
41 Toils away
44 Facilitate
48 Lab worker, at times
50 Cowboy's rope
51 Disney deer
52 Poseidon's purview
53 Part of UV
54 *Mary Tyler Moore Show* spinoff
58 Berra of baseball
60 Singer McEntire
61 PD dispatches
62 Ripped off
63 Condos and co-ops: Abbr.
66 Sawbuck

★ Guess Where

The capitalized words in the sentences below are all hidden in the diagram either across, down, or diagonally. The city being talked about is hidden also.

```
E Y E B U N A D Q R Y T I C
L T R I D I N G S D I E K F
E S R C O N C E R T H V A E
E A M O L I P I Z Z A N E R
H N R S T I S Y O L B P M R
W Y S E S R O H V A S R U I
T D C A S J E I C U B A S W
T N L A N I E H W N U T I B
I P E E T N R E C N R E C S
S S Z K N H N R A A G R N H
S E T A R B E L E C S E S F
H T I R J A O D V F H I A A
A O N I A O P I R P N M H M
R O H A H U S P E A O G O I
T F C C I I S T P U L X M L
S L S E T G S S S L I C E Y
```

This CITY SITS by the DANUBE RIVER at the FOOT of the ALPS.

It was the HOME of the HABSBURG DYNASTY.

You may VISIT the St. STEPHEN'S CATHEDRAL, the PRATER PARK with its GIANT FERRIS WHEEL, and the SPANISH RIDING SCHOOL with its LIPIZZANER HORSES.

You may also ENJOY a SCHNITZEL, followed by a SLICE of SACHERTORTE.

The FAMOUS ANNUAL NEW YEAR CONCERT CELEBRATES the MUSIC of the STRAUSS FAMILY.

INITIAL REACTION

Identify the well-known proverb from the first letters in each of its words.

E. D. H. H. D. _____

★★ Land of Lincoln

Enter the maze at bottom, pass through all the stars exactly once, then exit at the top. You may not retrace your path.

SAY IT AGAIN

What four-letter word can be either a piece of land or a piece of clothing?

—   —   —   —

★★ Frictionless by Fred Piscop

ACROSS

1 Jabs with a finger
6 Take a hike
10 Jazz phrase
14 Go-between
15 Soothing stuff
16 Demon's doing
17 Paper from the Returns Dept.
19 Sponge opening
20 Two fins, monetarily
21 Took the helm
23 Place to moor
25 With skill
26 Bogart's love
30 "¿Cómo __ usted?"
32 Metered vehicle
35 Autumn colour
36 Deck finish
37 Barn bird
38 Is regretful about
39 Beyond well-done
40 Hamster's home
41 LAX guess
42 Becker of tennis
43 Snaky shapes
44 Workout unit
45 Square footage
46 Hits hard
47 Lasting impression
49 After the buzzer
51 Accepts, as a challenge
54 Hook's crew
59 Actor Epps
60 Amusement-park feature
62 Baptism, e.g.
63 In perpetuity
64 Last Greek letter
65 Bad time for Caesar
66 Depend (on)
67 Former Green Party candidate

DOWN

1 Hostilities ender
2 Cruel sort
3 Sharp
4 Wraps up
5 Paint with dots
6 Stuff to discard
7 The whole shebang
8 Lane at *The Daily Planet*
9 Didn't give up
10 Ward off
11 West African republic
12 Hot stuff
13 Hightailed it
18 Slave away
22 Abba of Israel
24 Hung-jury result
26 Awl, for example
27 Sharp
28 Scrooge was one
29 Start of MGM's motto
31 __-serif typeface
33 "Shucks!"
34 Sanctify
36 Unerring
39 Library patron
40 CBS cop show
42 Flock calls
43 "Self-Reliance" essayist
46 Mix together
48 First asteroid discovered
50 Mimic's skill
51 Musical Amos
52 In the thick of
53 Church part
55 __ mater
56 Neck and neck
57 Upper hand
58 Blacken a bit
61 Address-book abbr.

★★ One-Way Streets

The diagram represents a pattern of streets. P's are parking spaces, and the black squares are stores. Find the route that starts at a parking space, passes through all stores exactly once, and ends at the other parking space. Arrows indicate one-way traffic for that block only. No block or intersection may be entered more than once.

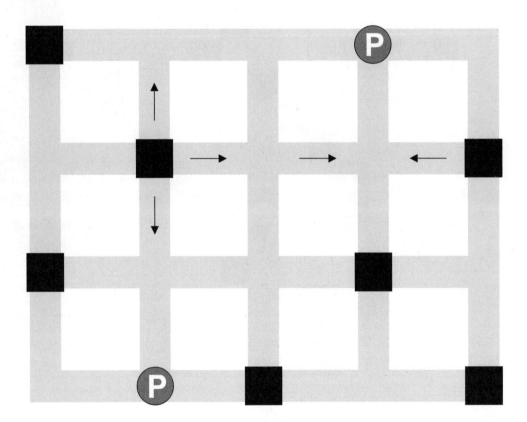

SOUND THINKING

The consonant sounds in the word FLAMES are F, L, M, and Z. What other six-letter word (not ending in S) is pronounced with the same consonant sounds in the same order?

_____

★★ 123

Fill in the diagram so that each rectangular piece has one each of the numbers 1, 2, and 3, under these rules: 1) No two adjacent squares, horizontally or vertically, can have the same number. 2) Each completed row and column of the diagram will have an equal number of 1's, 2's, and 3's.

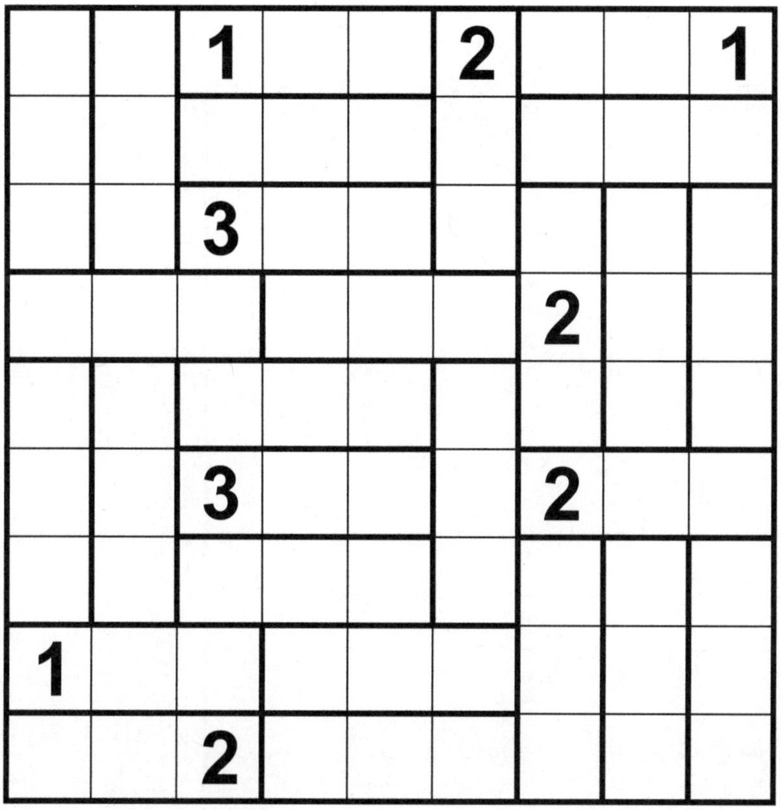

		1		2			1
		3					
					2		
		3			2		
1							
		2					

SUDOKU SUM

Fill in the missing numbers from 1 to 9, so that the sum of each row and column is as indicated.

	15	**14**	**16**
16		5	
11			3
18	6		

★★ **Line Drawing**

Draw two straight lines, each from one edge of the square to another edge,
so that the letters in each of the four regions form a word of a different length.

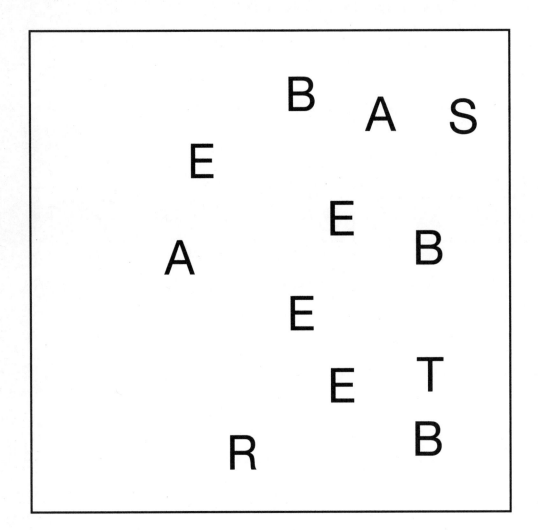

THREE OF A KIND

Find the three hidden words in the sentence that go together in some way.

There's no secret to teaching Earth Science.

★★ On Course by Kevin Donovan

ACROSS

1 Nightclub
6 Pointed weapon
11 Gift from 24 Down
14 More or less
15 Mandel of TV
16 Sense of self
17 Teddy Roosevelt's regiment
19 College website suffix
20 Lesson periods
21 At a quicker pace
23 Playfully evasive
24 Wild West hangouts
25 Big blockage
29 Family member
30 Spring time
31 People see through them
32 Classified listings
35 Swarm (with)
36 Board game of a sort
37 Take a powder
38 Compass reading
39 Craft for Columbus
40 Fabric fold
41 Ward workers
43 Pines (for)
44 Courtroom do-over
46 Mauna __ (Hawaiian peak)
47 Chinese philosophy book
48 Beach location
53 Newsman Dobbs
54 Skeet participant
56 Stately tree
57 Haunting
58 Putting into service
59 Society gal
60 Object of worship
61 Durango dough

DOWN

1 Graph components
2 Double-reed instrument
3 Notes promising payment
4 Pulls
5 On the up and up
6 Highly polished
7 Veggie holders
8 Farm female
9 Carriers' charges
10 Secondhand shop's business
11 Nondrinker
12 Utah city
13 Not mine
18 Space
22 Junior, to Senior
24 Chimney guy
25 Expected earlier
26 Amenable
27 Talent for gardening
28 Joseph Conrad title character
29 Actors' jobs
31 Group of experts
33 Senior member
34 Firms up
36 Clash
37 Marlins, on scoreboards
39 Put on paper
40 Fog, so to speak
42 Swiss canton
43 Affirmative answer
44 Vexed
45 Paris school
46 ... *Cuckoo's Nest* author
48 Skewer
49 Hydrant attachment
50 Big name in elevators
51 Silver State city
52 Work units
55 Onassis nickname

★★ Star Search

Find the stars that are hidden in some of the blank squares. The numbered squares indicate how many stars are hidden in the squares adjacent to them (including diagonally). There is never more than one star in any square.

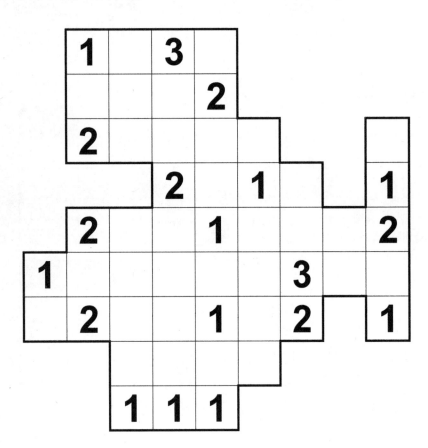

CHOICE WORDS

Form three six-letter words from the same category, by selecting one letter from each column three times. Each letter will be used exactly once.

B	A	A	A	D	Y	_ _ _ _ _ _
C	L	O	X	R	N	_ _ _ _ _ _
F	L	N	N	E	E	_ _ _ _ _ _

★★ Dicey

Group the dice into sets of two or more whose sums equal nine. The dice in each set must be connected to each other by a common horizontal or vertical side.

SMALL CHANGE

Change one letter in each of these two words, to form a common two-word phrase.

FUNNY NOTE

★★ Subterranean by Fred Piscop

ACROSS

1 Irish dances
5 Zhivago's love
9 Camel's backbreaker
14 Wrinkle remover
15 Top guns
16 Madrid art museum
17 Sun's position at twilight
20 Wind up
21 Take notice of
22 Reduces to bits
23 One on deck
25 Was really awful
27 Utah ski resort
29 Do something
30 Make a pick
33 Easily taken in
36 Hard work
38 Home to most
39 Out of sorts
42 Goofy or Daffy
43 Circle dance
44 Friars' fete
45 NBC show since '75
46 Sleep-stage acronym
47 It's typical
49 Basic principle
51 Mortar's mate
55 Jumbo
57 Salts' assents
59 Long, long time
60 Despicable
63 PC chip maker
64 Right-hand person
65 Copycat
66 Racket
67 Play a big part
68 Like Santa's cheeks

DOWN

1 Agrees
2 Goddess of peace
3 Meir of Israel
4 __-Cone (icy confection)
5 Hidden, as ability
6 Feel sore
7 Swamp plants
8 Hibachi residue
9 Top-speed run
10 Bit of magic
11 Tear to the ground
12 Commotions
13 Took home the jackpot
18 Ahab, for one
19 Delphic prophet
24 Expert
26 Taipei's land
28 Not on the road
30 Worker-safety org.
31 Slapstick ammo
32 Lip-puckering
33 Bar snacks
34 Ever and __
35 Inspirational figure
37 Francis Scott Key contraction
38 Molecule makeup
40 Bloggers' arena
41 Slap the cuffs on
46 Wine and dine
48 First game
49 Alder and elder
50 Quietly understood
52 Musical pace
53 Strides easily
54 Diary note
55 Late-night TV host
56 Voting no
58 Star Wars series sage
60 Trash holder
61 "Rumor __ it ..."
62 Musical gift

★★ Hyper-Sudoku

Fill in the blank boxes so that every row, column, 3x3 box, *and* each of the four 3x3 gray regions contains all of the numbers 1 to 9.

	4						2	
							3	
7	3	2		6		8		
	8			2		5	6	
5			1			9		
	7							1
			7					
	3				5	7	8	
6		7				1		2

MIXAGRAMS

Each line contains a five-letter word and a four-letter word that have been mixed together (the order of the letters in each word has not been changed). Unmix the two words on each line and write them in the spaces provided. When you're done, find a two-part answer to the clue by reading down the letter columns in the answers.

CLUE: Kind of driver

P H E U B A B Y S = _ _ _ _ _ + _ _ _ _

K A N Y I C A K E = _ _ _ _ _ + _ _ _ _

E P O K R O A C H = _ _ _ _ _ + _ _ _ _

F M I L E A K T Y = _ _ _ _ _ + _ _ _ _

★★ ABC

Enter the letters A, B, and C into the diagram so that each row and column has exactly one A, one B, and one C. The letters outside the diagram indicate the first letter encountered, moving in the direction of the arrow. Keep in mind that after all the letters have been filled in, there will be two blank boxes in each row and column.

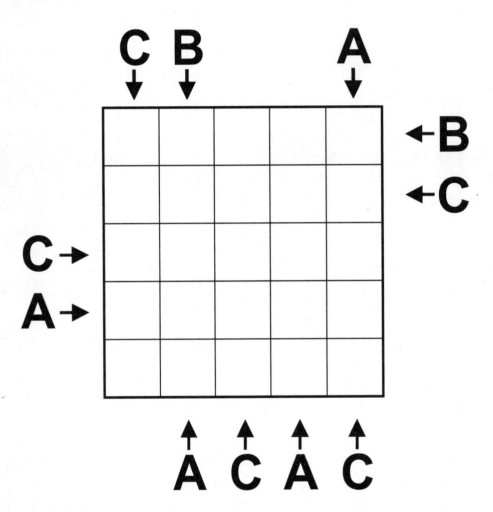

NATIONAL TREASURE

Find the one common six-letter word not ending in S that can be formed from the letters in SPANIARD.

__ __ __ __ __ __

★★ Elevating by Daniel R. Stark

ACROSS

1 Type of tooth
6 Slightly
10 Baby chick sound
14 Hacienda brick
15 Arizona city
16 Peeve
17 Installed ceramic
18 Campus figure, for short
19 Bad day for Caesar
20 Brontë hero
22 Small coin
23 Nationality ender
24 Wagner works
26 Miniature tree
30 2000 presidential candidate
32 Not in a whisper
33 Defied gravity
37 Willowy
38 Courteous
39 Verne captain
40 Set aside (for)
42 Once more
43 More frosty
44 Tips off
45 Fireplace frames
48 Spooky, maybe
49 Litter's smallest
50 Electric utility's concern
57 Arm bone
58 *Casablanca* role
59 Mr. Spock portrayer
60 Sedaka or Simon
61 Online auction site
62 Stale
63 Difficult journey
64 Criticizes
65 Assuaged

DOWN

1 Calculus, for example
2 Garfield pal
3 Singer Falana
4 Be a party to
5 Lucille Ball, e.g.
6 More than enough
7 Actress Hatcher
8 Starting
9 Vivid yellow
10 Comparison shopper's consideration
11 Pillow filler
12 Helen, in Spanish

13 Nuisances
21 CBS cop series
25 Household member
26 Foundation
27 __ podrida
28 Black: Fr.
29 High-level meeting
30 "When pigs fly!"
31 Zealous
33 Are fond of
34 Lacerate
35 Give off
36 Slips into
38 Less soggy

41 Top-rated
42 Firm, as pasta
44 Throw in
45 Pig's noise
46 One in charge
47 Sharpshooter Oakley
48 Signs off on
51 Island near Corsica
52 On the double
53 Oscar winner Sorvino
54 Left Bank chums
55 Written reminder
56 Changed the color of

★★ Knot or Not?

When the ships weigh anchor, which ropes will knot, and which will not?

BETWEENER

What four-letter word belongs between the word at left and the word at right, so that the first and second word, and the second and third word, each form a common compound word?

TOUCH __ __ __ __ GRADE

★★ Find the Ships

Determine the position of the 10 ships listed to the right of the diagram. The ships may be oriented either horizontally or vertically. A square with wavy lines indicates water and will not contain a ship. The numbers at the edge of the diagram indicate how many squares in that row or column contain parts of ships. When all 10 ships are correctly placed in the diagram, no two of them will touch each other, not even diagonally.

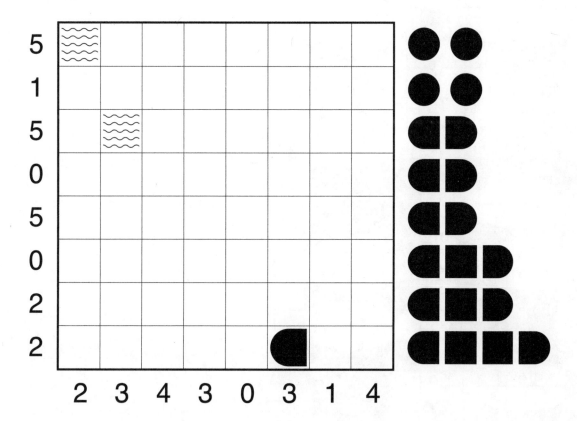

TWO-BY-FOUR

The eight letters in the word PERJURER can be rearranged to form a pair of common four-letter words in only one way. Can you find the two words?

— — — —　　— — — —

★★ Triad Split Decisions

In this clueless crossword puzzle, each answer consists of two words whose spellings are the same, except for the consecutive letters given. All answers are common words; no phrases or hyphenated or capitalized words are used. Some of the clues may have more than one solution, but there is only one word pair that will correctly link up with all the other word pairs.

TRANSDELETION

Delete one letter from the word DEFIANT and rearrange the rest, to get a two-word Hollywood term.

_____

★★ Rookies by Fred Piscop

ACROSS

1 Ritzy
5 Wearing loafers, say
9 Practices boxing
14 Utah ski resort
15 Cobbled together
16 Reef material
17 Frankenstein's helper
18 Teen fave
19 Still in the game
20 Factory input
23 Understand
24 Guitarist __ Paul
25 Show contrition
27 Completely wrecks
31 "Am not!" retort
33 Japanese dog
34 Auth. unknown
35 Govt. workplace watchdog
39 Dr. Seuss book
42 Novelist Paretsky
43 Tick off
44 Place for a pimiento
45 Snack with tea
47 Primitive fellows
48 Butter or oleo
51 "Unknown," on a sched.
52 Rainbow gradation
53 Party time
60 Hitting
62 Be hysterical
63 Dry as dust
64 MapQuest.com offering
65 Otherwise
66 "Well done!"
67 Sign up
68 Call for
69 Sharp as a tack

DOWN

1 Ark complement
2 Gymnast Korbut
3 Pack away
4 Rough up
5 Wallops, old-style
6 Styx locale
7 Fragrance
8 Supermarket section
9 Fish features
10 Officeholder
11 Crop up
12 Poe bird
13 Winter forecast
21 Poe's middle name
22 Concert venue
26 Popular pet
27 Gets to "it"
28 Gumbo veggie
29 Stadium section
30 Relaxing
31 Go for fish
32 Wine choice
34 Not "fer"
36 Leveling piece
37 Hold title to
38 Congregation comeback
40 Chip away at
41 Without face value
46 Horse's gait
47 Dropped off
48 Don't hog
49 Add, as weight
50 Show otherwise
51 Tied up in knots
54 Small songbird
55 Ivy League school
56 Dropped sharply
57 Toledo's lake
58 Bad habit
59 Idyllic place
61 Had

★★ 123

Fill in the diagram so that each rectangular piece has one each of the numbers 1, 2, and 3, under these rules: 1) No two adjacent squares, horizontally or vertically, can have the same number. 2) Each completed row and column of the diagram will have an equal number of 1's, 2's, and 3's.

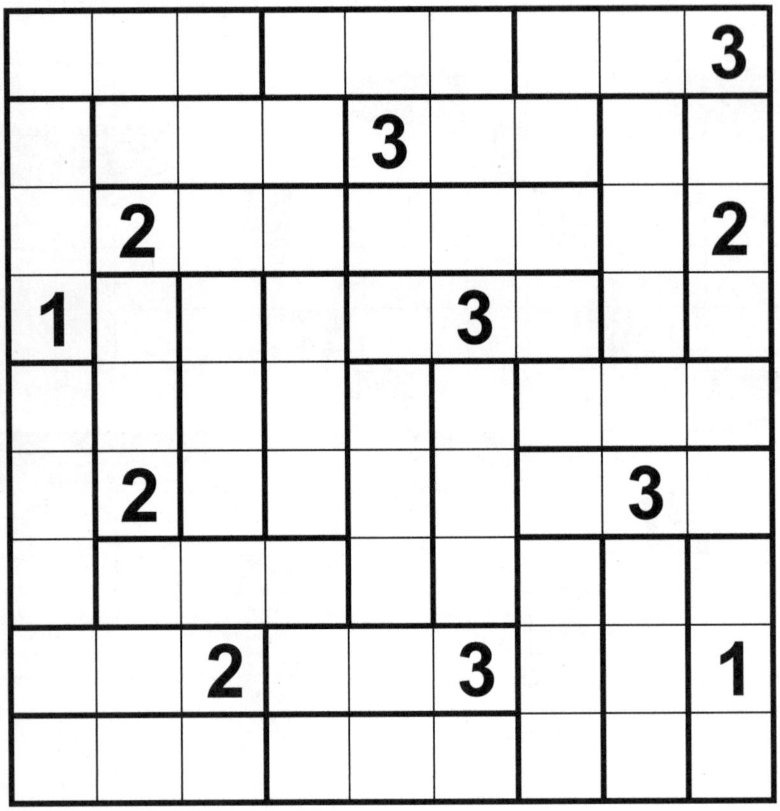

								3
				3				
	2							2
1				3				
	2						3	
		2		3				1

WRONG IS RIGHT

Which of these four words is misspelled?

A) mannequin   B) manatee

C) manouver   D) manganese

★ Square Routes

Fill in the blank circles so that every row, column, and path contains all of the numbers from 1 to 5.

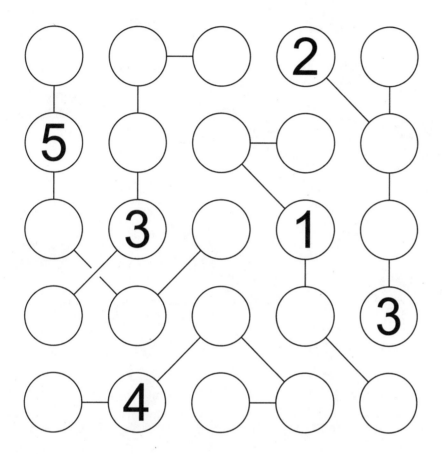

ADDITION SWITCH

Switch the positions of two of the digits in the incorrect sum at right, to get a correct sum.

```
  1 6 7
+ 3 2 9
-------
  5 2 3
```

★★ The Basics by Norma Steinberg

ACROSS

1 Alaska city
5 Bulgarian capital
10 Eagle's weapon
14 Imperfection
15 Skilled
16 Tune for a sitar
17 Be fond of
18 "Here's to you," e.g.
19 Laundry-room appliance
20 40 Down denizen
21 Backwards duplicate
23 International news service
25 "We __ not amused!"
26 Study, with "over"
27 Friendly
32 Coffeehouse order
34 Befits
35 Orbison or Rogers
36 Functions
37 Shirley Temple trademark
38 "You bet!"
39 __ Vegas
40 Sorrowful poem
41 Battled, as a blaze
42 Modern
44 Do, as dishes
45 Salesperson
46 People from Akron
49 Alternate title for the puzzle
54 Witnessed
55 Rooster, for one
56 Party hearty
57 Prima donna
58 Blueprint
59 Come up
60 Economist Smith
61 Summer and fall mo.
62 Global extremes
63 High-pitched bark

DOWN

1 Raven or Falcon
2 Popeye's girl
3 Absentee's exam
4 Lamb's parent
5 *Mad* magazine material
6 Kitchen emanations
7 Phobia
8 __ facto
9 Draws in
10 Black Sea peninsula
11 Actress __ Flynn Boyle
12 Slack-jawed
13 Opposite of wax
21 Simple
22 Spring flower
24 Preschoolers
27 Sudden increase
28 Slick
29 Dismiss disdainfully
30 Legends
31 Checked out
32 Whopper
33 At once
34 Bird food
37 Baloney
38 Fair to middlin'
40 Biblical garden
41 Nixon Chief of Staff
43 East
44 Largest mammals
46 Santa-like
47 Part of USNA
48 Overwhelm
49 Little devils
50 Yarn
51 Strike with the palm
52 Good guy
53 Wicked
57 Part of a week

★★ Find the Treasure

Enter the map through a road on one of the four sides. Use a road path that includes passing over exactly one bridge and making a right turn at the intersection (in either order); then leave the road, traveling east across the land until you reach a tree, where you should mark an X to indicate where the treasure is buried. No grid square may be visited more than once.

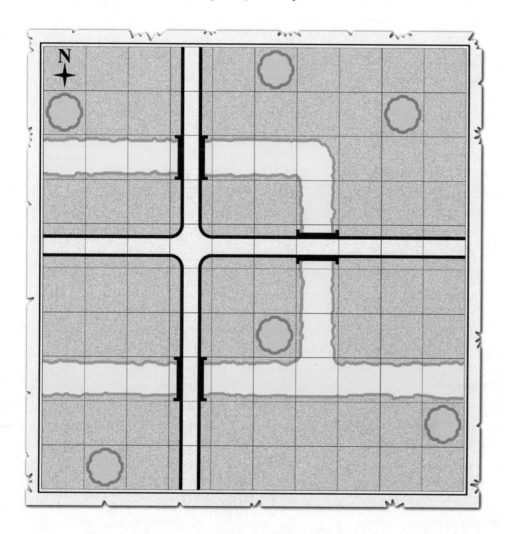

SAY IT AGAIN

What four-letter word can be either a direction or a past-tense verb?

— — — —

bRAin BREATHER
POUR IT ON! THE MANY USES OF BABY OIL

Just because there are no longer any babies living in your household, don't think that bottle of baby oil in the medicine chest has become superfluous. The tasks that can be eased with a few drops of this handy liquid are many and varied.

Slip off a stuck ring Is that ring jammed on your finger again? First, lubricate the ring area with a generous amount of baby oil. Then, swivel the ring around to spread the oil under it. You should be able to slide the ring off with ease.

Remove latex paint from skin Did you get almost as much paint on your face and hands as you did on the bathroom you just painted? You can quickly get latex paint off your skin by first rubbing it with some baby oil, and then following up with a good washing with soap and water.

Shine stainless steel sinks and chrome trim Pamper your dull-looking stainless steel sinks by rubbing them down with a few drops of baby oil on a soft, clean cloth. Rub dry with a towel and repeat if necessary. This is also a terrific way to remove stains on the chrome trim of your kitchen appliances and bathroom fixtures.

Polish leather bags and shoes Just a few drops of baby oil applied with a soft cloth can add new life to an old leather bag or pair of patent leather shoes. Don't forget to wipe away any oil remaining on the leather when you're done.

Make your own bath oil Do you have a favorite perfume or cologne? You can literally bathe in it by making your own scented bath oil. Simply add a few drops of your scent of choice to 1/4 cup baby oil in a small plastic bottle. Shake well and add it to your bath.

Remove a bandage You can eliminate—or at least significantly lessen—the "ouch" factor and subsequent tears, when removing a youngster's bandage by first rubbing some baby oil into the adhesive parts on top and around the edges. If you see the bandage working loose, let the child finish the job to help him/her overcome his/her fear. (Even "stoic" adults may want to try this one on themselves.)

Get scratches off dashboard plastic You can disguise scratches on the plastic lens covering the odometer and other indicators on your car's dashboard by rubbing over them with a bit of baby oil.

★ Never the Same

Find these "different" words that are hidden in the diagram, either across, down, or diagonally.

```
D D X W N K I T N E T N O C T        ASYMMETRY
R I N S P O Y T I S R E V I D        CHANGE
O S Y O A D I V E R G E N C E        CLASH
C S R O I L E T E X I L N U V        CONFLICT
C I T Y Q T C G I O S N L E A        CONTENTION
A M E C N A N O S S I D K E R        DEVIATION
S I M J H A E E N C O I F G I        DIFFERENCE
I L M Z H K D X T F L P C D A        DISACCORD
D A Y C C C I V C N L A P U T        DISPARITY
F R S B L A S L U E O I S O I        DISSIDENCE
P Q A A M R S W N G P C C Y O        DISSIMILAR
D I S P A R I T Y U J T R T N        DISSONANCE
C H A N G D D E V I A T I O N        DIVERGENCE
E C N E R E F F I D L U N O Z        DIVERSITY
D I S S I D E N C H A N G I N        EXCEPTION
                                     OPPOSITION
                                     UNLIKE
                                     VARIATION
```

WHO'S WHAT WHERE?

The correct term for a resident of Zürich, Switzerland, is:

A) Züricher   B) Zürichian

C) Zürichster   D) Zürichi

★★ Hyper-Sudoku

Fill in the blank boxes so that every row, column, 3x3 box, *and* each of the four
3x3 gray regions contains all of the numbers 1 to 9.

	2			9	1			
7				2	4	6		
	8	9						
								3
		6			5			
	3	8		7		9		
3			2	8			5	
							3	4
	1				9	2		7

MIXAGRAMS

Each line contains a five-letter word and a four-letter word that have been mixed together (the order of the letters in each word has not been changed). Unmix the two words on each line and write them in the spaces provided. When you're done, find a two-part answer to the clue by reading down the letter columns in the answers.

CLUE: It's between mouth and bowl

S O U P O T I L S	=	_ _ _ _ _	+	_ _ _ _
M I C E S N E R T	=	_ _ _ _ _	+	_ _ _ _
S E P A L S E I T	=	_ _ _ _ _	+	_ _ _ _
D E W M O R U R M	=	_ _ _ _ _	+	_ _ _ _

★★★ Let Us Illustrate by Hy Hickman

ACROSS

1 Monetary value
6 Grills, maybe
10 Breathe hard
14 Parting word
15 Hernando's hand
16 Footnote abbr.
17 Flavor of a place
19 Put the finger on
20 Soprano parts
21 Sent to the sidelines
23 Oxygen source
24 Japanese immigrant
25 Compass needles
28 Silent's successor
32 Max __ Sydow
33 Highlanders
35 Stannic
36 Declare solemnly
38 Vaults
40 Winged goddess
41 Greedy king of myth
43 Purse closers
45 Provided dinner for
46 Examiner
48 Needed a new washer
50 Garbage holders
52 Caviar
53 Fencing cry
56 Mariachi wear
60 Graceful wrap
61 Leave it to luck
63 Stretch across
64 __ Linda, CA
65 Novelist Glasgow
66 Toward sunrise
67 Painter Jan van __
68 Textile workers

DOWN

1 Cartoonist Kelly
2 Fragrance
3 Beans partner
4 Something to dunk
5 Shelling, as corn
6 Cookie man
7 "Gal" of song
8 Rounded handles
9 Most peeved
10 List tentatively
11 Four Corners state
12 Starlet's aspiration
13 Bolted
18 Breakfast fare
22 Well-groomed
24 Gas-pump platforms
25 62 Down offering
26 Battery terminal
27 Kickoff stands
29 Tarzan's weapon
30 Signed, as a contract
31 Watched carefully
32 Siren
34 Ship pole
37 Makeup, so to speak
39 Bell towers
42 Seal in the juices of
44 Had on
47 Puzzling question
49 Lustrous
51 Film director Mervyn
53 To be, to Brutus
54 Wine valley
55 Mardi __
56 Envelope acronym
57 Bleached-out
58 Decorative pitcher
59 FICA IDs
62 HBO alternative

★★ One-Way Streets

The diagram represents a pattern of streets. P's are parking spaces, and the black squares are stores. Find the route that starts at a parking space, passes through all stores exactly once, and ends at the other parking space. Arrows indicate one-way traffic for that block only. No block or intersection may be entered more than once.

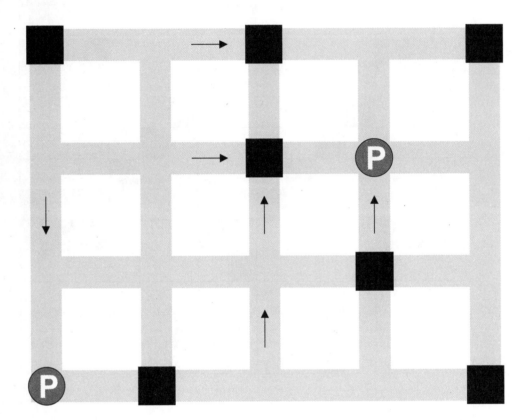

SOUND THINKING

Common words whose consonant sounds are G (as in "get"), N, and G (as in "get") include GONG and GOING. The consonant sounds of what six-letter word (that doesn't end in –ING) are G, N, and G, in that order?

_____

★★ Star Search

Find the stars that are hidden in some of the blank squares. The numbered squares indicate how many stars are hidden in the squares adjacent to them (including diagonally). There is never more than one star in any square.

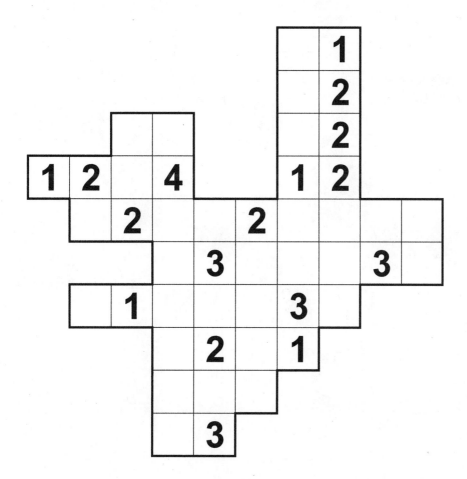

CHOICE WORDS

Form three six-letter words from the same category, by selecting one letter from each column three times. Each letter will be used exactly once.

C	E	C	E	R	M	_ _ _ _ _ _
E	A	T	A	E	D	_ _ _ _ _ _
R	S	G	H	E	T	_ _ _ _ _ _

★★★ Conduct Yourself by Shirley Soloway

ACROSS

1 Sounds of delight
5 Obliterate
10 Loose-limbed
14 Reputation spoiler
15 Becker or Badenov
16 Ballet bend
17 *The Alienist* author
18 Dress ornamentation
20 Mideast region
22 Bolt holder
23 Breadth
24 Rendered unreadable
26 Keats creations
27 Barbed remark
29 Wait
30 Barely defeat
31 Silent screen star?
34 When Operation Overlord began
38 Ring great
39 Ring-shaped reef
40 Wish undone
41 Optometric object
43 Lasso feature
44 Knitting stitch
45 Ceramic flaw
47 Nominal, at NASA
49 Schieffer successor
52 *King of Queens*, e.g.
54 Really get to
55 Publicity, so to speak
56 Pipsqueak
59 Transparent plastic
62 Singer Adams
63 Greet with acclaim
64 Element #5
65 Eats in the evening
66 Some amb. drivers
67 Casts forth
68 Small scrap

DOWN

1 Elementary stuff
2 Jai __
3 Being a busybody
4 Hard to explain
5 Subside
6 Tourney segment
7 Be difficult
8 River deposit
9 Compass reading
10 Caught with a fork
11 Preparations
12 High-pressure system
13 Assents
19 Raised
21 Water cooler
25 Branch of chemistry
26 Tempestuous
27 Enthusiastic emotion
28 Taking it easy
29 OPEC amts.
32 Surmounting
33 Milne marsupial
35 Got by hard work
36 Mystic glow
37 Cheerleading routine
42 Moves through a computer file
44 Great skill
46 Lone Ranger exclamation
48 Start of the fourth qtr.
49 Storehouse
50 Very early in the day
51 Darkened
52 Entangle
53 "No need to remind me"
55 Waffle House alternative
57 Morning TV host
58 Irritant
60 *American Masters* network
61 Recent USNA grad

★★ Dotty

Draw a line from square to square, moving either horizontally and vertically, so that all squares have been visited once. You may pass from one square to another only if it contains a dot of the same color and size. Note that many squares have small dots on top of large dots.

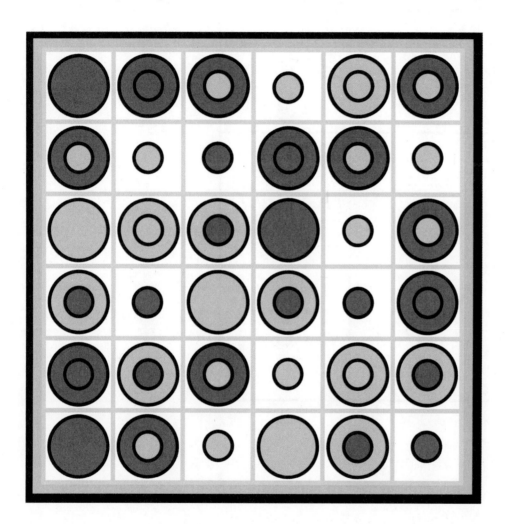

SMALL CHANGE

Change one letter in each of these two words, to form a common two-word phrase.

SHIRT STORM

★★ Sudoku

Fill in the blank boxes so that every row, column, and 3x3 box contains all of the numbers 1 to 9.

			8	7		5	1	6
5	9	6		1		2	7	8
7	1	8	6		5		3	
1			7	5	6	8		3
6	5			8		1	2	7
8		7				6		5
	8	1	3	6		7	5	
	7	4	5	9	8	3	6	
	6	5		4	7		8	

CENTURY MARKS

Select one number in each of the four columns so that the total adds up to exactly 100.

$$\boxed{\frac{26}{10}} + \boxed{\frac{59}{13}} + \boxed{\frac{22}{19}} + \boxed{\frac{50}{12}} = 100$$

★★★ Turkey Day by S.N.

ACROSS

1 Green course
6 Caspar and company
10 What a tartan may symbolize
14 First-class, so to speak
15 French state
16 Dixieland trumpeter
17 Felonious flames
18 Thoughtful one
19 Uneasy longing
20 Major Istanbul attraction
23 Storm center
24 Pampering, for short
25 *New World Symphony* composer
28 Warplane mission
30 Air pollution
32 Earlier
33 Hero sandwich
35 Unconfident attempt
36 Turkey was once part of it
41 Green expanse
42 Baltic nation
43 *Aladdin* prince
44 Indonesian island
46 Be firm
50 Make firmer
52 Bobbsey girl
53 Largest U.S. union
54 Adjective for Turkey
58 Electronic read
60 Ontario's provincial bird
61 Go away
62 Try for a goal
63 Beef cut
64 Compare
65 Babbles on
66 Just
67 Perfectly still

DOWN

1 Outpourings
2 Southwestern gully
3 Daffy Duck, e.g.
4 Frenzied
5 Raffle buy, perhaps
6 Corpsman
7 Surmounting
8 Festive occasion
9 "That's good enough"
10 Oldest of the Marxes
11 Intellectuals
12 It's measured in degrees
13 Ultimate
21 Fabric fold
22 Summary stat.
26 Ice-cream thickener
27 Japanese city
29 As compared to
30 Region east of Suez
31 Swimming event
34 Fish feature
35 Mineral springs
36 Spill a secret
37 Thornton Wilder alma mater
38 Hard bread
39 Town on Lake Geneva
40 *Cabaret* Oscar winner
44 Tampa NFLer
45 Leader of the Muses
47 Channel entrance
48 Mets Hall-of-Famer
49 Certain scout's concern
51 Informers
52 Yo-yo
55 When shadows are shortest
56 Arduous activity
57 Rhinelander's refusal
58 Telescope target
59 Spy org.

★★ Split Decisions

In this clueless crossword puzzle, each answer consists of two words whose spellings are the same, except for the consecutive letters given. All answers are common words; no phrases or hyphenated words are used. Some of the clues may have more than one solution, but there is only one word pair that will correctly link up with all the other word pairs.

TRANSDELETION

Delete one letter from the word CORRODE and rearrange the rest, to get something that may be broken.

_____

★★ Number-Out

Shade squares so that no number appears in any row or column more than once. Shaded squares may not touch each other horizontally or vertically, and all unshaded squares must form a single continuous area.

2	2	6	1	3	3
2	3	6	1	4	1
2	6	6	3	2	4
1	4	3	5	6	2
4	1	1	1	5	2
3	5	1	2	1	2

THINK ALIKE

Unscramble the letters in the phrase FRAME SHOP to form two words with the same or similar meanings.

_____   _____

★★★ Pour It On by Doug Peterson

ACROSS

1 Great divide
5 "Who's there?" response
10 Leave unmentioned
14 Mass declaration
15 Courteous
16 Decorative vessel
17 Jam cause
19 Land of leprechauns
20 Tampa gridder, briefly
21 Fourth person
22 Dior creation
23 Finger Lakes city
25 Sporty '55 debuts
28 Archie Andrews' pal
32 Arab League member
34 Sacramento's __ Arena
35 It sounds like "air"
36 Approximate
38 Charlie Parker's instrument
41 __ culpa
42 Transport
44 Fasts no more
45 Leafy carnivore
49 The Gong Show host
50 First electronic stock market
54 Spa treatments
56 Constitution St.
58 Hosp. section
59 Body of a boat
60 '20s DC scandal
63 Gathering dust
64 Back street
65 Fateful Forum date
66 Piquancy
67 Prophetic signs
68 Irritant

DOWN

1 Synagogue leader
2 Folder's phrase
3 Go get
4 Demolition compound
5 Sprain soother
6 Rake feature
7 More slender
8 Karaoke need, briefly
9 Leather used for moccasins
10 Take too far
11 Confusing mess
12 Mother of Horus
13 Till contents
18 Gap
22 NBA nickname
24 Iliad warrior
26 Kidman's mother in Birth
27 Inspirational figure
29 John Wayne film of '62
30 Well-known times
31 Census datum
32 "Dedicated to the __ Love"
33 Pasta topper
36 Brat
37 Moonstruck Oscar winner
39 Boarder
40 Feedbag morsels
43 Posh
46 Oval-shaped pill
47 Timecard stats.
48 Drives up the wall
51 Part of LED
52 High points
53 Knight work
54 Virtuoso
55 Churlish
57 Not buttoned
60 Chinese philosophical principle
61 Spreading tree
62 French __ (sort of sandwich)

★★ ABC

Enter the letters A, B, and C into the diagram so that each row and column has exactly one A, one B, and one C. The letters outside the diagram indicate the first letter encountered, moving in the direction of the arrow. Keep in mind that after all the letters have been filled in, there will be two blank boxes in each row and column.

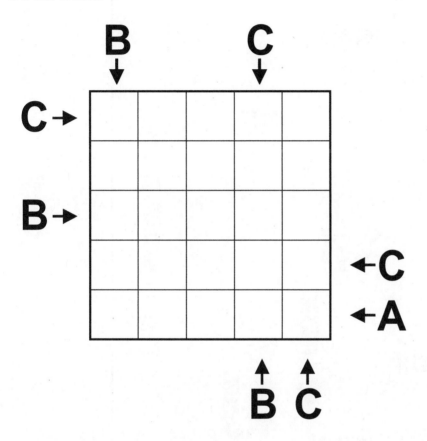

CLUELESS CROSSWORD

Complete the crossword with common uncapitalized seven-letter words, based entirely on the letters already filled in for you.

F		D	G			Y
U	■	I		Q	■	
R			C			
	■	P		■		■
I				T		
	■		■			■
R					R	M

★★ Bumper Crop

Draw a path for the ball so that it hits all bumpers exactly once. The ball must move straight ahead, horizontally or vertically, until it hits a bumper, after which it may turn left, turn right, or reverse its path. It is okay to retrace your path.

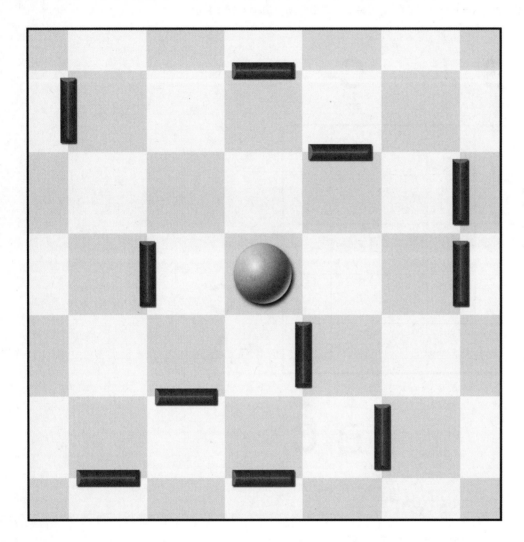

BETWEENER

What four-letter word belongs between the word at left and the word at right, so that the first and second word, and the second and third word, each form a common compound word?

VINE __ __ __ __ STICK

★★★ Line Drawing

Draw three straight lines, each from one edge of the square to another edge, so that the letters in each of the seven regions form a word.

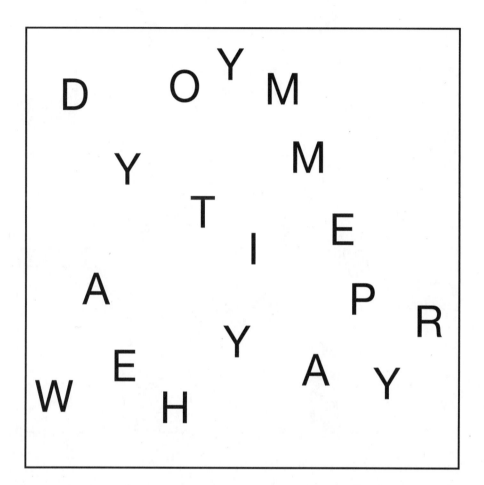

THREE OF A KIND

Find the three hidden words in the sentence that go together in some way.

He has to pave his green driveway with brown asphalt.

★★★ Table Talk by Shirley Soloway

ACROSS

1 Irving hero
5 Foundation
10 Chick's tail?
14 Poison-ivy soother
15 Overdo it on stage
16 Inflame
17 Flabbergasted
19 Book's ID
20 Cry of distress
21 Grabbed one's chance
23 Roll-call response
24 Plunders
27 False front
28 Pampered
30 "I should've thought of that!"
33 *Casablanca* set
36 Drudgery
37 Kid-lit gold source
39 __ squash
41 Halogen suffix
42 Lose, in a way
43 Digress
44 Get comfortable
46 Footnote abbr.
47 Solicit clarification
48 Police-book contents
51 Swim-meet units
53 Variety
54 Okra holder
57 Where to buy boots and bindings
60 Italian-style sandwiches
62 Bumblers
63 Print-shop employee
66 Chip in
67 Sea duck
68 Bicycle part
69 Nettlesome one
70 Cries out for
71 Fighting force

DOWN

1 Cameroon neighbor
2 Wahine's welcome
3 Rambunctious
4 Soccer great
5 It may be a "master"
6 I love: Lat.
7 Part of USSR
8 Topic of gossip
9 Señora's shawl
10 Taurus preceder
11 Distributed
12 Napoleon exile site
13 Counting-out word
18 Doc Holliday associate
22 Sidestep
25 Verbal disapproval
26 Most nasty
28 Blood fluids
29 Pearlike
31 Steak-rating agcy.
32 Bread-loaf end
33 *Residencia*
34 New Testament book
35 Warehouse equipment
38 Encouraging words
40 Mythological maiden
45 Capstones
49 Grand Slam tennis event
50 Work group
52 Account receivable, e.g.
54 Cheapskate
55 Small hour
56 Needing cleaning
57 Cleaning need
58 Welles role
59 Ballet bend
61 Dr. Jemison's former employer
64 Lime drink
65 Sam on *Cheers*

★★ Find the Ships

Determine the position of the 10 ships listed to the right of the diagram. The ships may be oriented either horizontally or vertically. A square with wavy lines indicates water and will not contain a ship. The numbers at the edge of the diagram indicate how many squares in that row or column contain parts of ships. When all 10 ships are correctly placed in the diagram, no two of them will touch each other, not even diagonally.

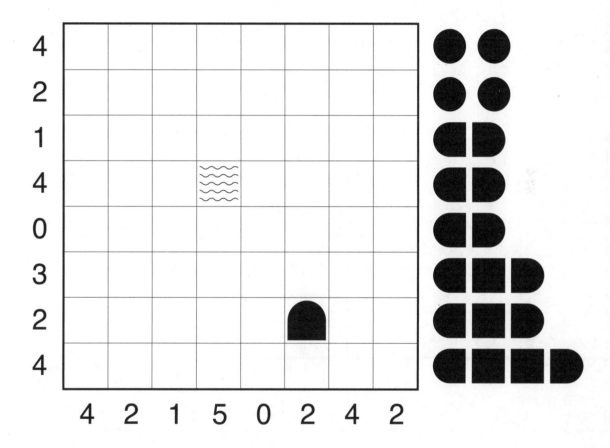

TWO-BY-FOUR

The eight letters in the word QUOTABLY can be rearranged to form a pair of common four-letter words in only one way, if no four-letter word is repeated. Can you find the two words?

— — — —　— — — —

★★★ Hyper-Sudoku

Fill in the blank boxes so that every row, column, 3x3 box, *and* each of the four 3x3 gray regions contains all of the numbers 1 to 9.

				2				
		7						9
	2	9		1		7	8	
2								
		6					5	1
	7		9		8	4		
1			5			2	9	
		2		6			7	
		8						

MIXAGRAMS

Each line contains a five-letter word and a four-letter word that have been mixed together (the order of the letters in each word has not been changed). Unmix the two words on each line and write them in the spaces provided. When you're done, find a two-part answer to the clue by reading down the letter columns in the answers.

CLUE: Traveler's time out

C L A R U S E T H = _ _ _ _ _ + _ _ _ _

D U D E C O T R Y = _ _ _ _ _ + _ _ _ _

P E G S A L M O S = _ _ _ _ _ + _ _ _ _

P I T I C H P E Y = _ _ _ _ _ + _ _ _ _

★★★ Watch Words by Doug Peterson

ACROSS

1 Bivouac
5 Seized auto
9 Extended families
14 Mixed bag
15 Merit
16 Distiller Walker
17 Cell-phone accessory
20 In readiness
21 Western national park
22 Eventful time
23 Like some appliances
26 Oil-platform worker
28 "Talking in Your Sleep" singer
32 Knee-slapper
33 Homer's exclamation
34 Jeweler's lens
38 Sort
39 New Jersey city
42 Auto-club service
43 Easy to comprehend
45 Jack of *Barney Miller*
46 Equivalent
47 Join forces
51 One filling shelves
54 Japanese "beef" city
55 Hosp. areas
56 Days before
58 Inundated
62 Gridiron setback
66 Public perception
67 Membership of a sort
68 Go wherever
69 Kitchen garment
70 Female empowerment org.
71 *October Sky* actress

DOWN

1 Salmon variety
2 Novelist Paton
3 '60s skirt
4 iTunes offering
5 Rink official
6 Order of corn
7 Ike, in the '50s
8 Five Nations tribe
9 Bedspread material
10 Actress Tyler
11 Sprite in *The Tempest*
12 Iridescent shell coating
13 Makeup mishap
18 Faction
19 Flat-bottomed boat
24 Anti-art art movement
25 Fill to excess
27 Zodiac predator
28 All the rage
29 Pack of pennies
30 Oxen holder
31 Pac-Man adversary
35 21 Across locale
36 Fleshy fruit
37 Decorative pitcher
39 Engineers' colleagues
40 Cubbyhole
41 Canceled, as a mission
44 Epitome of simplicity
46 Estate manager
48 St. Petersburg's river
49 Black-tie
50 Israeli statesman
51 Eastern European capital
52 Disney pooch
53 Jazz pianist Peterson
57 Depict unfairly
59 Natural balm
60 Headliner
61 Choir piece
63 It may be bruised
64 Fund-raising org.
65 Hellenic vowel

★★★ Square Routes

Fill in the blank circles so that every row, column, and path contains all of the numbers from 1 to 6.

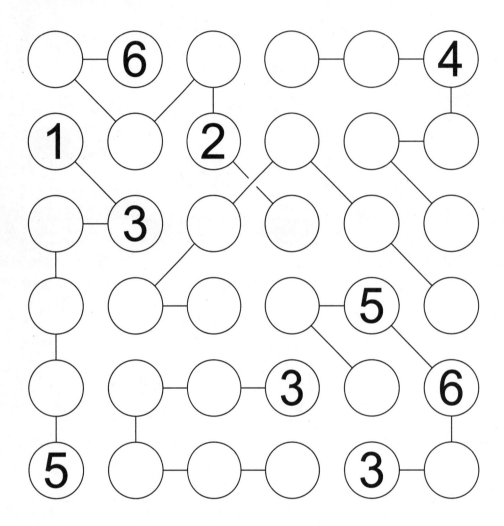

WRONG IS RIGHT

Which of these four words is misspelled?

A) château   B) charlatin

C) chassis   D) chameleon

★★ Sitting Bull

Enter the maze at bottom, pass through all the stars exactly once, then exit at top. You may not retrace your path.

SAY IT AGAIN

What four-letter word can mean either "intend" or "nasty"?

— — — —

★★ Number-Out

Shade squares so that no number appears in any row or column more than once. Shaded squares may not touch each other horizontally or vertically, and all unshaded squares must form a single continuous area.

3	3	1	6	2	4
4	3	6	1	2	5
6	3	5	3	2	2
5	5	4	1	3	6
5	2	4	4	4	1
5	1	2	3	6	3

THINK ALIKE

Unscramble the letters in the phrase STOP HORSE to form two words with the same or similar meanings.

_____   _____

★★★ In the Cards by Robert H. Wolfe

1 Bundle of loot
5 Plus
9 They're all true
14 *Hairspray* mom
15 Burn a bit
16 Maui greeting
17 Highway warning sign
19 Is worthy
20 Introduces
21 Puts down on paper
22 All ready
23 CV
24 "__ evil, hear ..."
25 One with a habit
26 "__ never work!"
27 Org. for Shaq
30 Political confrontation
33 Some suburbs
35 Green land
36 Atmosphere
37 Genie offering
38 Waiting-room reading
41 A lot
43 It means "a little"
44 "What __ For Love" (*A Chorus Line* song)
45 Disencumber
46 Worn away
48 Cry out loud
49 Photo
52 Mystery writer Christie
54 Get near
56 Silver or Scout
57 Homeric subject
58 Computer key
59 Soothing plant
60 Susan on *Desperate Housewives*
61 High, flat hills
62 Warning from Mom
63 Lyric poems

DOWN
1 Lends a hand
2 Dote on
3 Dried out, perhaps
4 Chemists' spots
5 Silly
6 Resulted in
7 Is droopy
8 Cal. neighbor
9 Studs Lonigan creator
10 French actor Delon
11 Seed separator
12 You, of old
13 Be impertinent

18 Disprove
21 Water source
24 Cooking direction
25 Barrie barker
26 Covered with plants, perhaps
28 Tops
29 Pale gray
30 Bruce Willis ex
31 Big times
32 Generous natures
34 Inspired with wonder
36 Have __ with (know well)

39 Stringed instruments
40 Notion
41 Type of plane
42 Zodiac sign
47 Floundering
48 Dish's companion
49 Touched clumsily
50 Phrase of concern
51 Rock of comedy
52 Throat-clearing sound
53 No longer here
54 Woody's son
55 Not taken in by
57 Abe's son

★★★ 123

Fill in the diagram so that each rectangular piece has one each of the numbers 1, 2, and 3, under these rules: 1) No two adjacent squares, horizontally or vertically, can have the same number. 2) Each completed row and column of the diagram will have an equal number of 1's, 2's, and 3's.

SUDOKU SUM

Fill in the missing numbers from 1 to 9, so that the sum of each row and column is as indicated.

	11	23	11
11		8	
20	7		
14			5

★★★ Find the Ships

Determine the position of the 10 ships listed to the right of the diagram. The ships may be oriented either horizontally or vertically. A square with wavy lines indicates water and will not contain a ship. The numbers at the edge of the diagram indicate how many squares in that row or column contain parts of ships. When all 10 ships are correctly placed in the diagram, no two of them will touch each other, not even diagonally.

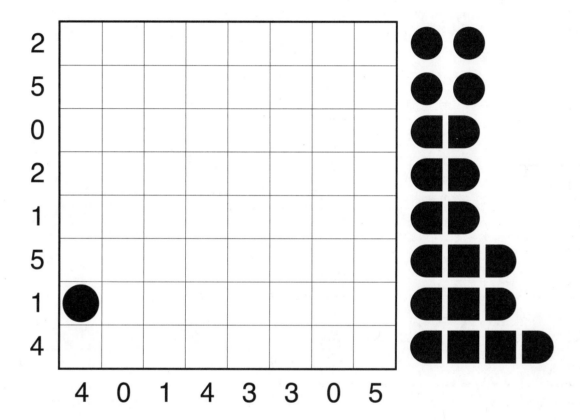

TWO-BY-FOUR

The eight letters in the word RUMINANT can be rearranged to form a pair of common four-letter words in only one way, if no four-letter word is repeated. Can you find the two words?

— — — —　— — — —

★★★ Fetch by Randall J. Hartman

ACROSS

1 Cuban dance
6 Grind to a halt
10 Former Milan money
14 Sports negotiator
15 Large quantity
16 River through Kazakhstan
17 Plotter's need
19 Candy shape
20 Sashimi fare
21 Glasgow girl
22 Southern NFL team
24 Skipper's spot
25 Window ledge
26 Balance-sheet entries
29 Horror-film scientist's cry
33 Close shave
34 Jogging gait
35 Genesis spot
36 *The Alienist* author
37 Gator cousins
38 Longtime West Virginia senator
39 Jai __
40 Sow's squeal
41 Have a cow
42 Some streamers
44 Cut down
45 "Had enough?"
46 Narrate
47 Fit to be tried?
50 Fish story
51 __ de deux
54 It's nothing
55 Cop club
58 Harness attachment
59 Small band
60 __-frutti
61 Church area
62 Out of the woods
63 Deep chasm

DOWN

1 Hamster's home
2 Fiend of folklore
3 *Hud* Oscar winner
4 Econ. indicator
5 One in training
6 Sudden twitch
7 Overturns
8 Bullring cheer
9 Keeps going
10 Early TV superstar
11 OPEC member
12 Carry on
13 Microbrewery offerings
18 Close associates
23 __ mode
24 Textile pattern
25 Inventory
26 Tin Pan Alley org.
27 Symbol of justice
28 Kitchen wrap
29 Golf-bag items
30 Pastoral poem
31 Pizazz
32 Done
34 Far from fresh
37 Buildings with cells
41 Glockenspiel relative
43 Have a bug
44 Pool-table material
46 Resort near Reno
47 Old Testament book
48 Hard to comprehend
49 Spring bloom
50 Weary worker's mantra
51 Feel bad for
52 Performs
53 Participates in the Super G
56 401(k) alternative
57 Clumsy boat

★ Serendipity

Find these "lucky" terms that are hidden in the diagram either across, down, or diagonally. (Individual words of multiple-word answers are hidden separately; ignore words in parentheses.) There's one additional nine-letter answer in the category, not listed below, that's also hidden in the diagram. What's that word?

```
B W Z S S U C C E S S F U L Y
H E P R O S P E R O U S F F L
O L N E W W F L Q C O E A A E
R V D E S S E L B H I N E V M
S E L P F L L T A T U L O I
E L V O F I I O R I T R R T
S P E O R O C S A M P R U E R
H O R T L S I I T E O O O D C
O F O O A C T L A D R P F S L
E M I M M N O K L L P P B U L
J S U O T I U T R O F O F U R
C L O V E D S T U H R E C G W
T N A H P M U I R T P K F W Y
E N V I A B L E N O Y P P A H
W I N N I N G X H G F R O L N
```

BENEFICIAL
BLESSED
CHARMED
ENVIABLE
FAVORED
FELICITOUS
FORTUITOUS
FORTUNATE
FOUR-LEAF CLOVER
HAPPY
HOPEFUL
LUCKY
MASCOT
(On a) ROLL
OPPORTUNE
PROMISING
PROPITIOUS
PROSPEROUS
SUCCESSFUL
TIMELY
TRIUMPHANT
WELL OFF
WINNING

IN OTHER WORDS

There is only one common uncapitalized word that contains the consecutive letters DKE. What is it?

_____

★★ Alternating Tiles

Starting at a red tile somewhere at top and moving either horizontally or vertically, draw a path through the tiles to the bottom. You may not pass through two tiles of the same color consecutively.

SMALL CHANGE

Change one letter in each of these two words, to form a common two-word phrase.

PEACH TOWER

_____

★★★ Star Search

Find the stars that are hidden in some of the blank squares. The numbered squares indicate how many stars are hidden in the squares adjacent to them (including diagonally). There is never more than one star in any square.

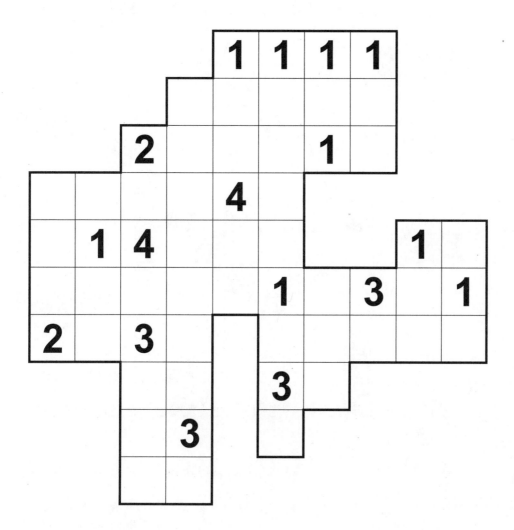

CHOICE WORDS

Form three six-letter words from the same category, by selecting one letter from each column three times. Each letter will be used exactly once.

G	E	B	E	O	N	_ _ _ _ _ _
T	O	R	P	E	T	_ _ _ _ _ _
T	U	A	L	E	T	_ _ _ _ _ _

★★★ Cutting Class by Donna Levin

ACROSS

1 Hindu ascetic
6 Tent openings
11 Moistened
14 Steakhouse order
15 Israeli resort
16 Blow away
17 Karate move
19 Gun
20 "à la vodka" pasta
21 If you please
23 Cosine reciprocals
26 A, for one
27 Made accountable for
28 Of an interruption
29 Astrological beast
30 Toad features
31 W. Va. clock setting
34 Guacamole and hummus
35 Intent looks
36 Intertwine
37 "Uh-huh!"
38 In good shape
39 "Don't hold your breath!"
40 Got together on the sly
42 Baltimore footballers
43 Stretches out
45 Many a Floridian
46 Our, to Umberto
47 Swan song's opposite
48 Fireworks watcher's exclamation
49 Succinctness principle
54 Site of the Tell legend
55 Lab-dish name
56 Pong creator
57 Recipe abbreviation
58 Favored earl of Elizabeth I
59 Advantage

DOWN

1 Mil. posts
2 Dancing with the Stars network
3 Fish in a Japanese garden
4 To the nth degree
5 Takes umbrage at
6 Plants with fronds
7 Be fond of
8 Larter of Heroes
9 Obsessive collectors
10 Caribbean island
11 Wally and Beaver's dad
12 The Seven Year Itch actor
13 "If I Were a Rich Man" singer
18 Cognizant of
22 Actress Vardalos
23 Disreputable
24 Kind of creepy
25 Gold Rush-era vessel
26 Made public
28 Made misty
30 Ebbs
32 Noisy spectacle
33 Not windy
35 Succeed
36 Perform a magic trick
38 Water-skier need
39 Unaffected
41 Long.'s counterpart
42 Yanks' opponents
43 Porky's nose
44 Standard partner
45 New version of an old song
47 Have the nerve
50 Small change: Abbr.
51 Move erratically
52 Tulsa sch.
53 Criticize

★★★ Sudoku

Fill in the blank boxes so that every row, column, and 3x3 box contains all of the numbers 1 to 9.

4	5						8	9
2								7
			5		8			
	9				7	8		
	2			6		5		
	7		2			6		
			9		3			
8								3
3	6						4	8

MIXAGRAMS

Each line contains a five-letter word and a four-letter word that have been mixed together (the order of the letters in each word has not been changed). Unmix the two words on each line and write them in the spaces provided. When you're done, find a two-part answer to the clue by reading down the letter columns in the answers.

CLUE: Where jerks work

S E M I B E D E R = _ _ _ _ _ + _ _ _ _

T H A K E F T E N = _ _ _ _ _ + _ _ _ _

G O L U C H O R Y = _ _ _ _ _ + _ _ _ _

P E S T R E L U M = _ _ _ _ _ + _ _ _ _

★★★ One-Way Streets

The diagram represents a pattern of streets. A and B are parking spaces, and the black squares are stores. Find the route that starts at A, passes through all stores exactly once, and ends at B. Arrows indicate one-way traffic for that block only. No block or intersection may be entered more than once.

SOUND THINKING

The consonant sounds in the word HURLED are H, R, L, and D. What other six-letter word (not ending in ED) is pronounced with the same consonant sounds in the same order?

_____

★★★ ABC

Enter the letters A, B, and C into the diagram so that each row and column has exactly one A, one B, and one C. The letters outside the diagram indicate the first letter encountered, moving in the direction of the arrow. Keep in mind that after all the letters have been filled in, there will be two blank boxes in each row and column.

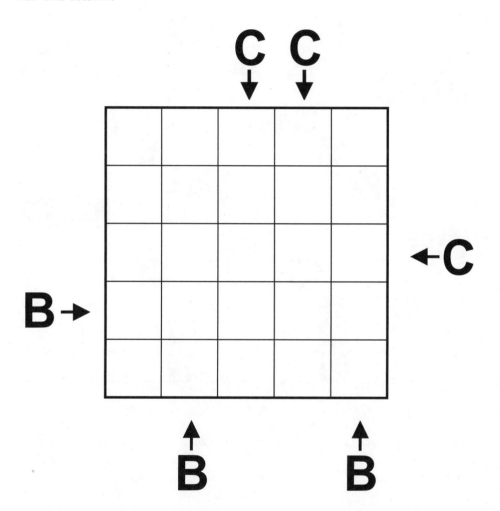

NATIONAL TREASURE

Rearrange the letters in ARGENTINE to get something edible.

— — — — — — —

★★★ Hard Sells by Doug Peterson

ACROSS

1 Fake drake
6 Warty critter
10 One-liner
14 Wed on the sly
15 Holy ring
16 Open, as knots
17 Highly excited state
19 Éclair finisher
20 Uniform
21 Bear in the air
22 "Swiss" entrée
23 Consequences
25 Long-snouted beast
27 Rhythm of little feet
31 Card con
34 Stuck on oneself
35 Many moons __
36 Sweet sandwich
37 Tollbooth location
39 Mediterranean fruits
40 Crew-team member
41 Gradually withdraw
42 Garden flower
43 Xylophone cousin
47 __ Series
48 Bullwinkle feature
52 Emulate Pac-Man
54 Ultimate
56 Run off
57 Plot flaw
58 Net profit or loss
60 Facts, briefly
61 "Dies __"
62 Sized up
63 Hammer end
64 Track figures
65 Slow-cooked courses

DOWN

1 Postpone
2 French student
3 Sheltered bays
4 Confide in
5 Suffix for law
6 Craving
7 Granola ingredient
8 Pen called "The Rock"
9 Outburst from Homer
10 "That's enough!"
11 Up in the air
12 Notion
13 Cuban sandwich ingredient
18 Shot that rolls
22 Wing measurement
24 Be false
26 Capital of Samoa
28 Dynasty actress
29 Easter purchase
30 Promising
31 Synthesizer name
32 Paperless test
33 Rex Stout character
37 Tangerine cover
38 Boardinghouse proprietor
39 Fail completely
41 Sitcom call letters
42 Classroom favorite
44 "Gimme a break!"
45 Works on a collage
46 Serious about
49 Chosen few
50 Freshen
51 Future flowers
52 Salsa scooper
53 Make keener
55 Not very much
58 Celeb's story
59 Miss, after matrimony

★★ Wheels and Cogs

When the bandit turns the handle as shown, is he rewarded with the dollars or the dynamite?

BETWEENER

What five-letter word belongs between the word at left and the word at right, so that the first and second word, and the second and third word, each form a common compound word?

STOP __ __ __ __ __ WORD

★★★ Find the Ships

Determine the position of the 10 ships listed to the right of the diagram. The ships may be oriented either horizontally or vertically. A square with wavy lines indicates water and will not contain a ship. The numbers at the edge of the diagram indicate how many squares in that row or column contain parts of ships. When all 10 ships are correctly placed in the diagram, no two of them will touch each other, not even diagonally.

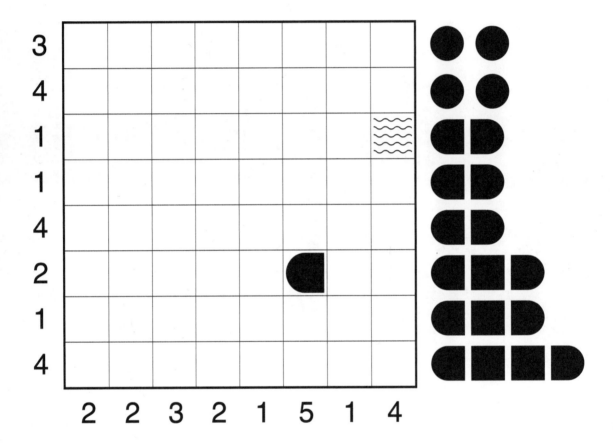

TWO-BY-FOUR

The eight letters in the word TATTOOED can be rearranged to form a pair of common four-letter words in two different ways. Can you find both pairs of words?

— — — —   — — — —

— — — —   — — — —

★★★ 123

Fill in the diagram so that each rectangular piece has one each of the numbers 1, 2, and 3, under these rules: 1) No two adjacent squares, horizontally or vertically, can have the same number. 2) Each completed row and column of the diagram will have an equal number of 1's, 2's, and 3's.

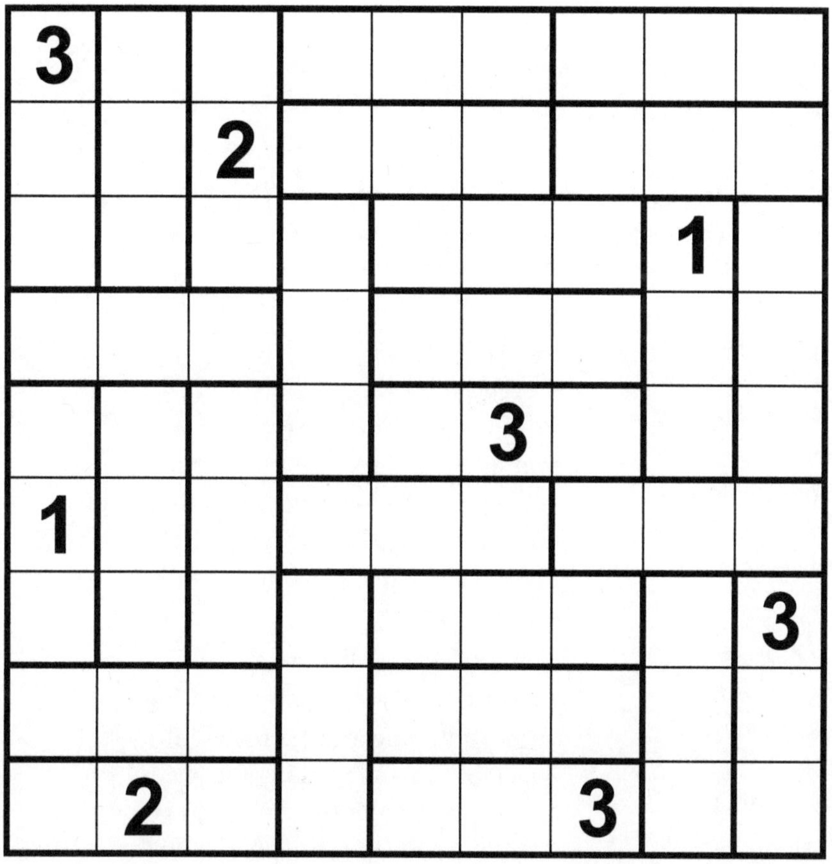

3								
		2						
							1	
					3			
1								
								3
	2					3		

ADDITION SWITCH

Switch the positions of two of the digits in the incorrect sum at right, to get a correct sum.

```
  808
+ 749
-----
  951
```

bRain BReatHeR
THE 411 ON STORING FRESH FOOD

Tired of having to toss out "fresh" food because its freshness is so fleeting? Try these tips for extending the life of the fresh foods you buy.

First things first: The truth about food-package dates Many perishable-food packages are stamped—by the FDA in the US, and the CFIA in Canada—with dates identified by terms such as "use by," "best before," etc. However, with very few exceptions, this information is useful only as a general guideline and is more about the food's peak freshness than about safety; most foods are quite safe well beyond the dates on their packaging.

TLC for the contents of vegetable crispers Line your fridge's crisper drawer with paper towels, which will absorb the excess moisture that's the bane of raw veggies. Replace the towels as they become damp. A similar method for dehumidifying the crisper is to place a couple of new kitchen sponges in the drawer, squeezing moisture out over the sink as needed.

Longer-lasting milk If you buy more milk than you can use before the expiration date, extend its life with a couple of pinches of baking soda. Baking soda reduces milk's acidity, thus staving off spoilage.

Vinegar and cheese To keep cheese fresh, wrap it in a piece of soft cloth dampened with vinegar. It should come as no surprise that cheesecloth is ideal for this purpose.

Celery Care 101 Celery is all about crispness, so when it starts to go limp, you might as well toss it—right? Not necessarily. Try putting sagging stalks in a bowl of cold water with a few slices of raw potato. After an hour or so in this starchy bath, the celery is likely to deliver the crunch you expect.

Oiled eggs Prolong the life of fresh eggs by dipping a paper towel into vegetable oil and rubbing the shells before storing the eggs in the fridge. The oil will keep the eggs fresh for an additional three to four weeks!

Get the most out of lemons When a recipe calls for a few drops of lemon, don't slice the lemon. Simply puncture the rind with a toothpick and gently squeeze out the small amount of juice you need. Then, cover the hole you made with a piece of tape and return the lemon to the fridge until you need it again.

★★★★ Letter Drops by Raymond Hamel

ACROSS

1 Party snack
5 Purse feature
10 Location
14 Resting upon
15 Leave wanting more
16 Use hip boots
17 Ravi Shankar offering
18 "Rubber Duckie" singer
19 White House worker
20 *Beagle* passenger
23 Large sea duck
24 Where to get *Lost*?
26 Fringe groups
29 __ Jima
31 Dolly's cry
33 Hybrid fruit
34 "Dream Lover" singer
38 Space
39 New York city
40 Aims (for)
41 Is concerned
43 __ Royale National Park
44 Erie-to-Philadelphia dir.
45 Start of MGM's motto
46 Antiknock fuel
47 Rough journey
49 Excessive excitement
52 Forrest Gump's friend
58 Jackie's couturier
60 Stood for
61 January caucus state
62 "Sure!"
63 *The Taming of the Shrew* setting
64 Works by Horace
65 Artist's quarters
66 Common sense
67 Snack

DOWN

1 Bust maker
2 Jazz home
3 Imperial attire of old
4 Leisure hours
5 Trusty horse
6 Brief
7 Break from work
8 Hong Kong's location
9 Marquess, e.g.
10 Beau
11 Palette toucher
12 Strange
13 Stand with a concave head
21 __ *for Lawless*
22 Ax target
25 As Narcissus would
26 Sudden increase
27 Narcissus, for one
28 Highway feature
29 Construction piece
30 "The Perfect Fool"
32 Photographer Adams
34 Male badger
35 Reo eponym
36 Arthur of TV
37 Washing-machine action
42 Rice beverage
46 Article in *Der Spiegel*
48 Edith Head's Oscar count
49 General at Antietam
50 Invalidate
51 Of birth
53 Strike callers
54 Colts or Broncos
55 Pigeon's erstwhile kin
56 Deeply moves
57 *A Beautiful Mind* subject
58 Popeye's pal
59 Sign of summer

★★★ Square Routes

Fill in the blank circles so that every row, column, and path contains all of the numbers from 1 to 6.

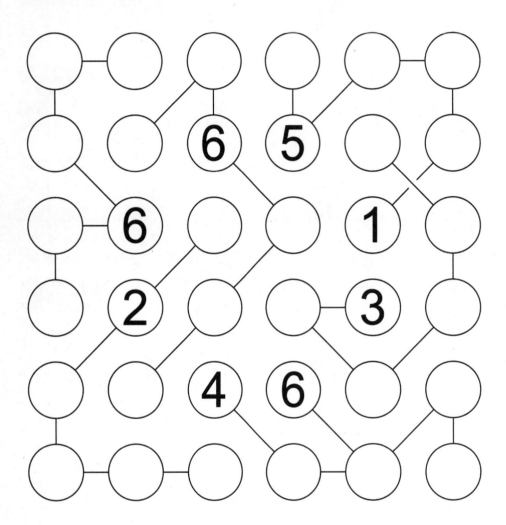

WRONG IS RIGHT

Which of these four words is misspelled?

A) spaghetti   B) sphygmomanometer

C) spesious   D) spigot

★★★ Number-Out

Shade squares so that no number appears in any row or column more than once. Shaded squares may not touch each other horizontally or vertically, and all unshaded squares must form a single continuous area.

2	5	3	3	6	4
3	5	6	5	4	2
4	6	1	1	1	5
1	3	5	4	2	3
4	2	4	6	5	2
5	4	4	6	1	2

THINK ALIKE

Unscramble the letters in the phrase RELINE RUG to form two words with the same or similar meanings.

_____   _____

★★★★ All the Way by Rich Silvestri

ACROSS

1 Almost a majority
5 Abound
9 Bernie's songwriting partner
14 Theater award
15 The A of TAE
16 Start a set
17 Great Pyramid site
18 Transvaal settler
19 Show contempt
20 Surprising folk tale
23 Be situated
24 Jeer at
25 Points in time
29 American seismologist
33 City near Los Angeles
34 Model's asset
36 Like
37 Makes a memo
38 Tootler's need
39 Cape Cod, essentially
40 Early afternoon
41 *Bewitched* aunt
42 Derisive
43 Beef or lamb
45 Stuck with a stick
47 Hand and foot
49 Foul caller
50 Captain Kirk's pay
57 French river
58 Criticizes
59 "Now __ me down ..."
60 Zeal
61 Soissons state
62 Frank casing
63 Chews (on)
64 Test model
65 Green feature

DOWN

1 Monopolizes
2 Minimally
3 Judy's eldest
4 Intrepid
5 Gelcap alternative
6 *Time Machine* people
7 Long jump, e.g.
8 Cantina concoctions
9 Basic nature
10 Duration
11 House site
12 Cookie cooker
13 Social outcast
21 *What's Love Got to Do With It* name
22 Oscar actress Rainer
25 Student's choice
26 Threatened layer
27 Toned down
28 Made a mess, in a way
30 Long-snouted mammal
31 Skip, as a syllable
32 Sized up
35 Paternoster beginning
38 Natural talent
39 Irritable
41 Convergence points
42 Final Four game
44 *See It Now* host
46 Asks of
48 "Good" person
50 Smeltery refuse
51 Unable to choose
52 Radames' love
53 Unwanted e-mail
54 Nevada city
55 Get the goods on
56 Force measure

★★★ Pirate Ship

Enter the maze where indicated at bottom, pass through all the stars exactly once, then exit where indicated at bottom. You may not retrace your path.

BETWEENER

What five-letter word belongs between the word at left and the word at right, so that the first and second word, and the second and third word, each form a common compound word?

TURN __ __ __ __ __ CLOTH

★★★ Hyper-Sudoku

Fill in the blank boxes so that every row, column, 3x3 box, *and* each of the four
3x3 gray regions contains all of the numbers 1 to 9.

	1				2		5	
5	6				9	8		
						7		
	7				5			
					3			
	8		4					
	5	4						
		6				3		
1	2		9		6	4		7

MIXAGRAMS

Each line contains a five-letter word and a four-letter word that have been mixed together (the order of the letters in each word has not been changed). Unmix the two words on each line and write them in the spaces provided. When you're done, find a two-part answer to the clue by reading down the letter columns in the answers.

CLUE: What milk may do

```
K N A T I S A L S  =  _ _ _ _ _  +  _ _ _ _
I T O U R C H O N  =  _ _ _ _ _  +  _ _ _ _
E S E R M U M U S  =  _ _ _ _ _  +  _ _ _ _
O M Y N U R A S H  =  _ _ _ _ _  +  _ _ _ _
```

★ Speak Up

Find these languages and terms related to languages that are hidden in the diagram either across, down, or diagonally.

```
E V K D N N G N T G Y Q G N E
S A E M I A O I A E Q I O O N
P W G R E A R R S C B I Y G G
E O E L N K L E S B S R N R L
R L I R S A L E E E N U I A I
A C G N B A C R C X A G R J S
N A A N H E I U H T A N A T H
T S W G O S H O L J K O D L E
O M N F H T S D U A I T N A T
V I V O C A B U L A R Y A T N
S O N I P I L I F R F C M I O
T A G A L O G E T G A S T B R
G R E E K E U G N O T A X H S
G I B B E R I S Z T L A T I P
```

AFRIKAANS
ARGOT
DIALECT
ENGLISH
ESPERANTO
ETRUSCAN
FILIPINO
GAELIC
GIBBERISH
GREEK
HEBREW
JARGON
LATIN
MANDARIN
NORSE
SANSKRIT
SINGHALESE
TAGALOG
TONGUE
VERNACULAR
VOCABULARY
XHOSA

INITIAL REACTION

Identify the well-known proverb from the first letters in each of its words.

I. N. R. B. I. P. _____

★★★★ Four-H Club by Fred Piscop

ACROSS

1 DJ's inventory
4 Scratches, perhaps
8 *The Nanny* name
12 Former Big Apple ballpark
13 Double reed
14 Playbill listings
16 Conversation interrupter
19 Peanut product
20 Can't stomach
21 Tear into
22 Flat land
24 Pleasingly pretty
25 Roof covering
26 Close-knit group
27 Chocolate unit
30 Big-mouthed reptiles
33 Links cry
34 Gabrielle Chanel's nickname
35 Dressy footwear
38 Friend in battle
39 Dental photo
40 Easy mark
41 Kicker's prop
42 Marquee name
43 Race official
44 Author Silverstein
45 Emergency situation
49 Nucleus part
52 Ten C-notes
53 Doc bloc
54 '60s veep
57 "Uncle!"
58 Partner
59 Dynamic start
60 Goes to visit
61 Was behind
62 Give it a shot

DOWN

1 Group in a loft
2 Mason's helper
3 Bummed out
4 Angora fabric
5 Tail off
6 Repetitive pattern
7 Ready
8 Citrus ruiners
9 Fire up
10 Pond organism
11 *M*A*S*H* drink
12 Visit an e-tailer
15 Cardinal cap letters
17 Defeat soundly
18 Took by truck
23 Like a bug bite
24 '90s pop-music sensation
26 Opposite in character
27 Kick out
28 Air heroes
29 Optimistic
30 Cyber-exchange
31 Fire up
32 Make eyes at
33 Unbroken
34 Rub roughly
36 Full range
37 Hit the gas
42 Resort settings
43 Shared a flat (with)
44 Malcolm Forbes' son
45 Water-park slide
46 Harder to locate
47 Abrasive stuff
48 Belafonte tune
49 Key word
50 Floor covers
51 Stage award
52 Reduction in tension
55 Patient care grp.
56 Something to tip

★★ Triad Split Decisions

In this clueless crossword puzzle, each answer consists of two words whose spellings are the same, except for the consecutive letters given. All answers are common words; no phrases or hyphenated or capitalized words are used. Some of the clues may have more than one solution, but there is only one word pair that will correctly link up with all the other word pairs.

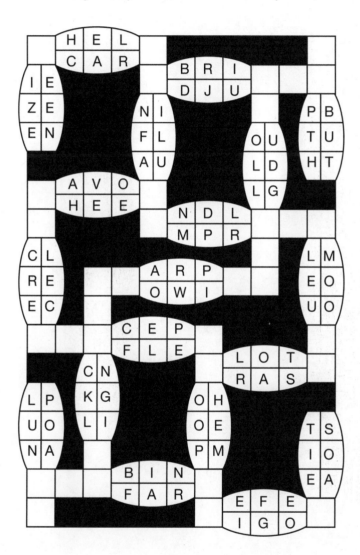

TRANSDELETION

Delete one letter from the word REFILTER and rearrange the rest, to get a farming term.

_____

★★★ One-Way Streets

The diagram represents a pattern of streets. A and B are parking spaces, and the black squares are stores. Find the route that starts at A, passes through all stores exactly once, and ends at B. Arrows indicate one-way traffic for that block only. No block or intersection may be entered more than once.

SOUND THINKING

What is the shortest common uncapitalized word whose only consonant sounds are two J's?

_____

★★★★ Off Your Chest by Merle Baker

ACROSS

1 Inhibit
6 Like some chances
10 Nautical pole
14 Lothario
15 Greenhorn
16 Steering wheel
17 *Sesame Street* misanthrope
18 Bands together, in a way
20 Worker with a chisel
22 Looked through casually
23 Comic bane
27 Connecticut campus
28 Some loaves
30 Reliever's quest
31 Grassland
33 Watch readouts, briefly
36 Microwave
37 Words from Ecclesiastes
40 Transmit telephonically
42 Arctic ice
43 Will Smith film
44 Turned red, maybe
46 Caspian Sea feeder
48 Irving character
52 Brush up on
55 Office gadget
57 Source of scores
59 Disrespectful
62 Parboil
63 Farm sound
64 __'acte
65 Try
66 Shade trees
67 Freudian mediators
68 Bar figs.

DOWN

1 A *That's Entertainment!* host
2 Oration stations
3 "O.K. with me"
4 Have good intentions
5 Sponge parts
6 Robust
7 *Fatal Attraction* director
8 Isle of Man locale
9 Lodge member
10 Goofs off
11 Dispenser candy
12 Tap choice
13 Apt. divisions
19 Japanese computer giant
21 Go astray
24 Not assiduous
25 "Little" '60s singer
26 Good name, for short
29 Young eel
32 Mischievous kid
34 *CSI* setting
35 French contraction
37 Jump on the ice
38 Test measurement
39 Striped pet
40 White House monogram
41 Voter's choice
45 Enticements
47 Changes
49 Orioles' div.
50 Land and buildings
51 Bluenoses
53 Comics bark
54 U.S. Grant foe
56 Rhymes of music
58 Fascinated by
59 Honour given to J.K. Rowling
60 Web browser entry
61 Highlands hat

★★★ Tile Maze

Find the shortest path through the maze from the bottom to the center, by passing over color tiles in this order: red, blue, yellow, red, blue, etc. It is okay to retrace your path.

SAY IT AGAIN

What five-letter word can be either a short street or a sports venue?

— — — — —

★★★ Star Search

Find the stars that are hidden in some of the blank squares. The numbered squares indicate how many stars are hidden in the squares adjacent to them (including diagonally). There is never more than one star in any square.

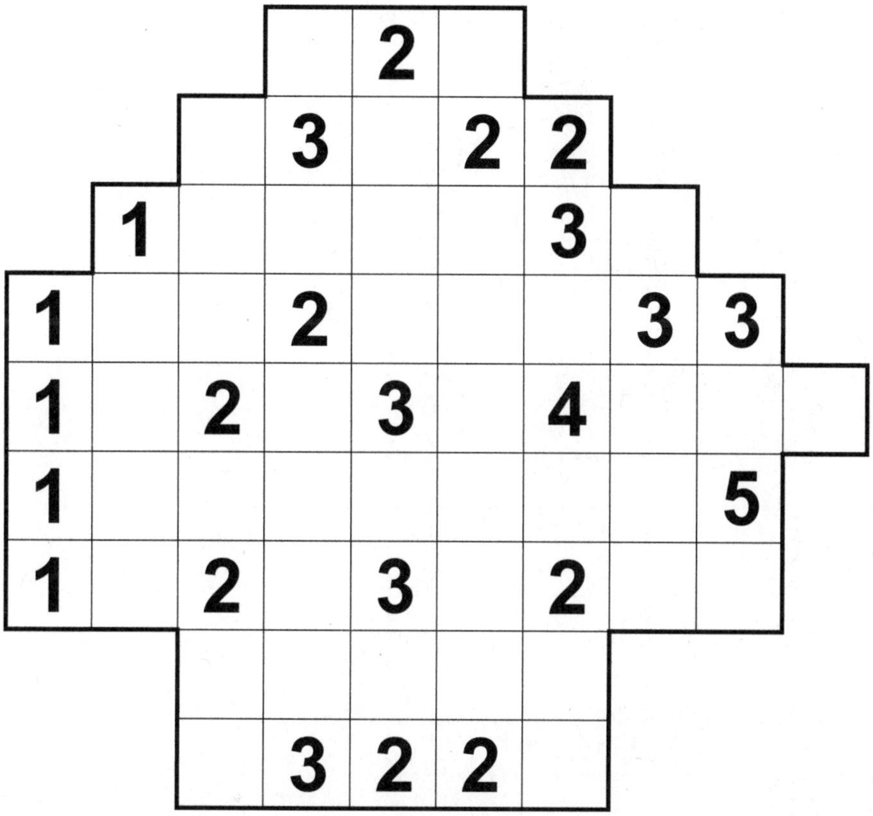

CHOICE WORDS

Form three six-letter words from the same category, by selecting one letter from each column three times. Each letter will be used exactly once.

E	E	T	A	G	E
R	E	G	A	R	N
S	N	C	U	I	E

_ _ _ _ _ _
_ _ _ _ _ _
_ _ _ _ _ _

★★★ Sudoku

Fill in the blank boxes so that every row, column, and 3x3 box contains all of the numbers 1 to 9.

1	9	3						
							5	
	6				4			7
		1				6		3
7				4				9
2		8			7			
5			6			2		
	8							
					9	1	3	

CENTURY MARKS

Select one number in each of the four columns so that the total adds up to exactly 100.

$$\boxed{\begin{matrix}14\\19\end{matrix}} + \boxed{\begin{matrix}28\\29\end{matrix}} + \boxed{\begin{matrix}27\\21\end{matrix}} + \boxed{\begin{matrix}25\\26\end{matrix}} = 100$$

★★★★ Silver Bullets by Ray Hamel

ACROSS

1 Sampling undoer
5 Threatening word
9 Low-paying employment
14 Leave a deep impression
15 Gangster's gal
16 Yellowish cheese
17 Sonic comeback
18 Milk container
19 Tunnel creators
20 He was stopped by a silver bullet
23 Customary act
24 JFK and RFK, e.g.
25 Haunt
27 Formulated idea
30 __ sprach Zarathustra
32 Distinctive air
33 Irascible *St. Elsewhere* doctor
34 Hardworking boat
37 Site of the Silver Bullet roller coaster
41 Shaker marking
42 How crates may be set
43 Jackie Robinson school
44 Twelve Oaks neighbor
45 No more than
47 Petulance
51 Bounty rival
52 Last name in spydom
53 User of silver bullets
59 Melancholy poem
61 Sink or swim
62 Deal (with)
63 Greeting word or parting word
64 "Major" constellation
65 Listen to
66 Petulant
67 Synthesizer name
68 Brings to bear

DOWN

1 Borscht veggie
2 Restless longing
3 Rue the run
4 End-zone dancer, say
5 Take advantage of
6 Lounges
7 Shed some weight
8 Spanish "she"
9 *Gigi* studio
10 With 50 Down, product with Silver Bullet Train ads
11 *Carousel* heroine
12 *Golden Boy* playwright
13 They may be loaded
21 Boston Bruins great
22 Polite refusal
26 Hobgoblin
27 Gate profits
28 Barbarous group
29 Child of Aphrodite
30 Pro sports venue
31 Cooking material
33 Semi driver, often
34 Tex-Mex snack
35 Web addresses
36 GRE relative
38 Airplane carry-on
39 Show one's teeth
40 Fictional criminal genius
45 Car-safety item
46 Dam org.
47 Use a crib, perhaps
48 Handel's birthplace
49 Triple-layer treats
50 See 10 Down
51 Page two, for one
54 Haploid cell
55 *Quo Vadis* ruler
56 Exits
57 Blunt weapon
58 Warren Beatty movie
60 Spectator's cheer

★★★ ABC

Enter the letters A, B, and C into the diagram so that each row and column has exactly one A, one B, and one C. The letters outside the diagram indicate the first letter encountered, moving in the direction of the arrow. Keep in mind that after all the letters have been filled in, there will be two blank boxes in each row and column.

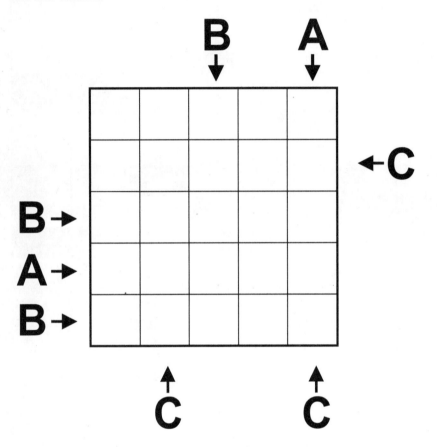

CLUELESS CROSSWORD

Complete the crossword with common uncapitalized seven-letter words, based entirely on the letters already filled in for you.

★★★ Find the Ships

Determine the position of the 10 ships listed to the right of the diagram. The ships may be oriented either horizontally or vertically. A square with wavy lines indicates water and will not contain a ship. The numbers at the edge of the diagram indicate how many squares in that row or column contain parts of ships. When all 10 ships are correctly placed in the diagram, no two of them will touch each other, not even diagonally.

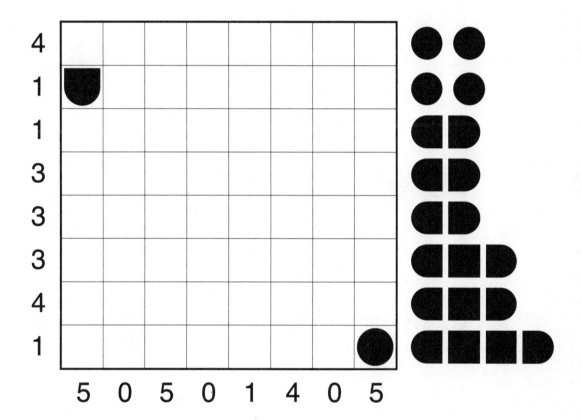

TWO-BY-FOUR

The eight letters in the word UNBROKEN can be rearranged to form a pair of common four-letter words in three different ways. Can you find them all?

— — — —   — — — —   — — — —   — — — —

— — — —   — — — —

★★★★ Chief Cities by Alex Vaughn

ACROSS

1 Facial center
4 Biography subtitle, perhaps
9 Catherine in a Tudor home
13 Alley trailer
14 __ vivendi
15 Wee hr.
17 Eponymous figure in four state capitals' names
19 "Uncle!"
20 Leander's love
21 Quintessential villain
22 "OK!"
23 Flawed, in mfg.
25 One of four (see 17 Across)
27 Backyard amenities
30 Kappa preceder
31 Melodiously
32 Tribe of Israel
33 Toe's neighbor
36 One of four (see 17 Across)
40 __ Boys (Alcott novel)
41 Extreme
42 Ashe Stadium event
43 In __ (where it first was)
45 Uncontrived
46 One of four (see 17 Across)
50 Mag mogul's moniker
51 Use
52 Animal with 54 Across
54 Fine feathers
57 Word before "words"
58 One of four (see 17 Across)
60 Shearing music?
61 Aura
62 Bendable element
63 Nile denizens
64 Not leave alone
65 "Sprechen __ Deutsch?"

DOWN

1 History 201 taker, perhaps
2 Gaze earnestly
3 Before-dinner drinks
4 Friend of a Francophile
5 California wine center
6 Guides for the high-minded
7 Mold and mildew
8 Language akin to Finnish
9 Belgian sleuth
10 Zambia neighbor
11 Tut's tenure
12 Bird seen on totem poles
16 Insignificant
18 In a way
24 Trick
26 Think likewise
27 Certain pilgrimage
28 Two-tone cookie
29 Hereditarily occupying
32 Simpsons shout
33 Graphic-design choices
34 City on the Skunk River
35 Hoodwinks
37 Fall guy?
38 Narrow strip of land: Abbr.
39 El Greco home
43 Tasseled top, often
44 Cays and such
45 My Life __ ('85 film)
46 Window piece
47 St. Teresa's place
48 Weaves, as a chair seat
49 Stiller's partner
53 Fava look-alike
55 When DDE oversaw the ETO
56 Striped billiard ball
59 Cal. column

★★ Dot to Dot

Draw five squares in the diagram so that each corner of each square is on a dot.
The squares may be at any angle. Dots may be used for more than one square,
or not be used at all.

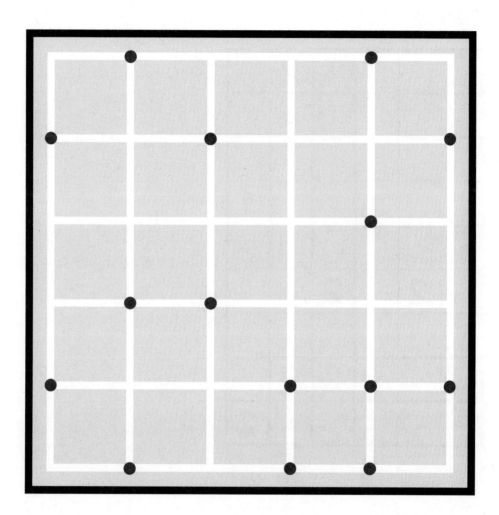

SMALL CHANGE

Change one letter in each of these two words, to form a common two-word phrase.

SHOW COOLER

★★★ 123

Fill in the diagram so that each rectangular piece has one each of the numbers 1, 2, and 3, under these rules: 1) No two adjacent squares, horizontally or vertically, can have the same number. 2) Each completed row and column of the diagram will have an equal number of 1's, 2's, and 3's.

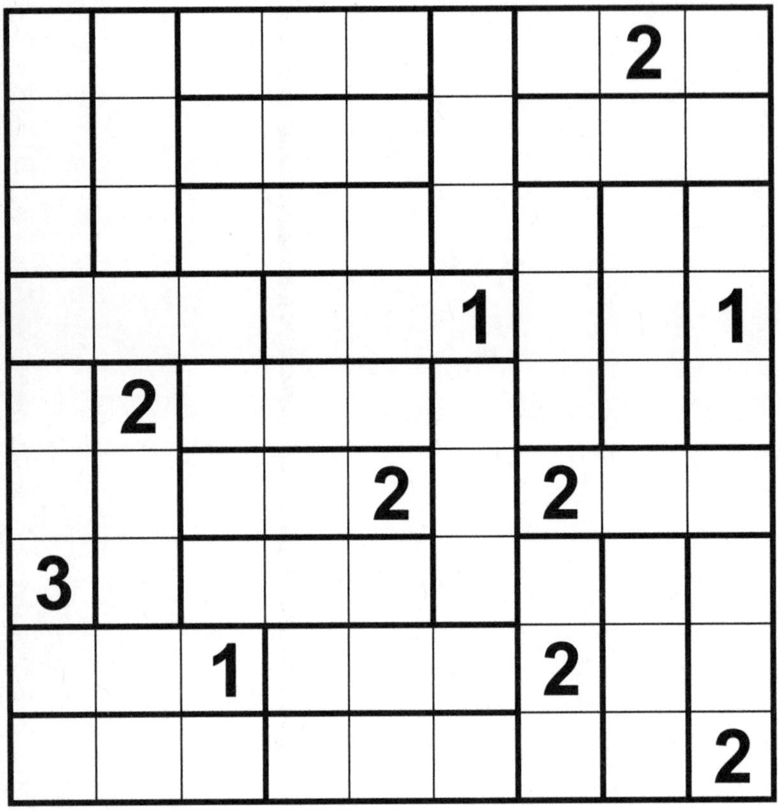

SUDOKU SUM

Fill in the missing numbers from 1 to 9, so that the sum of each row and column is as indicated.

	17	14	14
19			7
14	8		
12		1	

★★★ Square Routes

Fill in the blank circles so that every row, column, and path contains all of the numbers from 1 to 6.

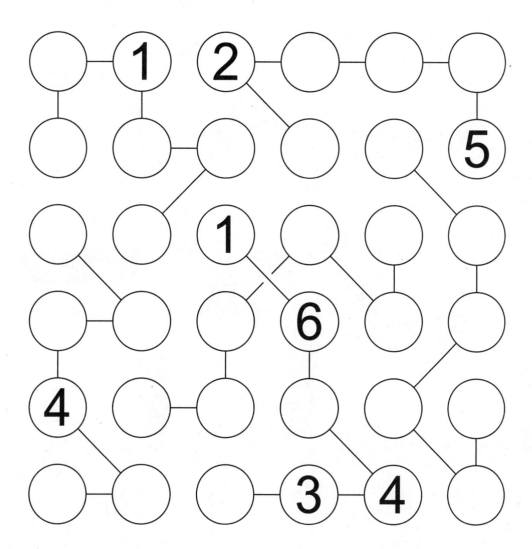

<u>**WRONG IS RIGHT**</u>

Which of these four words is misspelled?

A) homily

B) hominny

C) hombre

D) homogenize

★★★★ Mexican Menu by S.N.

ACROSS

1 Have a bawl
5 600 Home Run Club member
9 Biblical prophet
14 Mideast airline
15 Butterfingers' comment
16 Uncle Sam's land
17 Rick's old flame
18 Remark of disbelief
19 Pub orders
20 "Fajitas," literally
23 *Merrick* character
24 Seam material
25 Check for food
28 New York college
31 Odysseus' home
33 "The Man Who Owned Broadway"
37 Times
39 Cools down
40 "Enchilada," literally
43 Hit with hail
44 Particular
45 Tiny quantities
46 Oscar winner as Disraeli
48 Exam for some college srs.
50 One opposed
51 UN Day month
53 *Iliad* advisor
58 "Guacamole," literally
61 Tehran tongue
64 Kuwaiti ruler
65 Canadian Indian
66 *Brady Bunch* housekeeper
67 Succotash morsel
68 Shade of black
69 River bend
70 Garlic kin
71 Keeps

DOWN

1 "Mack the Knife" composer
2 *Dallas* mama
3 Bridge positions
4 *Bulworth* star
5 South African region
6 Sounds impressed
7 Tiff
8 Jetsons' dog
9 One of several Oz characters
10 Egyptian goddess
11 One opposed
12 To the rear
13 Keeps
21 "High Noon" singer
22 From Cork
25 Unstated
26 Amtrak high-speed train
27 Justification
29 Pond swimmer
30 Shakespearean sprite
32 Informal greeting
33 TV debut of '79
34 Mozart genre
35 Rolling
36 Show starter
38 Card-activated devices
41 '70s music
42 Quotes
47 Communist council
49 Cold-weather wear
52 Antigen attacker
54 '20s anarchist
55 *Pleading Guilty* author
56 Large quantity
57 Staggers
58 *The Nazarene* novelist
59 Cannes confidante
60 FDR's place
61 Swell
62 "Rumble in the Jungle" winner
63 Assemble, with "up"

★★★ Hyper-Sudoku

Fill in the blank boxes so that every row, column, 3x3 box, *and* each of the four 3x3 gray regions contains all of the numbers 1 to 9.

		2		3	6			5
		6			5			4
5			4	8			3	
9		8				1		
						7		
6								
						5		
8		9			7			
			3		4			7

MIXAGRAMS

Each line contains a five-letter word and a four-letter word that have been mixed together (the order of the letters in each word has not been changed). Unmix the two words on each line and write them in the spaces provided. When you're done, find a two-part answer to the clue by reading down the letter columns in the answers.

CLUE: Walk after this

B U F O R N A L T = _ _ _ _ _ + _ _ _ _

A W O L A R E D O = _ _ _ _ _ + _ _ _ _

L U R O T N U S S = _ _ _ _ _ + _ _ _ _

L A R U B I N E L = _ _ _ _ _ + _ _ _ _

★★ Split Decisions

In this clueless crossword puzzle, each answer consists of two words whose spellings are the same, except for the consecutive letters given. All answers are common words; no phrases or hyphenated or capitalized words are used. Some of the clues may have more than one solution, but there is only one word pair that will correctly link up with all the other word pairs.

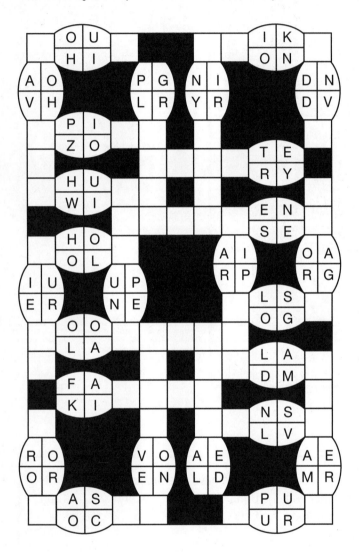

TRANSDELETION

Delete one letter from the word PORTALED and rearrange the rest, to get something spotted at the zoo.

_____

★★★★ Family Films by Merle Baker

ACROSS

1 Absorbed
5 Lost it
11 Part of RSA
14 Diva's notes
15 Pond denizen
16 Away
17 Sask. neighbor
18 Swayze film of '93
20 Wrapped up
21 Guitar feature
22 Steak selection
23 Reagan film of '38
26 Comics bulldog
27 Second word of
   A Tale of Two Cities
28 Theory
30 Rare gas
33 Culkin film of '89
39 Harvard deg.
40 Go astray
42 Curly companion
43 Maggie Smith film
   of '92
45 Stowe character
47 Shade source
48 Some AL batters
49 '40s White House
   resident
52 Russell film of '58
59 Certain naval officers
61 Roulette bet
62 Kimono sashes
63 Heston film of '82
65 Agrees, in a way
66 Argentine article
67 Assumed
   appearances
68 __ ranch
69 Alphabet string
70 Bear witness
71 Underworld river

DOWN

1 Music genre
2 Fire
3 André Watts'
   instrument
4 Second shot
5 Social errors
6 Horoscope columnist
7 Carrier
8 Bombay-born
   conductor
9 *Simpsons* grandpa
10 Sudden movement
11 In progress
12 Where armies meet
13 Calgary Stampede
   is one
19 Cold War concern
24 *Water Music*
   composer
25 Joust
29 Do a slow burn
30 Some times
31 World Series stat
32 Empty talk
33 Katie Couric
   alma mater
34 Cage, familiarly
35 Medical acronym
36 Tennis judge
37 Trig. function
38 Pivotal
41 *Cope Book* aunt
44 Train
46 Utah group
48 Most dreadful
49 Longest bone in the
   body
50 Neural transmitters
51 "__, c'est moi"
53 Still to be burned
54 Lariat loop
55 Meteorology
   concerns
56 In the vicinity
57 Annapolis student
58 County in England
60 Nintendo
   competitor
64 Furrow

★★★ Solitaire Poker

Group the 40 cards into eight poker hands of five cards each, so that each hand contains two pairs or better. The cards in each hand must be connected to each other by a common horizontal or vertical side.

BETWEENER

What five-letter word belongs between the word at left and the word at right, so that the first and second word, and the second and third word, each form a common compound word?

THERE __ __ __ __ __ THOUGHT

★★★ Number-Out

Shade squares so that no number appears in any row or column more than once. Shaded squares may not touch each other horizontally or vertically, and all unshaded squares must form a single continuous area.

5	2	4	4	1	3
6	5	3	2	1	5
2	3	5	1	6	2
3	3	6	2	2	2
1	4	5	3	5	6
4	5	2	6	4	3

THINK ALIKE

Unscramble the letters in the phrase SEWS SPOONS to form two words with the same or similar meanings.

_____   _____

★★★ One-Way Streets

The diagram represents a pattern of streets. A and B are parking spaces, and the black squares are stores. Find the route that starts at A, passes through all stores exactly once, and ends at B. Arrows indicate one-way traffic for that block only. No block or intersection may be entered more than once.

SOUND THINKING

Common words whose consonant sounds are K, S, and T include CAST and COAST. What eight-letter word is pronounced with the same consonant sounds in the same order?

★★★★ Take the Plunge by Doug Peterson

ACROSS

1 "My Heart Will Go On" singer
5 Squirrel away
10 On a grand scale
14 Ben's mom
15 Apology prompter
16 Places
17 Squandered
18 Collect, as cash
19 Home-decor giant
20 Start of a Shirley Chisholm quote
23 Bank charges
24 Informant
27 Acapulco article
28 Go past
30 British "bub"
31 Very small computers
33 Old character
34 Comedian Kaplan
35 Middle of quote
38 NBA team locale
39 Frowned-upon contraction
40 Churchill successor
41 Storage acronym
42 No-nonsense judge
43 Down
44 Easily attachable
46 Laugh riots
50 End of quote
53 Negligible amount
55 Informal instrument
56 Tar
57 Anise-flavored drink
58 Commuter's community, perhaps
59 Island off Tuscany
60 Do as told
61 American Dance Theater founder
62 Lunar regions

DOWN

1 Middle of a Flintstone yell
2 Firth, for one
3 Late bedtime
4 Unexpected tidings
5 Parade honorees
6 Paperless tests
7 Desiccated
8 Santa __, CA
9 More formal
10 Yale who endowed Yale
11 World Series event
12 Motel freebie
13 Grp. with moles
21 Savage sort
22 Outdo
25 Like Desi Arnaz
26 All square
28 Cheerful
29 Nautical unit
31 Climber's spike
32 Adapt for the stage
33 Incursion
34 Venus et al.
35 Astor's line
36 Home of the Keck Observatory
37 All in
42 Cup's contents
43 With 53 Down, toon canine
45 New Orleans sandwich
46 Rumble in the night
47 Dickens title starter
48 Australian soprano
49 Mex. misses
51 Fleet member
52 Blue, in Bogotá
53 See 43 Down
54 Buff

★★★ Sudoku

Fill in the blank boxes so that every row, column, and 3x3 box contains all of the numbers 1 to 9.

		2	8	6				4
		4	9				3	
6			2				1	
1	2	5						
					5	8	7	
	8				6			2
	5				1	3		
9				2	8	7		

MIXAGRAMS

Each line contains a five-letter word and a four-letter word that have been mixed together (the order of the letters in each word has not been changed). Unmix the two words on each line and write them in the spaces provided. When you're done, find a two-part answer to the clue by reading down the letter columns in the answers.

CLUE: Where some deals are made

R O A R B I M N Y = _ _ _ _ _ + _ _ _ _

P R O H A U S E T = _ _ _ _ _ + _ _ _ _

E T A C O N K S Y = _ _ _ _ _ + _ _ _ _

B A S M U K E R G = _ _ _ _ _ + _ _ _ _

★★★ Star Search

Find the stars that are hidden in some of the blank squares. The numbered squares indicate how many stars are hidden in the squares adjacent to them (including diagonally). There is never more than one star in any square.

		1		2			
	4	1					
			2	3	3	1	
1	2		3				2
					2		
1		1	4	5		3	
	1	2		2			

CHOICE WORDS

Form three six-letter words from the same category, by selecting one letter from each column three times. Each letter will be used exactly once.

B	A	N	H	O	E
F	I	S	H	E	M
M	U	T	U	T	L

_ _ _ _ _ _

_ _ _ _ _ _

_ _ _ _ _ _

★★★★ Flyday Puzzle by Shirley Soloway

ACROSS

1 Energetic
5 Taken-back merchandise
9 Latin music
14 Latin bird
15 Thought
16 Blunted weapons
17 Buttercup relatives
19 Auspices
20 "The most merciful"
21 Souvenir
23 Region bordering the Rhine
26 __ Tomé and Principe
27 Fate
28 Wise, man
31 Ancient navigator
33 Rightful
35 Questionnaire question
37 Narrow passage
40 Well into the night
41 Barrel of laughs
43 Seat of the Mughal Empire
44 Hans Christian Andersen's hometown
46 Groups of petals
48 Marching grp.
49 School 007 attended
50 Two sharp turns
51 Ministry of Defence div.
53 Stretch (out)
55 Humbles, in a way
57 Snobs
60 Gather up
64 Temporary *Tonight Show* name
65 Engulf
68 Family man
69 Masterson colleague
70 Actress Reid
71 Do some tailoring

72 Acctg. periods
73 Center cuts of beef

DOWN

1 Celebratory
2 Sort of circular
3 Brownie, for one
4 Herr Schindler
5 Split open
6 URL suffix
7 Special privilege
8 Retreats
9 Cruise-ship stop
10 Copies
11 Hotshot defender
12 Timex alternative

13 Goodwill, e.g.
18 Big name in Florida football
22 Admits one's mistake
24 Nags
25 European capital
28 Symbol of purity
29 Old-style "Yikes!"
30 *Network* Oscar winner
32 Boundary marker
34 Russian river
36 City on I-80
38 Portfolio holdings
39 Soviet news source
42 Scintilla

45 Women's Hall of Fame member
47 Suns star
51 Come back
52 Singularly
54 Footnote abbr.
56 Struck down
58 Unlikely story
59 With 61 Down, repel
61 See 59 Down
62 Agreeable response
63 Hydromassage facilities
66 Opposite of dep.
67 Yard-sale staples

★★★ Your Turn

Entering at bottom and exiting at top, find the shortest path through the maze, following these turn rules: You must turn right on red squares, turn left on blue squares, and go straight through yellow squares. Your path may retrace itself and cross at intersections, but you may not reverse your direction at any point.

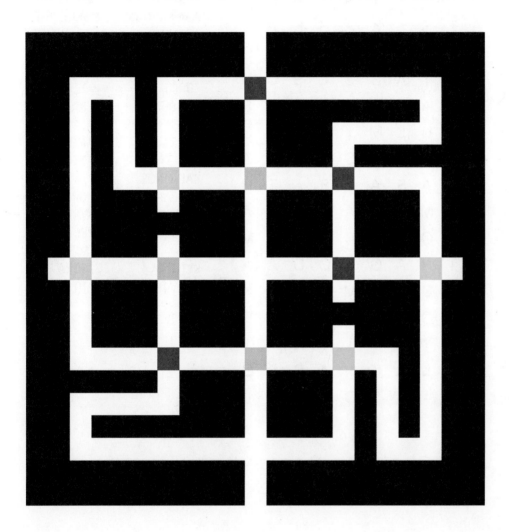

SAY IT AGAIN

What five-letter word can be either a small animal or a computer accessory?

— — — — —

★★★ Greek Island Cruise

Starting with KARPATHOS, move up, down, left, or right one letter at a time, to trace a path of these Greek islands. Every letter will be used exactly once.

```
A  T  S  S  R  P  I  O  S  I  S  T  A  D  O
I  H  O  K  O  A  Z  S  S  K  A  S  K  A  N
K  O  L  A  O  F  O  N  I  I  M  O  I  D  O
S  N  E  F  R  A  H  T  A  S  O  L  S  O  U
A  I  K  E  T  S  K  A  G  O  R  E  P  B  S
A  R  P  A  N  R  Y  U  L  M  I  L  E  S  S
K  C  S  T  A  O  P  O  A  T  S  I  X  I  A
R  O  O  H  Z  S  I  A  S  A  T  E  A  T  H
F  U  S  A  L  A  M  M  O  P  A  R  P  K  A
A  S  O  R  I  A  F  O  S  C  H  I  A  A  M
E  G  K  A  H  D  T  R  A  G  E  O  D  A  A
N  I  I  A  T  E  S  S  N  I  M  S  F  K  K
A  L  A  K  Y  S  M  O  N  S  O  R  E  L  R
H  A  T  S  A  S  I  Y  M  I  T  I  N  I  I
Y  P  Y  L  A  O  L  L  A  K  N  A  S  S  O
D  R  A  E  F  O  N  I  S  S  O  S  T  I  L
```

AEGINA	LESBOS
AGATHONISSI	MAKRI
ASTAKIDA	MEGANISI
ASTYPALAIA	MILOS
CHIOS	PATMOS
CORFU	PAXI
DONOUSSA	PERISTERA
ELAFONISSOS	SALAMIS
HYDRA	SAMOS
ITHAKA	SANTORINI
KALYMNOS	SKIATHOS
~~KARPATHOS~~	SKORPIOS
KEFALONIA	SKYROPOULA
KIMOLOS	STROFADES
KOS	TILOS
KYTHIRA	ZAFORA
LEFKADA	ZANTE

WHO'S WHAT WHERE?

The correct term for a resident of the Mexican state of Veracruz is:

A) Veracruzaño   B) Cruziano

C) Veraiso   D) Jarocho

★★★ ABC

Enter the letters A, B, and C into the diagram so that each row and column has exactly one A, one B, and one C. The letters outside the diagram indicate the first letter encountered, moving in the direction of the arrow. Keep in mind that after all the letters have been filled in, there will be two blank boxes in each row and column.

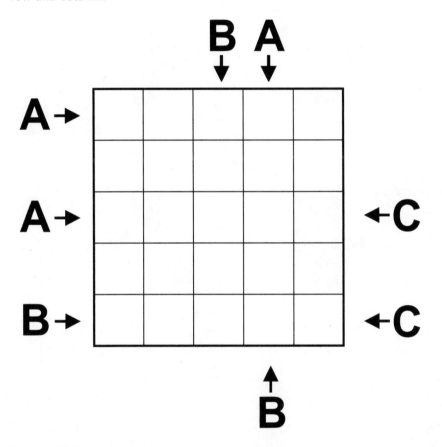

CLUELESS CROSSWORD

Complete the crossword with common uncapitalized seven-letter words, based entirely on the letters already filled in for you.

★★★★★ Themeless Toughie by Daniel R. Stark

ACROSS

1 Miscreant
7 Signora del Giocondo
15 Flammable gas
16 Thought
17 Undercover operations
18 Was contingent (on)
19 Silver, for one
20 Auel heroine
21 Band handout
22 Sitcom planet
23 Embankment
25 Poetic time
26 People
28 Remark of approval
30 Chances
31 Kudrow's mother on *Friends*
33 Filch
35 Orderly manners
36 Throw around
40 Navajo foe
41 Unpricey wine
42 Heat __
45 Five-time Masters champ
47 Pinch
48 __ roll
49 Euro adopter in January 2008
51 Sew up
52 This, south of San Diego
54 Chipper
55 Paganini's hometown
57 Cut out
59 Performers
60 Certain pots
61 Individually
62 Cut out
63 Flirted with

DOWN

1 Gets a new take from
2 Mouthpiece
3 Goldbricks
4 Preserves, perhaps
5 Kindly sort
6 __ *Liaisons Dangereuses*
7 Early summer or so
8 Diner order
9 County east of Sonoma
10 Grow up
11 Singer on a 50-kronor note
12 Without a doubt
13 Looked
14 Riders
20 Says decidedly
24 Canine coat
27 Evince interest
29 Hidden
30 Ended the agonizing
32 Hear clearly
34 Meal source
36 With regrets
37 They may be on probation
38 Nestle
39 Not freshly made
41 Put it threateningly
42 Flowing off the page, maybe
43 Shaky
44 __ of honor
46 Dominion
50 Wide open
53 Miller et al.
54 Moselle tributary
56 "The South-Sea House" byline
58 Company, supposedly
59 Needle work, for short

bRain BReatHer
CARPE DIEM: SEIZE THE DAY

Herewith, some advice on how to make the most of the opportunities life offers us.

If I had to live my life again, I'd make the same mistakes, only sooner.
—TALLULAH BANKHEAD

Life loves to be taken by the lapel and told, "I'm with you, kid. Let's go."
—MAYA ANGELOU

Enjoy life. There's plenty of time to be dead.
—STEVE ALLEN

The words printed here are concepts. You must go through the experiences.
—SAINT AUGUSTINE

Mix a little foolishness with your prudence: It's good to be silly at the right moment.
—HORACE

I would rather regret the things that I have done than the things that I have not.
—LUCILLE BALL

We could never learn to be brave and patient, if there were only joy in the world.
—HELEN KELLER

A life spent making mistakes is not only more honorable but more useful than a life spent in doing nothing.
—GEORGE BERNARD SHAW

When you're through changing, you're through.
—BRUCE BARTON

The great pleasure in life is doing what people say you cannot do.
—WALTER BAGEHOT

★★★★ Find the Ships

Determine the position of the 10 ships listed to the right of the diagram. The ships may be oriented either horizontally or vertically. A square with wavy lines indicates water and will not contain a ship. The numbers at the edge of the diagram indicate how many squares in that row or column contain parts of ships. When all 10 ships are correctly placed in the diagram, no two of them will touch each other, not even diagonally.

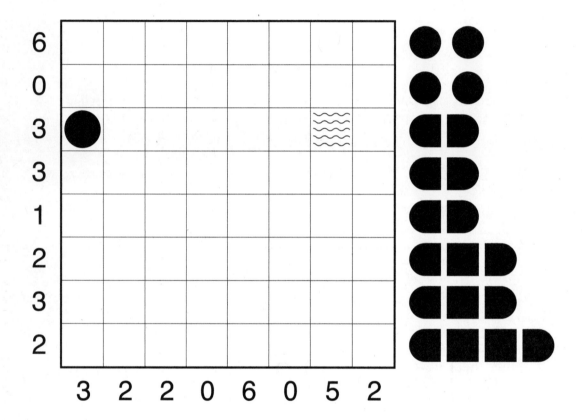

TWO-BY-FOUR

The eight letters in the word VALIDITY can be rearranged to form a pair of common four-letter words in two different ways, if no four-letter word is repeated. Can you find both pairs of words?

— — — —   — — — —

— — — —   — — — —

★★★★ Hyper-Sudoku

Fill in the blank boxes so that every row, column, 3x3 box, *and* each of the four 3x3 gray regions contains all of the numbers 1 to 9.

4			2					
6		9		4	1			
	8					7		
8							9	
						8		
		8				6		
		3	5		7	4		
					4	2	5	

BETWEENER

What six-letter word belongs between the word at left and the word at right, so that the first and second word, and the second and third word, each form a common compound word?

PICK __ __ __ __ __ __ BOOK

★★★★★ Themeless Toughie by Merle Baker

ACROSS

1 Fedora feature
9 Metamorphic rock
15 All of us
16 Right away
17 Waiting to be found
18 Confederate group
19 Fairy-tale sister
20 When books are closed
21 Retirement spot
22 Hardly husky
23 Allen successor
26 Propel
27 Batter
30 Not too thin-skinned
35 For all to hear
36 Early radio part
37 Arlington ___, IL
38 ___ told (comply)
39 Numbers game
40 Hard-boiled
42 Diner order
44 Newspaper listings
47 Big brother portrayer
51 Don't forget
52 '07 debate regular
53 Divine revelation
54 Pacts
55 Type of truck
56 End

DOWN

1 Push
2 It's inadvisable
3 Bldg. units
4 Pointers, perhaps
5 Ostentation
6 Tore
7 Made sure of
8 ___ school
9 Shining
10 Spooky sound
11 Far from innovative
12 Pulitzer dramatist of '53
13 Shock
14 Driven obliquely
20 Mainers, e.g.
22 Calendrical correction
23 Software update
24 Cancel
25 McBeal et al.
26 Botanist's runners
27 Circuit
28 City on the Cuyahoga
29 One way to Constitution Hall
31 Retaliation, so to speak
32 Gloomy
33 Pro
34 Finagler's activity
40 Digs less than satisfactory
41 Sheer fabric
42 Broods
43 Small arm
44 Hurry
45 Mame's pal
46 South Park kid
47 30 Rock name
48 Figures
49 Folks
50 Fleeting trace
52 Firm up

★★ Floor It

Which one of the numbered pieces will fit into the tiled floor?

SMALL CHANGE

Change one letter in each of these two words, to form a common two-word phrase.

GRANT TONAL

★★★★ Square Routes

Fill in the blank circles so that every row, column, and path contains all of the numbers from 1 to 7.

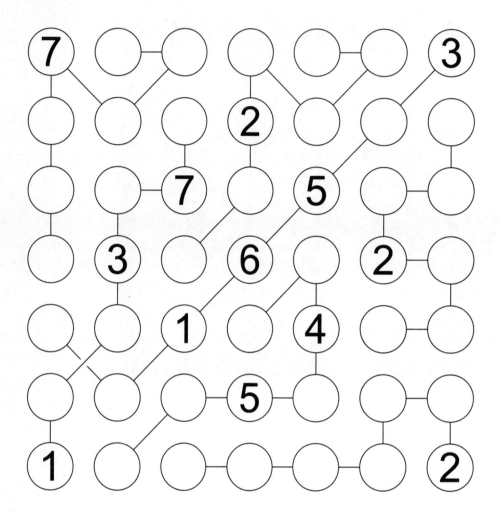

ADDITION SWITCH

Switch the positions of two of the digits in the incorrect sum at right, to get a correct sum.

$$
\begin{array}{r}
2\,8\,3 \\
+\,6\,1\,7 \\
\hline
4\,6\,0
\end{array}
$$

★★★★★ Themeless Toughie by Doug Peterson

ACROSS

1 Berth place
10 Carries on
15 Type of top
16 Means
17 Margarita ingredient
18 Word on Montana's state flag
19 Exceptional sight
20 Like creosote
21 Pinched
22 Stop arguing
24 2006 Kennedy Center honoree
26 News
27 "__ yours!"
29 Echolocation user
31 Short stop?
32 Archer's partner
35 Ones starting actions
36 Electric __
37 Free
40 Russian chessmaster
41 Mary and Mike
42 Realizes
43 RN assignment
44 Treat with heat
45 Dump
46 Spruce up
48 Catch
50 Concessions
54 "No problem"
56 HBO medium
58 Abe Vigoda, in *The Godfather*
59 Ritz alternative
60 Yellowish green
62 Put in
63 Tossed-off remarks
64 Chimney nester
65 Humorist on a 2002 stamp

DOWN

1 More pertinent
2 From Bergen
3 Round holders
4 Jaunt
5 1952 Winter Olympics site
6 French coronation city
7 House divider
8 Oval activity
9 Series ender
10 Absorbed
11 Visibly elated
12 Entrée with asparagus
13 Think about
14 Flags
21 Oath starter
23 Tendency
25 Queue component
28 Backpack fillers
30 Long suit
32 Sends up
33 Feng shui concern
34 Brings up, sort of
35 Body style
38 Work with feet
39 Foots
45 Resolve
47 Mix feature
49 Knocked down, in Norwich
51 *Ulysses* actor
52 Braces
53 Flounder in the water
55 One of the Channel Islands
57 Unsuccessful
60 Cutesy add-on
61 Cooper's spot

★★★★ 123

Fill in the diagram so that each rectangular piece has one each of the numbers 1, 2, and 3, under these rules: 1) No two adjacent squares, horizontally or vertically, can have the same number. 2) Each completed row and column of the diagram will have an equal number of 1's, 2's, and 3's.

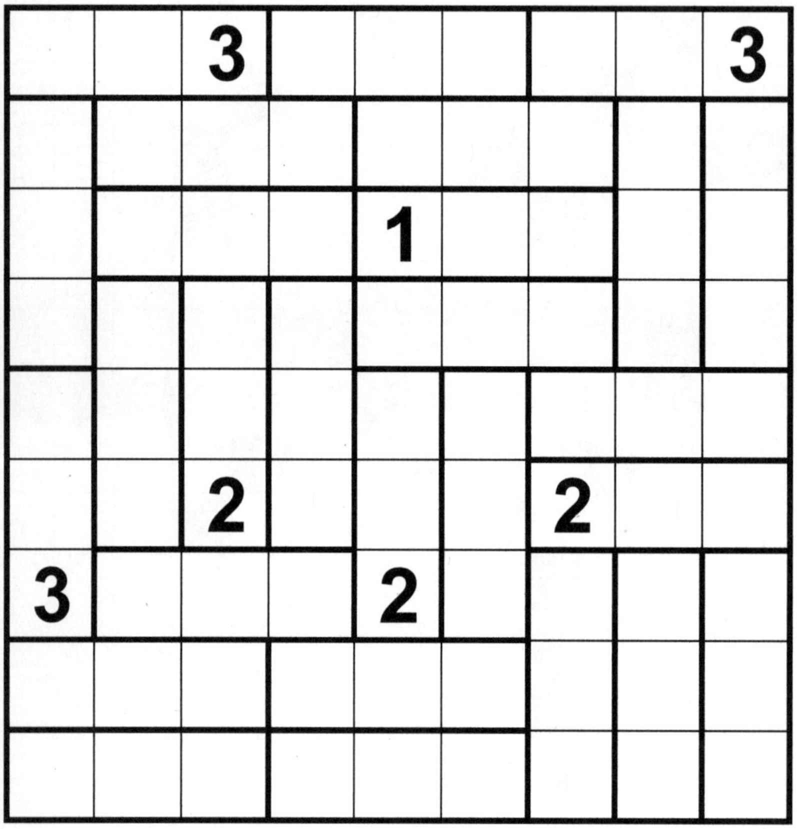

		3						3
				1				
		2				2		
3				2				

WRONG IS RIGHT

Which of these four words is misspelled?

    A) souvenir   B) dossier

    C) couturier   D) gondalier

★★★ Number-Out

Shade squares so that no number appears in any row or column more than once. Shaded squares may not touch each other horizontally or vertically, and all unshaded squares must form a single continuous area.

2	2	2	6	5	1
3	5	1	2	6	6
4	5	5	5	1	1
6	4	2	1	2	5
1	3	4	3	6	2
6	6	2	4	3	3

THINK ALIKE

Unscramble the letters in the phrase SHORN PEAHEN to form two words with the same or similar meanings.

_____   _____

★★★★★ Themeless Toughie by Anna Stiga

ACROSS

1 Close
5 Swiss-born physician/firebrand
10 Fling
14 Zola novel
15 Cruise-ship fixture
16 Nestlé brand
17 Jeffrey Archer title character
18 Restraint
20 Bower buy
22 Iconic queen
23 Relaxed
25 Mass movement
26 Flowed
27 Balneotherapy site
30 Dorothy Parker employer
34 What 1000 may stand for
36 Phrase of resignation
37 It's on the Red Sea
39 Nickname for José
40 Grind
42 Eternally frustrating
44 Out there
45 "For loan __ loses both itself and friend": Shak.
47 Something comparable
48 Honeybunch
53 Road to recovery
56 Great Pumpkin originator
57 Cutting corners?
59 Catalysts, for short
60 Rounds, for example
61 Easily addled
62 Kid-lit detective
63 Honey bunch
64 Made lighter
65 Mythical waterway

DOWN

1 Sound surly
2 Not to mention
3 Independent
4 Fjord adjunct
5 Ted Turner purchase of '86
6 With us
7 Copland ballet
8 Blackmun's predecessor
9 Patron of Spain
10 Spiteful
11 Others, long ago
12 Place
13 Collette of filmdom
19 Fail to be
21 *Scream* name
24 Appetites
27 Deriding
28 Bishop of Roma
29 Truly
30 Not open
31 Head-slapper's remark
32 Grand Slam event locale
33 Reagan def. program
35 One of the Epistles
38 "Blue" group
41 Weed whackers
43 Become separated
46 Window dressing
48 Lengthy meals
49 Presents, with "out"
50 Pick up
51 Like some bumpy roads
52 English county
53 Memorable Gregory Peck role
54 Price of __
55 Spell
58 Chaplin nickname

★★★ Opera Jigsaw

Find these operas that are arranged in jigsaw puzzle shapes in the diagram.
One piece is shown to get you started.

ALBERT HERRING
BILLY BUDD
BOCCACCIO
BORIS GODUNOV
CINDERELLA
DIDO AND AENEAS
DON GIOVANNI
EUGENE ONEGIN

FAIR MAID OF PERTH
~~FALSTAFF~~
GRISELDA
HUGH THE DROVER
INTERMEZZO
LA BOHÈME
LUCREZIA BORGIA
LULU

MANON LESCAUT
MERRIE ENGLAND
MERRY MOUNT
NEBUCHADNEZZAR
PARSIFAL
PERSEPHONE
PETER GRIMES
PORGY AND BESS

PRINCE IGOR
RIGOLETTO
SIEGFRIED
TALES OF HOFFMAN
THE MAGIC FLUTE
THREEPENNY OPERA
WOZZECK

IN OTHER WORDS

There is only one common uncapitalized word that contains the consecutive letters EKO.
What is it?

_____

★★★ Color Paths

Find the shortest path through the maze from the bottom to the center, by using paths in this color order: red, blue, yellow, red, blue, etc. Change path colors through the white squares. It is okay to retrace your path.

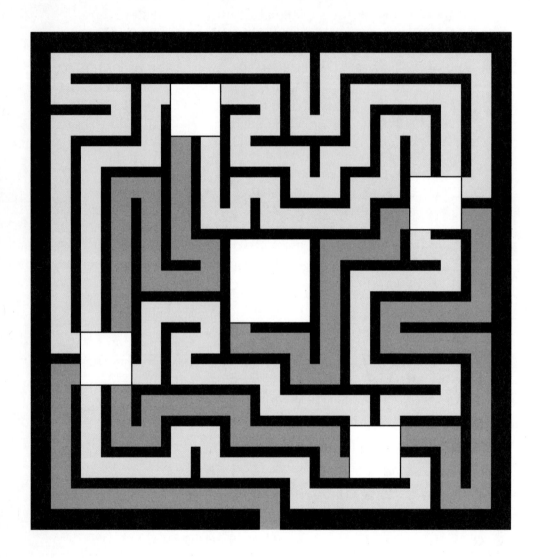

SAY IT AGAIN

What six-letter verb can mean either "overexert" or "filter?"

— — — — — —

★★★★★ **Themeless Toughie** by Daniel R. Stark

ACROSS

1 Got into
9 Not as bright
15 Less smooth
16 Full sway
17 Corn product
18 Small fowl
19 Fish-house choice
20 Shrewdness
22 "__ Beso" (Anka tune)
23 Stay-at-home surfers
25 Conducted
26 Move like a popinjay
28 City on the Indian Ocean
29 Cyrus' realm, today
31 One-in-a-million
32 Candy-stripers
34 Works with a written address
36 Willow-bark extract
39 Most promptly
40 Body-shop offering
41 Drawback
42 Troubadour accompanier
43 Sharp
45 Tall flowers
49 States peremptorily
51 Self-survival centers
52 Professional duds
53 Urge
54 On the spot
56 Sloth spot
57 Emcee's job
59 Make too thin
63 Part of the family
64 Naive progressive
65 Facilitate
66 Supermarket devices

DOWN

1 Is bratty
2 Stop straddling
3 One who plays on ice
4 Acrobat, e.g.
5 Certain runner
6 Part of a certain "response"
7 Sushi staple
8 Kids with crayons
9 Obligation
10 Cosby alma mater
11 ICU worker
12 Knowledgeable
13 Blank spaces, perhaps
14 Opposite of proximate
21 Snake River loc.
24 Pacino's sister in *The Godfather*
25 Encumbrance
27 Interpretive work
30 One preceder
33 Vileness
35 Trying
36 Putting to rest
37 Mug, maybe
38 Land, over 500 times
39 Remains inactive
41 Capra hero
44 Aura
46 Wear off
47 Mike Myers *SNL* character
48 Directs
50 Track __
55 Latin I verb
58 American Marconi acquirer
60 Soft shoe
61 Ottoman official
62 Take for a ride

★★★★ ABCD

Enter the letters A, B, C, and D into the diagram so that each row and column
has exactly one A, one B, one C, and one D. The letters outside the diagram
indicate the first letter encountered, moving in the direction of the arrow. Keep
in mind that after all the letters have been filled in, there will be two blank
boxes in each row and column.

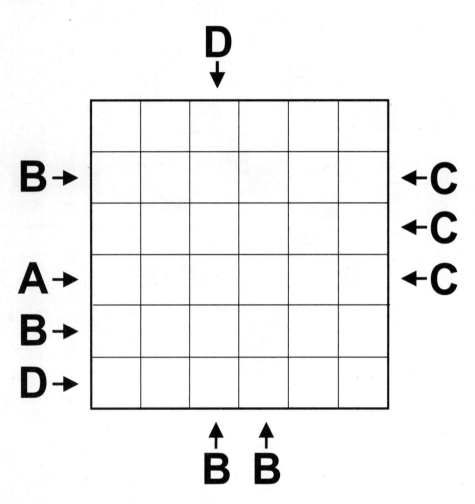

NATIONAL TREASURE

The words ARIA, RANK, and RUIN can be formed from the letters of what European language?

_____

★★★★ Sudoku

Fill in the blank boxes so that every row, column, and 3x3 box contains all of the numbers 1 to 9.

6				4				
	1		5					
		7		3		8		
	5				6			
1		2				3		8
			9				7	
		8		1		4		
					2		6	
				7				2

MIXAGRAMS

Each line contains a five-letter word and a four-letter word that have been mixed together (the order of the letters in each word has not been changed). Unmix the two words on each line and write them in the spaces provided. When you're done, find a two-part answer to the clue by reading down the letter columns in the answers.

CLUE: Forties' outfit

G H O R A Z E S T	=	_ _ _ _ _	+	_ _ _ _
B I F E S O U N D	=	_ _ _ _ _	+	_ _ _ _
V E A L I L O L Y	=	_ _ _ _ _	+	_ _ _ _
U N C H T U T O E	=	_ _ _ _ _	+	_ _ _ _

★★★★★ Themeless Toughie by Merle Baker

ACROSS

1 Ancient symbols of royalty
5 In other days
9 Wooden wear
14 *NYPD Blue* setting
16 About two dozen sheets
17 Tore
18 Not necessary
19 They move with great care
20 Makes a straw mat
22 Dutch master
23 Some sides
24 Saddler's device
27 Desk-calendar shapes
30 Sluggish
34 *Children of the Tenements* author
35 One found among the reeds
36 Least interesting
38 Federal agcy. since 1964
39 Cheap
43 Take advantage of
45 German spa
46 "But when thou ___ alms ...": Matthew
47 Drive
52 Drop off
54 Lung protectors
55 Vociferous
57 Stopped
59 Beyond help
60 Withstanding successfully
61 Inclines
62 Draft choices
63 Foil alternative

DOWN

1 Vulcanology subject
2 Beans
3 Racetrack figure
4 Wrapped clothing
5 Some are high-grade
6 Green light
7 Pope piece
8 Put
9 Make uncomfortable, in a way
10 Maiden ___
11 Recognizes, finally
12 Tulsa sch.
13 Site for some shots
15 Oktoberfest attire
21 Plaintiff, sometimes
23 New Left grp.
25 Watch starter
26 Holds on
28 Discharge
29 Albion neighbor
30 Songwriters Hall of Fame member
31 Alongside
32 Moderates
33 Thrill
37 Rutgers' river
40 Sucrose derivative
41 Perfumery staple
42 Grade E-1
44 Blazons
48 Lose one's identity
49 Patient place
50 Arise
51 Vanilla or chocolate order
53 Loot
54 Certain skimmers
55 Dictionary abbr.
56 Potential perch
58 Gray lines

★★★★ One-Way Streets

The diagram represents a pattern of streets. P's are parking spaces, and the black squares are stores. Find the route that starts at a parking space, passes through all stores exactly once, and ends at the other parking space. Arrows indicate one-way traffic for that block only. No block or intersection may be entered more than once.

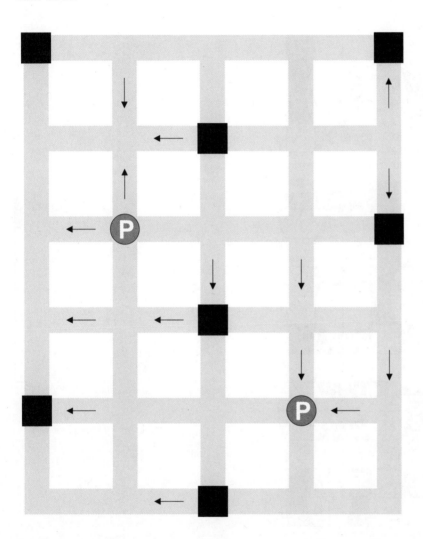

SOUND THINKING

The consonant sounds in the word LIGNITE (a type of coal) are L, G, N, and T. What more common seven-letter word is pronounced with the same consonant sounds in the same order?

_____

★★ Split Decisions

In this clueless crossword puzzle, each answer consists of two words whose spellings are the same, except for the consecutive letters given. All answers are common words; no phrases or hyphenated or capitalized words are used. Some of the clues may have more than one solution, but there is only one word pair that will correctly link up with all the other word pairs.

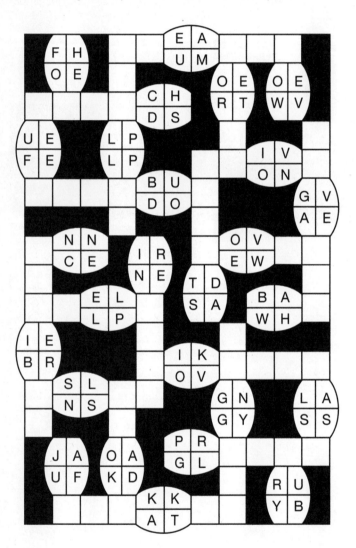

TRANSDELETION

Delete one letter from the word PREGATHER and rearrange the rest, to get a two-word golf term.

_____

★★★★★ Themeless Toughie by Daniel R. Stark

ACROSS

1 Went easy on
7 Flight paths
15 Esoteric
16 Man or beast
17 Magic charm
18 Chicken addition
19 Vinegary
20 Just bought
22 *YM* workers
23 Speeds up
24 Meditate
25 Rocky rubble
27 Gilbert and Sullivan soprano
28 Most spacious
30 Business concern
31 Place
32 March time
33 __ sort
35 Remains
37 Goes slyly
40 Decide on close ones
41 All-purpose vehicles
42 Some tag players
44 Goldie's Oscar role
47 Cultured fare
49 Business-card letters
50 Straight up
52 Elbow neighbor
53 To __ (just so)
54 Bill
55 Baseball, basketball and hockey term
57 Marching band's music holder
58 Close one
60 Cold covering
62 Geometric figures
63 Lack of power
64 Say again
65 Better organized

DOWN

1 Fly-drive vacations
2 Went first
3 Turn on
4 Unscrupulous recruitment
5 Tennis center
6 Make more comfortable, maybe
7 Impeaches
8 Work at the Getty Museum
9 Chateaubriand novella
10 Makes shore
11 __ discount
12 *Dos*, for one
13 Undermines
14 Feels
21 Some posers
26 Reunion attendees
28 Bug
29 Forbearance
34 Punch need
36 __-a-brac
37 Floors
38 Tot's companion
39 Lowest class
41 Worst behaved
43 Kind of car
44 Not as cool
45 Meadowlark kin
46 Literally, "cloud"
48 Removal
51 Forces down
53 Wife of Prince Valiant
56 Epistolary courtesy
59 Garden *fleur*
61 Prompt

★★★★ Pig Races

Enter the maze at bottom, pass through all the stars exactly once, then exit at left. You may not retrace your path.

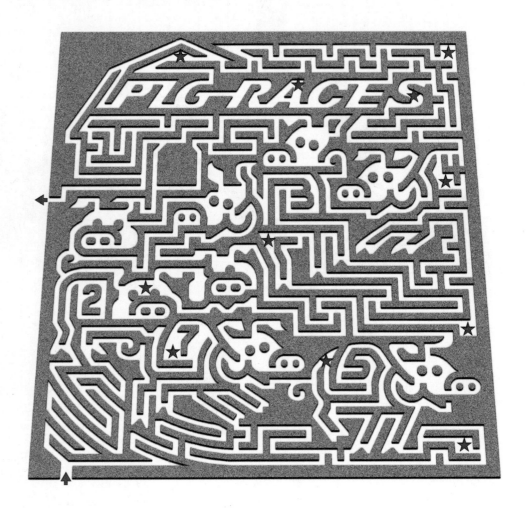

SAY IT AGAIN

What six-letter word can mean either "ban" or "criminal"?

— — — — — —

★★★★ Star Search

Find the stars that are hidden in some of the blank squares. The numbered squares indicate how many stars are hidden in the squares adjacent to them (including diagonally). There is never more than one star in any square.

	1			2	2		1		
		2				2			
2			4			3		3	
				2	2				
		1				4		2	
1		1		3			3		2
		2		4	5		3		
	1								

CHOICE WORDS

Form three six-letter words from the same category, by selecting one letter from each column three times. Each letter will be used exactly once.

G	L	E	E	Z	Y	_ _ _ _ _ _
S	N	U	E	P	Y	_ _ _ _ _ _
S	R	E	M	P	Y	_ _ _ _ _ _

★★★★★ Themeless Toughie by Doug Peterson

ACROSS

1 Study aid
9 Exhilarate
15 Excessive interest, slangily
16 Oppressor
17 "You might say that"
18 Certain skinners
19 Cloud-chamber particles
20 Specialty
22 Frozen formations
23 Soothing phrase
25 Desert landforms
29 "It's a possibility"
30 Creator of Caractacus
32 Bring up again
33 Brat Pack name
34 1974 Peace Nobelist
35 Key-lock creation
38 Ranch calls
39 Sm., med. and lg.
40 Percipient
41 Wake Forest's grp.
42 Hindi relative
43 Stick with a pocket
44 Soup morsel
47 Prefix for linear
48 Rooter's remark
49 Close to shut
53 Self-absorption
55 *Kiss Me Kate* character
57 Electronic control system
58 Going for
59 Sanction
60 Football-helmet features

DOWN

1 LIII times XIX
2 Lad of La Mancha
3 Former Big Apple archbishop
4 Green shade
5 Rush discovery
6 Large pianistic spreads
7 Send out
8 Dessert topping
9 Masked man
10 Swell
11 *Law of the Lash* star
12 Confounds completely
13 Testy ones
14 Angel Clare's love
21 Foreign women
23 Midway Isl., for one
24 Keep tabs on, perhaps
25 Dutch island
26 Markets differently
27 Charge holders
28 Hustles
31 *Una dirección*
33 Cool cat
34 Town on the Vire River
36 Caution
37 Take in
42 Concert
43 Less gritty
45 Offensive
46 Historic plane name
47 Badlands feature
49 Cher, e.g.
50 *Gunsmoke* set
51 Elizabeth I's mother
52 Directives, in brief
54 Centennial St. setting
56 Training ctr.

★★★★ Number-Out

Shade squares so that no number appears in any row or column more than once. Shaded squares may not touch each other horizontally or vertically, and all unshaded squares must form a single continuous area.

1	2	2	4	4	5
5	2	6	3	1	3
2	4	1	1	6	6
4	5	3	5	6	1
2	5	2	6	6	4
3	3	4	2	5	1

THINK ALIKE

Unscramble the letters in the phrase ULTRA FAUCET to form two words with the same or similar meanings.

_____   _____

★★★★ Line Drawing

Draw three straight lines, each from one edge of the square to another edge, so that the letters in each region form a word. Then, add the same letter to each region so that a new word can be formed from the letters in each region.

TWO-BY-FOUR

The eight letters in the word WRECKAGE can be rearranged to form a pair of common four-letter words in three different ways. Can you find them all?

___ ___ ___ ___   ___ ___ ___ ___   ___ ___ ___ ___   ___ ___ ___ ___

___ ___ ___ ___   ___ ___ ___ ___

★★★★★ Themeless Toughie by Anna Stiga

ACROSS

1 Gibbon, for one
10 Give up
15 Away for a while
16 SAG Life Achievement honoree of '01
17 Evidence of freshness
18 Photo finish
19 Union-vote facilitator
20 First responders, at times
21 Land on the Euphrates
22 Xbox participant
24 Drudge
26 Hole-in-the-wall fixture
27 Gets by
29 Sharp attack
32 JFK, once
33 Former AT&T rival
35 Portion of corn?
36 __ dance
37 Dance
38 *Speak, Memory* autobiographer
41 Sound of annoyance
42 Place for bargains
45 Acre people
47 Symbol of power
49 Caribbean locale
50 *St. Elmo's Fire* star
52 Quick cries
53 German surrealist
56 Hot stuff
58 Inexperienced one
59 Goose
60 Unscientific
62 City near Saint Bonaventure
63 Face-off spot
64 Bugs
65 Amen alternative

DOWN

1 Watering holes
2 Opposite of "free"
3 Declaration signer from Connecticut
4 Broke down
5 Gary Collins predecessor, 1980-81
6 Get on
7 Victoria Beckham, née __
8 Frisked, with "down"
9 Marching order
10 Good source of B6
11 Essex exclamation
12 Get on
13 Last Beatles film
14 Visionary
23 Updated version
25 Unconventional
28 Head of a violin
30 Appetizing
31 George V approved its flag
34 Sacrosanctness
36 Sort of stole
38 Words of appeasement, perhaps
39 More often than not
40 Dmitri Karamazov portrayer
42 New Mexico's official neckwear
43 Set
44 Got comfy
46 Gershwin's first successful song
48 Preserve, in a way
51 Equalizes
54 Put something over on
55 Fair pair
57 Musical starter
61 Hideout

★★ Triad Split Decisions

In this clueless crossword puzzle, each answer consists of two words whose spellings are the same, except for the consecutive letters given. All answers are common words; no phrases or hyphenated or capitalized words are used. Some of the clues may have more than one solution, but there is only one word pair that will correctly link up with all the other word pairs.

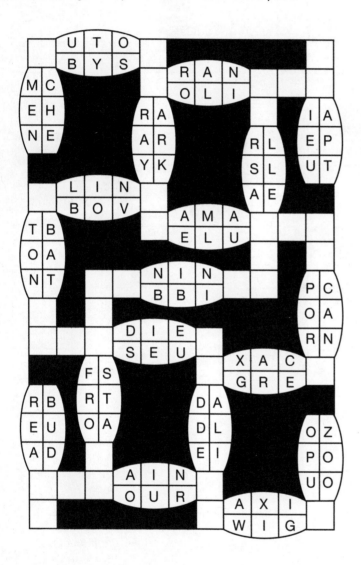

TRANSDELETION

Delete one letter from the word SAUCEPLATE and rearrange the rest, to get something you do mentally.

_____

★★★ Piece It Together

Fill in the blue design using pieces with the same shape outlined in black. Some pieces are "mirror-image" versions of the shape shown.

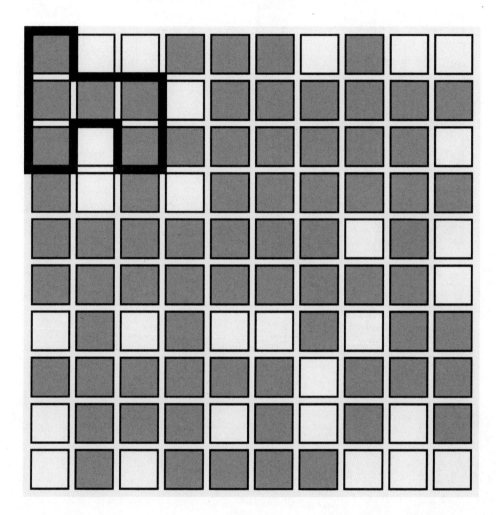

SMALL CHANGE

Change one letter in each of these two words, to form a common two-word phrase.

FLEW MARKER

★★★★★ Themeless Toughie by Daniel R. Stark

ACROSS

1 Cover stories
7 Least reputable
15 Not like at all
16 Annie's song
17 Pseudopod possessor
18 Ecclesiastical honorific
19 Spirit you can hear
21 A as in Austria
22 Anecdotal assembly
23 They'll darken your door
24 Hurdle for some seniors
25 Lid
26 For one
27 With zeal
28 Lyric words
29 Checked out
31 Red head
32 Brought out
34 As expected
37 Scull
38 Check mark
39 Studio workplace
41 Some correspondence
44 Whey-faced
45 Connect
46 Isn't timely
47 Banner headlines
50 Give __ rest
51 Furnace input
52 They may go down the tubes
54 Culmination
56 Beauty mag
57 Code
58 Cheerleader's exhortation
59 Oil source
60 Evinces unhappiness

DOWN

1 Buffalo hunter
2 Stand product
3 Cut off
4 Burpee's Golden, for one
5 Out, maybe
6 Best replacement
7 Soaked
8 Not as cold
9 Off
10 Cautionary note
11 Atl. isl.
12 Physicist Rutherford
13 Mixer
14 Score
20 Appeared overwhelmed
24 Appear ahead
27 Pay attention
29 Branch of biol.
30 Topiary tree
31 Soft shoe
33 *O'Hara's Choice* author
34 Like I
35 Geometry calculation
36 One who hates to act
38 Unenviable outfit
40 Lures
41 Runs off
42 Canton inductee of '05
43 Auspices
44 Fleeced
47 Drink named for a Yemeni city
48 Symbols of October
49 Hair __
52 Preserve, perhaps
53 Pivot
55 Something to write with

PAGE 17

Duplications

W	I	P	E	S		C	A	R	T		S	T	I	R
P	R	I	M	A		A	R	I	A		A	W	R	Y
M	A	T	C	H	S	T	I	C	K		B	I	K	E
	S	T	E	A	M		D	E	E	P	E	N	S	
			E	R	A	S			T	O	R	E		
A	N	D		A	R	T	S	H	O	W		N	B	C
P	O	O	L		T	R	E	E		E	A	G	E	R
P	L	U	T	O		I	D	A		R	A	I	S	E
L	I	B	R	A		P	A	R	T		A	N	T	S
E	E	L		S	C	E	N	T	E	D		E	S	T
		E	V	I	L			H	A	R	E			
	E	P	I	S	O	D	E		S	E	M	I	S	
A	L	A	S		C	O	P	Y	E	D	I	T	O	R
C	A	R	E		K	N	E	E		G	R	I	M	E
E	L	K	S		S	T	E	T		E	S	S	E	S

PAGE 18

Starbursts

CENTURY MARKS
40, 26, 18, 16

PAGE 19

Power Play

INITIAL REACTION
Money Talks

PAGE 20

Sudoku

4	6	5	1	9	3	7	2	8
3	7	1	8	5	2	6	4	9
9	8	2	4	6	7	3	5	1
8	5	9	6	7	1	4	3	2
7	4	6	2	3	8	9	1	5
1	2	3	9	4	5	8	6	7
5	3	8	7	2	6	1	9	4
6	1	4	5	8	9	2	7	3
2	9	7	3	1	4	5	8	6

MIXAGRAMS

A	L	O	F	T		O	P	U	S
I	N	G	O	T		S	O	L	O
F	I	E	R	Y		E	X	A	M
W	H	E	E	L		A	C	R	E

PAGE 21

Look Sharp

O	S	L	O		S	P	A	R		S	P	L	A	T
P	L	O	D		H	A	L	E		T	I	A	R	A
T	O	G	O		I	R	A	S		A	N	V	I	L
S	W	O	R	D	F	I	S	H		I	S	A	A	C
			I	T	S		A	U	N	T				
S	A	M	P	L	E		A	P	R		R	U	T	S
A	F	I	E	L	D		M	E	N		I	B	E	T
T	I	N	N	Y		C	O	D		S	P	O	R	E
E	R	I	C		C	O	N		A	T	E	A	S	E
D	E	S	I		N	A	G		B	E	S	T	E	D
			L	E	N	T		A	D	E				
V	O	T	E	S		R	A	Z	O	R	T	H	I	N
I	P	O	D	S		A	L	U	M		R	O	D	E
E	E	R	I	E		C	O	R	E		O	L	E	S
W	R	E	N	S		K	E	E	N		T	E	A	S

PAGE 22

Square Routes

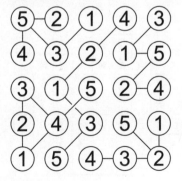

WRONG IS RIGHT
Effrontory (should be *effrontery*)

PAGE 23

Line Drawing

LAPEL, PAPER, PLAZA, VALET, A

THREE OF A KIND
<u>NOW</u>, LET'S HAVE N<u>ONE</u> OF
YOUR ET<u>ERNAL</u> MA<u>LARKE</u>Y.

PAGE 24

Veggie Surprise

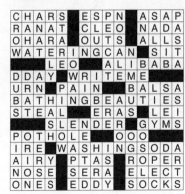

Unlisted word is CAULIFLOWER

WHO'S WHAT WHERE?
Barbadian

PAGE 25

All Wet

C	H	A	R	S		E	S	P	N		A	S	A	P
R	A	N	A	T		C	L	E	O		N	A	D	A
O	H	A	R	A		O	U	T	S		A	L	L	S
W	A	T	E	R	I	N	G	C	A	N		S	I	T
			L	E	O			A	L	I	B	A	B	A
D	D	A	Y		W	R	I	T	E	M	E			
U	R	N		P	A	I	N			B	A	L	S	A
B	A	T	H	I	N	G	B	E	A	U	T	I	E	S
S	T	E	A	L			E	R	A	S		L	E	I
			S	L	E	N	D	E	R		G	Y	M	S
P	O	T	H	O	L	E			O	O	O			
I	R	E		W	A	S	H	I	N	G	S	O	D	A
A	I	R	Y		P	T	A	S		R	O	P	E	R
N	O	S	E		S	E	R	A		E	L	E	C	T
O	N	E	S		E	D	D	Y		S	O	C	K	S

PAGE 26
Number-Out

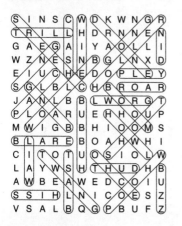

3	5	3	1	3
1	4	1	5	3
2	4	4	4	1
5	3	1	2	5
5	1	3	3	3

THINK ALIKE
PULL, TUG

PAGE 27
Seven Circles

SMALL CHANGE
TOP DOG

PAGE 28
Able-Bodied

L	I	N	T		J	E	S	T		A	C	R	E	S
A	N	E	W		O	B	O	E		T	H	U	M	P
S	T	R	O	N	G	B	O	X		E	A	G	E	R
S	O	D		A	G	E	N	T		A	N	G	R	Y
		T	I	E	D		B	A	S	T	E			
	C	H	I	L	D		C	O	D	E		D	E	W
P	L	U	M	S		H	O	E		S	P	A	R	
R	O	S	E		T	R	E	K	S		P	A	V	E
O	A	K	S		R	O	E		E	A	T	E	N	
S	K	Y		T	E	A	R		T	A	C	H	S	
	V	O	W	E	D		D	I	R	E				
D	R	O	N	E		S	P	E	N	T		B	U	S
R	A	I	S	E		T	O	U	G	H	L	U	C	K
A	R	C	E	D		E	N	C	E		I	S	L	E
B	E	E	T	S		R	Y	E	S		T	H	A	W

PAGE 29
One-Way Streets

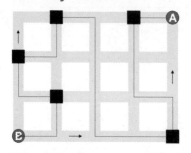

SOUND THINKING
UNISON

PAGE 30
Split Decisions

TRANSDELETION
CALF, FOAL

PAGE 31
Star Search

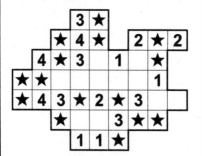

CHOICE WORDS
RACKET, SERVER, VOLLEY

PAGE 32
Make Some Noise

S	I	N	S	C	W	D	K	W	N	G	R
T	R	I	L	L	H	D	R	N	N	E	N
G	A	E	G	A	I	Y	A	O	L	L	I
W	Z	N	E	S	N	B	G	L	N	X	D
E	I	U	C	H	E	D	O	P	L	E	Y
S	G	L	B	L	C	H	B	R	O	A	R
J	A	N	L	B	B	L	W	O	R	G	T
P	L	O	A	R	U	E	H	H	O	U	P
M	W	I	G	B	B	H	I	O	O	M	S
B	L	A	R	E	B	O	A	H	W	H	I
C	I	T	O	T	U	O	S	I	O	L	W
L	A	Y	W	S	H	T	H	U	D	H	B
A	W	B	E	A	W	E	D	C	O	I	U
S	S	I	H	L	N	I	C	O	E	S	Z
V	S	A	L	B	Q	G	P	B	U	F	Z

IN OTHER WORDS
CLOAKROOM

PAGE 33
Fond Four

C	N	B	C		T	A	S	T	E		S	P	A	S
O	A	T	H		A	F	T	E	R		A	R	C	H
I	D	E	A		N	O	O	N	E		F	I	R	E
F	A	N	C	Y	G	O	W	N		D	A	Z	E	D
			H	A	L	T	S		T	I	R	E		
S	C	R	A	P	E		T	H	R	I	F	T		
O	R	E	S		S	H	E	E	T		I	O	U	
D	E	L		B	A	L	O	N	E	Y		G	R	R
A	M	I		A	G	E	N	T		S	H	A	G	
	E	S	P	I	E	D		T	E	E	T	H	E	
		H	U	T	S		N	E	R	V	E			
W	A	T	T	S		L	O	V	E	A	P	P	L	E
E	U	R	O		H	A	V	E	N		A	R	I	A
S	T	A	N		A	M	E	N	D		G	E	N	T
T	O	Y	S		M	E	L	T	S		E	Y	E	S

PAGE 34
Hyper-Sudoku

6	4	3	5	9	1	2	7	8
2	8	5	4	3	7	6	1	9
1	9	7	6	8	2	5	3	4
5	2	1	3	7	8	4	9	6
4	7	9	2	1	6	3	8	5
8	3	6	9	5	4	1	2	7
3	5	2	8	4	9	7	6	1
9	1	4	7	6	3	8	5	2
7	6	8	1	2	5	9	4	3

MIXAGRAMS

W	H	E	A	T		O	G	R	E
C	A	M	E	L		N	O	O	K
A	R	M	O	R		P	A	C	E
E	D	I	C	T		T	A	K	E

PAGE 35

Looking Back
#6

BETWEENER
HOP

PAGE 36

123

2	3	1	2	1	3
3	1	2	3	2	1
1	2	3	1	3	2
3	1	2	3	2	1
1	2	3	1	3	2
2	3	1	2	1	3

SUDOKU SUM

9	4	5
6	2	1
3	8	7

PAGE 37

Physics 101

S	C	A	R	F		E	D	I	T		E	M	I	T
P	A	L	E	R		M	A	S	H		L	I	N	E
A	R	E	N	A		O	S	L	O		A	N	T	E
S	E	C	O	N	D	T	H	E	M	O	T	I	O	N
			C	E	E			A	P	E				
B	A	R	R	E	N		P	S	S	T		P	E	A
A	L	A	I		S	I	L	O		I	D	E	A	S
B	U	N	D	L	E	S	O	F	E	N	E	R	G	Y
A	M	A	S	S		E	T	A	L		M	I	L	E
R	S	T		A	G	E	S		V	I	O	L	E	T
		S	T	Y			H	E	N					
S	A	L	E	S	R	E	S	I	S	T	A	N	C	E
I	R	O	N		A	R	I	D		A	L	O	H	A
T	E	A	S		T	I	L	E		C	O	N	I	C
S	A	F	E		E	E	L	S		T	E	E	T	H

PAGE 38

ABC

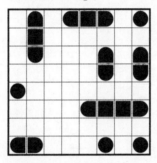

CLUELESS CROSSWORD

D	U	T	I	F	U	L
E		W		R		O
P	R	O	S	A	I	C
O		S		Z		U
S	N	O	O	Z	E	S
I		M		L		T
T	E	E	T	E	R	S

PAGE 39

Find the Ships

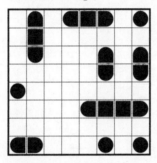

TWO-BY-FOUR
LEND, RICH

PAGE 40

"C" in the Kitchen

Missing answer is COUNTER

INITIAL REACTION
Familiarity Breeds Contempt

PAGE 41

Flabbergasted

C	P	A	S		A	D	O	S		P	O	S	E	S
L	A	S	T		N	E	S	T		E	V	E	N	T
A	R	I	A		T	A	C	O		R	E	E	D	Y
S	T	A	G	G	E	R	A	R	O	U	N	D		
S	E	N	S	E			R	E	D			C	O	W
Y	D	S		T	O	P		S	E	A	P	O	R	T
			P	L	A	I	D			M	A	R	E	S
	F	L	O	O	R	C	O	V	E	R	I	N	G	
F	O	O	L	S			C	O	R	A	L			
D	I	N	E	T	T	E		W	A	D		C	O	S
A	L	E			A	S	S			I	C	A	N	T
		S	H	O	C	K	A	B	S	O	R	B	E	R
A	S	T	I	R			I	L	I	E		E	A	S	E
S	P	A	R	E		M	A	R	T		A	N	E	W
P	A	R	E	S		O	D	D	S		M	A	C	S

PAGE 42

Missing Links

SMALL CHANGE
BEAR HUG

PAGE 43

Square Routes

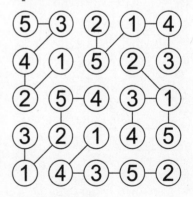

WRONG IS RIGHT
Burgandy (should be *burgundy*)

PAGE 44
Still in the Box

```
J G I G V U N W P M O D D B R
H T F D U S U Y E N R E V N A
C A O X U E D W E G H H D D N
T U N T U I O P Q P N B Z W E
N C U O H D N E O E U N W A F
A F T H E D Q R O L J T D E T N C
L H F D Z B P Q M I I G A X Z
C B L A T H U P T N G D R Y T
D F T S E S O T H Y T U N H S
F D P Q K L D A B C X D N A L
O R J H K H E T W S S L E D L
G I D K U N S M N R E V C Z N
I N O E I O P L J H D Z J U S
L A R Q L E D S L O T L N I T
G E K H F A E Y B C B N U R F
```

WHO'S WHAT WHERE?
Mainer

PAGE 45
Fruit Openers

```
T R A S H  C U T S  R D S
O U N C E  P R O M  O A T S
M E D I A  A N T I D O T E S
      F L U    E L E M E N T
B E F I T S    A M E N  L O S
L X I  H A N G  S I S I
I A G O  G O E S  A I N T
P L U M B E R S H E L P E R S
  T R A Y  M A I L  S N I P
    I N R E  G N A T  B T U
S I N  O N T O  T R A C E D
E N G R A V E    E A R
C L O U D I E S T  N E I G H
T A U T  E U R O  C A T E R
  W T S  S P A T  E S S E S
```

PAGE 46
Sudoku

```
6 2 3 4 7 9 8 5 1
1 9 4 6 5 8 7 3 2
7 8 5 3 2 1 9 6 4
2 7 9 8 4 5 3 1 6
8 5 1 9 6 3 4 2 7
4 3 6 7 1 2 5 9 8
3 1 7 5 8 6 2 4 9
9 6 8 2 3 4 1 7 5
5 4 2 1 9 7 6 8 3
```

MIXAGRAMS
```
H E R O N   W E N T
I N N E R   T O O T
G R U E L   U P O N
H E I S T   G O N E
```

PAGE 47
123

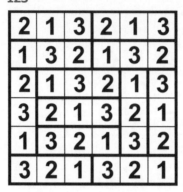

```
2 1 3 2 1 3
1 3 2 1 3 2
2 1 3 2 1 3
3 2 1 3 2 1
1 3 2 1 3 2
3 2 1 3 2 1
```

ADDITION SWITCH
218 + 302 = 520

PAGE 48
Rhyme Time

```
H A S A T  N A S A  S M O G
E L A T E  E L A L  H A L O
R A N O N  W E N T  A I D E
S I G N  J A C K H O R N E R
    E M I T    O D E S
G O S T A G  L A U D  T A M
A V O I D  P A N G  A R L O
F A R M E R I N T H E D E L L
F L E E  E N D S  A H E A D
E S L  E L K S  P R E T T Y
    O I L Y    P A N S
M I S S M U F F E T  I P O D
A D E S  P I E S  E V A D E
P E R U  O R E O  M E L O N
S A S E  N E T S  U S E R S
```

PAGE 49
One-Way Streets

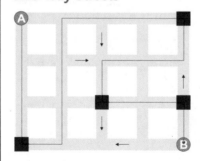

SOUND THINKING
ZINNIA

PAGE 50
No Three in a Row

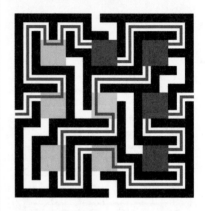

SAY IT AGAIN
BAY

PAGE 51
Star Search

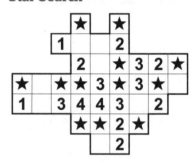

CHOICE WORDS
AMOUNT, CHARGE, TARIFF

PAGE 52
Put It Together

```
A F E W  M O A T  M O G U L
R O M E  A R C H  O B E S E
T I M E F R A M E  R A T E S
S L Y  L I T E R  A M I S S
    C A N E  M I L A N
  A W A R E  B A S E  S H E
T W I C E  O L E  S H O W
O A T H  T E R S E  T A M E
R I C E  A Y E  P A P E R
N T H  S L E D  M A L E S
    C R E E D  H I L L
A P R O N  R A I S E  V I A
B E A S T  O R D E R F O R M
R E F E R  P I E R  A T O M
A N T S Y  S A S S  R E N O
```

PAGE 53

Keyword

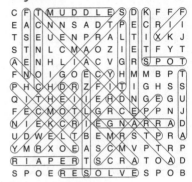

Keyword is FIX

IN OTHER WORDS
BYGONE

PAGE 55

Line Drawing

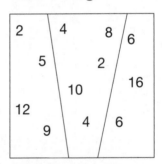

THREE OF A KIND
THE MIDNIGHT TRAIN TO
THAILAND LEAVES NOW.

PAGE 56

ABC

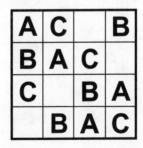

NATIONAL TREASURE
YANK

PAGE 57

That's the Price

PAGE 58

Five by Five

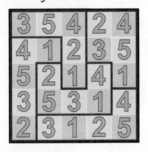

BETWEENER
COB

PAGE 59

Shopping Center Whodunit

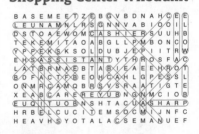

Perdita the personal shopper
did it, with a coat hanger, in
the fitting room

INITIAL REACTION
Don't Change Horses In
Midstream

PAGE 60

Find the Ships

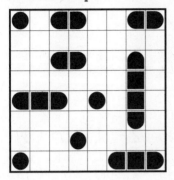

TWO-BY-FOUR
TELL, MANY (or MYNA)

PAGE 61

Sudoku

3	4	9	1	8	7	6	5	2
2	7	5	4	3	6	1	9	8
6	1	8	5	9	2	7	3	4
1	8	6	9	7	5	4	2	3
7	3	2	6	4	8	9	1	5
5	9	4	3	2	1	8	6	7
9	2	3	8	1	4	5	7	6
4	6	1	7	5	3	2	8	9
8	5	7	2	6	9	3	4	1

MIXAGRAMS

S	H	A	F	T		O	P	E	N
S	Y	L	P	H		P	A	P	A
A	D	O	P	T		F	R	E	E
D	E	M	U	R		S	K	I	M

PAGE 62

Down the Tubes

B	O	G	S		D	O	F	F	S		M	A	A	M
O	K	L	A		J	U	L	I	A		A	L	T	O
T	R	E	X		S	T	U	N	G		C	L	O	P
H	A	N	O	I		D	O	E	S		H	O	L	E
			P	R	I	O	R			L	O	W	L	Y
C	A	S	H	I	N		E	D	G	E				
A	C	C	O	S	T		S	N	O	O	P	E	R	S
S	T	A	N		R	E	C	A	P		E	V	E	S
T	I	R	E	S	O	M	E		A	R	R	E	S	T
			A	S	S	N		S	T	I	N	T	S	
Q	U	A	R	T			T	O	T	E	S			
U	N	D	O		H	A	L	O			S	C	R	A	M
A	T	O	P		A	M	A	Z	E		O	A	H	U
F	I	R	E		L	I	M	E	S		P	I	E	S
F	E	E	S		L	A	P	S	E		E	L	M	S

PAGE 63
Square Routes

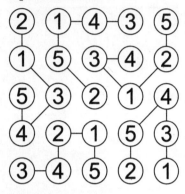

WRONG IS RIGHT
Sourkraut (should be *sauerkraut*)

PAGE 64
Triad Split Decisions

TRANSDELETION
PLEAD

PAGE 65
123

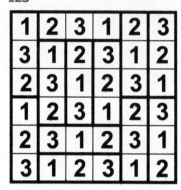

SUDOKU SUM

6	2	8
9	5	4
1	7	3

PAGE 66
Jury Duty

F	O	R	E		T	H	I	N		S	T	A	M	P
A	V	I	V		R	E	D	O		E	E	R	I	E
D	A	L	I		A	L	O	T		W	A	I	S	T
S	L	E	D		D	E	L	I	B	E	R	A	T	E
		E	D	E	N			E	D	U				
C	A	N	N	E	D		C	P	R		P	S	S	T
E	R	I	C	A		F	R	E	E	D		O	U	R
D	E	F	E	N	S	E	A	T	T	O	R	N	E	Y
A	N	T		S	O	R	T	S		L	E	A	D	S
R	A	Y	S		N	N	E		S	E	C	R	E	T
	O	U	I			S	I	D	E					
T	R	A	N	S	C	R	I	P	T		S	H	I	P
H	O	R	N	E		O	D	E	S		S	A	F	E
A	L	T	E	R		B	E	A	U		E	L	S	E
N	E	S	T	S		E	A	R	P		D	O	O	R

PAGE 67
Number-Out

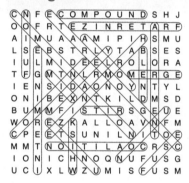

THINK ALIKE
PLOY, RUSE

PAGE 68
Looped Path

SAY IT AGAIN
SAW

PAGE 69
Get-Together

WHO'S WHAT WHERE?
Cantonian

PAGE 70
Portions

T	A	B	L	E		A	B	C	D		C	O	B	S
U	S	U	A	L		P	A	N	E		E	D	E	N
N	O	T	H	E	L	P	I	N	G		N	I	N	A
A	F	T		V	O	L	T		R	A	T	E	D	G
			C	A	S	E		W	E	R	E			
A	L	C	O	T	T		C	H	E	E	R	E	D	
V	A	L	U	E		T	O	E	S		P	R	E	P
I	C	O	N		W	O	E			I	O	T	A	
D	E	N	T		B	I	L	L		S	E	D	E	R
	D	E	E	P	E	N	S		D	I	C	E	R	S
		R	O	S	E		M	U	L	E				
C	A	R	P	E	T		S	E	E	K		A	H	S
A	R	E	A		M	A	K	E	T	H	E	C	U	T
P	I	E	R		A	B	I	T		A	R	E	N	A
S	A	L	T		N	E	T	S		T	A	S	T	Y

PAGE 71
One-Way Streets

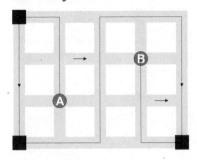

SOUND THINKING
OBEDIENT

PAGE 72
Hyper-Sudoku

4	2	5	9	6	1	3	8	7
8	9	1	7	4	3	5	6	2
7	3	6	2	5	8	9	4	1
3	4	8	5	9	2	7	1	6
5	6	7	1	3	4	2	9	8
2	1	9	8	7	6	4	5	3
6	7	3	4	8	9	1	2	5
9	5	2	6	1	7	8	3	4
1	8	4	3	2	5	6	7	9

CENTURY MARKS
31, 21, 25, 23

PAGE 73
Star Search

		1		★		
	2	★	4	3	3	
	★	3		★	★	2	★
	1		★		3		
		3	★			★	2
★	2	★			2	3	★
		1		1	★	

CHOICE WORDS
BADGER, HARASS, NETTLE

PAGE 74
Punctuation Piece

B	U	S	T		T	O	A	S	T		S	P	A	T
A	N	T	I		A	G	R	E	E		H	O	B	O
T	R	A	M		C	R	A	W	L		O	R	S	O
B	I	T	E	T	H	E	B	U	L	L	E	T		
O	P	E	R	A				P	E	G		R	A	P
Y	E	S		M	O	O	S		R	E	P	A	I	R
			S	P	I	R	I	T			L	I	M	O
	M	E	T	A	L	B	R	A	C	K	E	T	S	
G	A	L	A			S	E	C	O	N	D			
R	U	B	B	L	E		N	O	T	I		T	W	O
R	I	O		E	A	R			F	U	R	O	R	
	W	A	I	T	I	N	G	P	E	R	I	O	D	
A	M	P	S		E	V	I	L	S		A	B	L	E
L	E	A	K		R	A	C	E	S		L	E	E	R
E	N	D	S		S	L	E	E	T		S	S	N	S

PAGE 75
ABC

CLUELESS CROSSWORD

B	E	H	O	L	D	S
A		O		E		P
N	I	R	V	A	N	A
A		I		F		R
N	O	Z	Z	L	E	S
A		O		E		E
S	E	N	A	T	O	R

PAGE 76
Sequence Maze

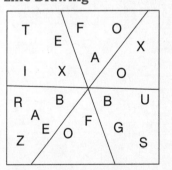

BETWEENER
BOX

PAGE 77
Sudoku

3	9	4	2	1	5	8	6	7
6	8	1	7	3	9	5	2	4
7	2	5	8	6	4	1	3	9
4	3	2	6	8	1	9	7	5
9	1	7	5	2	3	6	4	8
8	5	6	9	4	7	2	1	3
2	6	9	4	7	8	3	5	1
1	7	8	3	5	2	4	9	6
5	4	3	1	9	6	7	8	2

MIXAGRAMS

L A D L E   W A R D
A S S E T   O U C H
S C E N T   R E S T
T I D A L   D U E T

PAGE 78
In Place

O	P	E	C		A	L	T	O	S		S	S	T	S
N	A	D	A		B	E	A	U	T		O	P	A	L
T	W	I	N		S	A	R	G	E		S	A	L	E
O	N	T	O	P	O	F	T	H	E	W	O	R	L	D
			E	E	L			T	R	I				
D	E	S		A	U	D	I		S	N	A	P	A	T
E	R	E	I		T	I	N	E		C	U	R	V	E
M	I	D	D	L	E	O	F	T	H	E	R	O	A	D
O	C	A	L	A		N	O	N	E		A	M	I	D
S	A	N	E	S	T		R	A	Y	S		S	L	Y
			S	A	T			T	U	G				
B	O	T	T	O	M	O	F	T	H	E	H	E	A	P
A	R	E	A		A	D	O	R	E		A	L	L	I
G	E	N	T		L	O	N	E	R		N	A	M	E
S	O	D	A		E	S	T	E	E		A	L	A	S

PAGE 79
Line Drawing

```
  T      F    O
    E         X
           A
  I    X      O

  R   B     B   U
    A      F
  Z   E  O    G
                S
```

EXIT, OAF, OX, ZEBRA, OF, BUGS

THREE OF A KIND
TO OUR DISMAY, BEDLAM
ENSUED WHEN OUR EYES
OPENED.

PAGE 80

Find the Ships

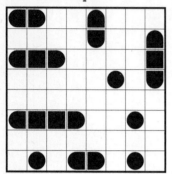

TWO-BY-FOUR
BOIL, TINY

PAGE 81

Square Routes

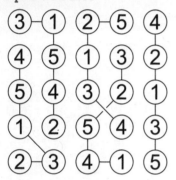

ADDITION SWITCH
4 6 3 + 2 1 5 = 6 7 8

PAGE 82

Noisemakers

G	E	T	S		C	A	S	K		B	Y	L	A	W
R	A	R	E		O	R	E	O		L	E	A	S	E
A	R	I	Z		L	A	M	A		T	A	C	K	S
S	N	O	W	M	O	B	I	L	E		R	E	S	T
		H	E	R		S	A	L	T	S				
A	M	M	O	N	I	A			F	R	A	C	A	S
R	O	E		N	C	O	S		I	G	A	V	E	
G	A	R	B	A	G	E	D	I	S	P	O	S	A	L
U	N	I	O	N		S	E	A	T		T	I	E	
E	S	T	A	T	E		M	U	S	S	E	L	S	
		T	E	E	T	H		M	O	N				
U	S	E	R		L	E	A	F	B	L	O	W	E	R
M	O	R	A	L		A	B	E	L		R	A	V	E
P	R	I	C	E		S	I	T	E		E	D	E	N
S	T	E	E	D		E	T	A	S		S	E	N	T

PAGE 83

Mail Call
Cat, Stinker; Matt, Rover; Nat, Rex; Pat, Fido

SMALL CHANGE
TEST TUBE

PAGE 84

123

1	3	2	3	1	2	3	1	2
2	1	3	1	2	3	1	2	3
3	2	1	2	3	1	2	3	1
1	3	2	1	2	3	1	2	3
3	1	3	2	1	2	3	1	2
1	2	1	3	2	3	2	3	1
2	3	2	1	3	1	3	1	2
3	2	3	1	2	1	2	3	1
2	1	3	2	3	1	2	3	1

WRONG IS RIGHT
Pursuade (should be *persuade*)

PAGE 85

Number-Out

2	2	5	1	4
1	2	3	1	5
5	2	4	3	3
5	5	5	2	3
3	4	2	5	3

THINK ALIKE
HUT, SHACK

PAGE 86

Piano Parts

PAGE 87

Tanks a Lot

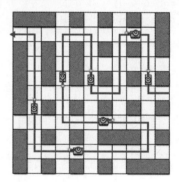

SAY IT AGAIN
OUT

PAGE 88

Split Decisions

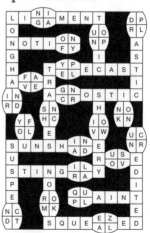

TRANSDELETION
READER

PAGE 89

Hyper-Sudoku

1	7	4	3	6	8	9	5	2
3	5	9	4	2	1	8	6	7
6	8	2	7	9	5	3	4	1
4	3	6	1	8	9	7	2	5
7	2	8	5	4	6	1	3	9
9	1	5	2	7	3	6	8	4
2	4	3	8	1	7	5	9	6
5	6	7	9	3	2	4	1	8
8	9	1	6	5	4	2	7	3

MIXAGRAMS

STORM HOBO
PENNY DAIS
RAVEN ZERO
AMEBA LADY

PAGE 90

Let It Snow

CASK GAZE TILES
PLEA ARIA ANODE
AMEN FENS LARGE
SANG FACEPOWDER
APES ENE
SCARES BANS GRR
ARBOR REIN FREE
DOYOUGETMYDRIFT
TOSS RATS ROPER
OKS SOLE WINERY
SAW CAPT
CORNFLAKES DASH
UNTIE DENT OHIO
BEEPS ANTE OOZE
ASSET MOSS RYES

PAGE 91

Put-Ons

Unlisted word is OUTFIT

IN OTHER WORDS
DUCTWORK

PAGE 93

One-Way Streets

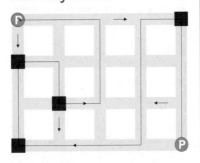

SOUND THINKING
DIAPHANOUS

PAGE 94

Put Up with It

B	L	A	S	T		D	A	S	H		T	O	P	S
A	U	D	I	O		O	B	O	E		A	P	O	P
S	T	A	N	D	S	T	I	L	L		K	A	L	E
H	E	M		D	U	E	T		P	E	E	L	E	D
	S	L	E	D		M	E	S	A					
B	A	T	T	E	D		D	I	R	E	C	T	S	
E	R	R	O	R		F	A	N	S		H	O	H	O
E	D	A	M		A	N	D		A	R	E	A		
S	O	D	A		A	B	C	S		E	N	T	E	R
R	E	C	Y	C	L	E		F	A	C	E	T	S	
	H	E	R	E		C	O	R	E					
P	O	T	A	T	O		M	A	L	L		S	P	A
A	L	E	C		B	E	A	R	D	O	W	N	O	N
Y	E	A	H		A	C	R	E		B	E	A	S	T
S	O	M	E		T	O	E	S		E	D	G	E	S

PAGE 95

Sets of Three

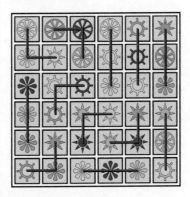

SMALL CHANGE
LOOK SHARP

PAGE 96

Star Search

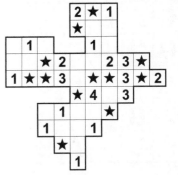

CHOICE WORDS
MOLARS, PALATE, TONGUE

PAGE 97

Triad Split Decisions

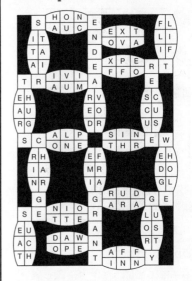

TRANSDELETION
ANGOLA

PAGE 98

Wee Ones

R	O	T	C		C	E	D	A	R		G	L	I	B
I	D	O	L		A	D	O	B	E		R	O	L	E
M	I	N	I	A	T	U	R	E	P	O	O	D	L	E
S	E	E	P	S		A	L	E	R	T	E	S	T	
	A	P	I	E			A	C	T					
S	E	A	R		S	M	A	L	L	H	O	U	R	S
T	A	F	T		L	I	L	O		I	S	S	U	E
E	G	O		R	E	L	I	V	E	D		H	I	T
E	L	O	P	E		I	B	I	S		D	E	N	T
P	E	T	I	T	P	O	I	N	T		E	R	G	O
	L	O	A		G	A	U	L						
A	S	S	O	O	N	A	S		S	I	N	A	I	
L	I	T	T	L	E	N	E	C	K	C	L	A	M	S
E	L	I	E		L	A	R	V	A		A	T	T	N
C	O	R	D		S	T	A	I	N		H	O	S	T

PAGE 99

ABC

C	A	B		
B		A	C	
A			B	C
	B	C		A
		C	A	B

NATIONAL TREASURE
ACID

PAGE 100

Find the Ships

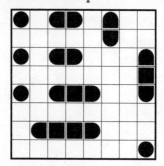

TWO-BY-FOUR
FORE, FEND; FOND, FREE
(or REEF)

PAGE 101

Piecework

S	P	E	E	D		S	T	R	O	P		C	A	P
E	A	G	L	E		K	O	A	L	A		O	N	E
A	T	O	M	S	M	A	S	H	E	R		D	I	S
		S	P	A	T	S		R	H	E	T	T
T	N	T		I	C	E		A	M	O	E	B	A	S
H	A	R	A	S	S		S	L	A	T	E	R
E	D	U	C	E		S	P	I	N		L	E	O	S
R	I	S	E		G	O	R	G	E		T	A	P	A
M	A	T	T		A	G	I	N		C	A	K	E	S
	B	A	D	E	G	G		P	A	P	E	R	S
A	C	U	T	E	L	Y		B	A	S		R	A	Y
L	A	S	E	R		S	U	I	T	S
O	P	T		M	E	A	T	G	R	I	N	D	E	R
O	R	E		A	R	I	A	S		L	O	U	S	E
F	I	R		L	A	R	R	Y		E	B	B	E	D

PAGE 102

Two Pairs

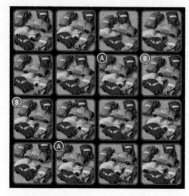

BETWEENER
CAKE

PAGE 103

Sudoku

8	3	1	2	4	5	9	7	6
9	7	4	6	1	3	8	5	2
5	6	2	8	9	7	1	4	3
2	1	6	4	5	9	7	3	8
7	8	5	3	2	6	4	1	9
4	9	3	1	7	8	2	6	5
6	4	9	5	8	1	3	2	7
1	5	8	7	3	2	6	9	4
3	2	7	9	6	4	5	8	1

MIXAGRAMS

S	E	V	E	R	V	I	A	L
D	R	A	K	E	S	A	C	S
A	R	S	O	N	D	U	A	L
A	D	U	L	T	H	E	R	O

PAGE 104

Square Routes

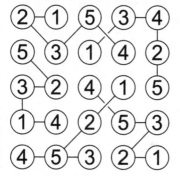

WRONG IS RIGHT
Innoculate (should be
inoculate)

PAGE 105

Sounds Correct

B	O	O	N		E	D	G	E		A	B	E	T	S
E	A	V	E		N	O	E	L		M	A	R	I	A
T	H	E	R	I	T	E	O	F	S	P	R	I	N	G
A	U	R	O	R	A			A	S	S	E	S	S	
			E	N	A	M	E	L
B	L	E	D		G	H	O	S	T	W	R	I	T	E
L	O	R	E		L	A	D	S		A	I	R	E	S
I	C	I	C	L	E			A	D	V	E	N	T
M	A	C	R	O		M	A	P	S		A	N	T	E
P	L	A	Y	W	R	I	G	H	T		L	E	S	S
			E	X	O	D	U	S
T	R	A	C	E	D			T	U	M	U	L	T
R	I	G	H	T	O	N	T	H	E	M	O	N	E	Y
A	T	E	I	N		B	O	I	L		S	T	O	P
P	A	S	T	A		C	O	P	Y		T	O	N	E

PAGE 106

Number-Out

1	3	5	5	5	4
1	2	4	6	5	3
5	1	6	3	2	1
6	1	4	3	4	2
4	1	3	3	1	2
2	6	2	1	3	2

THINK ALIKE
BOAT, SHIP

PAGE 107

Hyper-Sudoku

2	4	7	8	6	5	9	1	3
9	8	5	2	1	3	6	4	7
6	1	3	7	4	9	2	8	5
8	9	4	6	3	7	1	5	2
7	6	2	1	5	4	8	3	9
5	3	1	9	2	8	4	7	6
4	7	8	5	9	2	3	6	1
3	2	6	4	7	1	5	9	8
1	5	9	3	8	6	7	2	4

CENTURY MARKS
18, 29, 42, 11

PAGE 108
Music Boxes

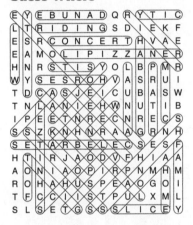

H	E	A	P	S		A	L	O	T			R	A	P
E	R	N	I	E		P	E	S	O		S	A	M	E
L	I	T	T	L	E	R	O	C	K		O	D	E	R
P	E	S	T	E	R		S	A	L		R	I	N	K
			N	O	D		R	A	M	R	O	D	S
F	L	U	B	A	D	U	B		S	A	Y
L	O	L	A		E	R	A	S		P	S	A	T	S
A	B	A	B		D	E	L	L	S		O	L	E	O
K	E	N	Y	A		R	E	A	L		U	S	E	R
		B	I	T		S	T	A	L	L	O	N	E
B	O	U	L	D	E	R		E	V	A
A	C	L	U		S	H	Y		E	R	R	A	T	A
M	E	T	E		T	O	O	T	S	I	E	P	O	P
B	A	R	S		E	D	G	E		A	B	B	O	T
I	N	A		R	A	I	N		T	A	S	K	S

PAGE 109
Guess Where

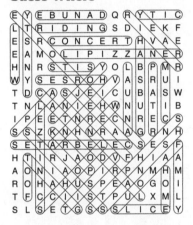

Unlisted answer is VIENNA

INITIAL REACTION
Every Dog Has His Day

PAGE 110
Land of Lincoln

SAY IT AGAIN
CAPE

PAGE 111
Frictionless

P	O	K	E	S		W	A	L	K		R	I	F	F
A	G	E	N	T		A	L	O	E		E	V	I	L
C	R	E	D	I	T	S	L	I	P		P	O	R	E
T	E	N	S	P	O	T		S	T	E	E	R	E	D
			P	I	E	R		A	B	L	Y
B	A	C	A	L	L		E	S	T	A		C	A	B
O	C	H	R	E		S	T	A	I	N		O	W	L
R	U	E	S		B	U	R	N	T		C	A	G	E
E	T	A		B	O	R	I	S		E	S	S	E	S
R	E	P		A	R	E	A		S	M	I	T	E	S
	S	C	A	R		L	A	T	E
T	A	K	E	S	O	N		P	I	R	A	T	E	S
O	M	A	R		W	A	T	E	R	S	L	I	D	E
R	I	T	E		E	V	E	R		O	M	E	G	A
I	D	E	S		R	E	L	Y		N	A	D	E	R

PAGE 112
One-Way Streets

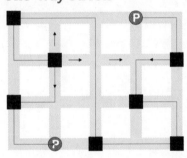

SOUND THINKING
FLIMSY

PAGE 113
123

1	3	1	2	3	2	3	2	1
2	1	2	3	1	3	1	3	2
3	2	3	1	2	1	3	2	1
2	3	1	2	1	3	2	1	3
3	1	2	1	3	2	1	3	2
1	2	3	2	1	3	2	1	3
2	3	1	3	2	1	3	2	1
1	2	3	1	3	2	1	3	2
3	1	2	3	2	1	2	1	3

SUDOKU SUM

2	5	9
7	1	3
6	8	4

PAGE 114
Line Drawing

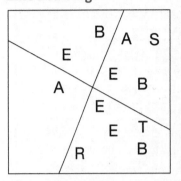

A, BE, BASE, BERET

THREE OF A KIND
THERE'S <u>NO</u> <u>SEC</u>RET TO
TEA<u>CHING</u> <u>EARTH</u> SCIENCE.

PAGE 115
On Course

B	O	I	T	E		S	P	E	A	R		T	O	Y
A	B	O	U	T		H	O	W	I	E		E	G	O
R	O	U	G	H	R	I	D	E	R	S		E	D	U
S	E	S	S	I	O	N	S		F	A	S	T	E	R
			C	O	Y		S	A	L	O	O	N	S
L	O	G	J	A	M		P	A	R	E	N	T
A	P	R	I	L		P	A	N	E	S		A	D	S
T	E	E	M		D	A	R	T	S		F	L	E	E
E	N	E		P	I	N	T	A		P	L	E	A	T
	N	U	R	S	E	S		Y	E	A	R	N	S
R	E	T	R	I	A	L		K	E	A
I	C	H	I	N	G		S	E	A	S	H	O	R	E
L	O	U		T	R	A	P	S	H	O	O	T	E	R
E	L	M		E	E	R	I	E		U	S	I	N	G
D	E	B		D	E	I	T	Y		P	E	S	O	S

PAGE 116
Star Search

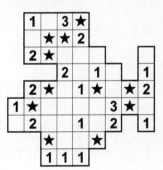

CHOICE WORDS
BLONDE, CANARY, FLAXEN

PAGE 117

Dicey

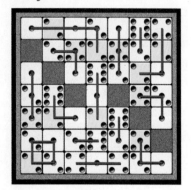

SMALL CHANGE
RUNNY NOSE

PAGE 118

Subterranean

J	I	G	S			L	A	R	A		S	T	R	A	W
I	R	O	N		A	C	E	S			P	R	A	D	O
B	E	L	O	W	T	H	E	H	O	R	I	Z	O	N	
E	N	D		H	E	E	D		R	I	C	E	S		
S	E	A	M	A	N		S	T	A	N	K				
		A	L	T	A		A	C	T		O	P	T		
N	A	I	V	E		T	O	I	L		A	S	I	A	
U	N	D	E	R	T	H	E	W	E	A	T	H	E	R	
T	O	O	N		H	O	R	A		R	O	A	S	T	
S	N	L		R	E	M		N	O	R	M				
		T	E	N	E	T		P	E	S	T	L	E		
L	A	R	G	E		A	Y	E	S		E	O	N		
B	E	N	E	A	T	H	C	O	N	T	E	M	P	T	
I	N	T	E	L		A	I	D	E		A	P	E	R	
N	O	I	S	E		S	T	A	R		R	O	S	Y	

PAGE 119

Hyper-Sudoku

9	4	8	5	1	3	6	2	7
1	6	5	7	8	2	4	3	9
7	3	2	4	6	9	8	1	5
4	8	1	9	2	7	5	6	3
5	2	6	1	3	4	9	7	8
3	7	9	8	5	6	2	4	1
8	5	4	2	7	1	3	9	6
2	1	3	6	9	5	7	8	4
6	9	7	3	4	8	1	5	2

MIXAGRAMS

H U B B Y   P E A S
K A Y A K   N I C E
E P O C H   O K R A
M I L K Y   F E A T

PAGE 120

ABC

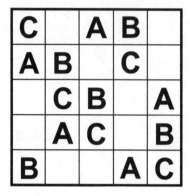

NATIONAL TREASURE
SPRAIN

PAGE 121

Elevating

M	O	L	A	R		A	T	A	D		P	E	E	P
A	D	O	B	E		M	E	S	A		R	I	L	E
T	I	L	E	D		P	R	O	F		I	D	E	S
H	E	A	T	H	C	L	I	F	F		C	E	N	T
			E	S	E		O	P	E	R	A	S		
B	O	N	S	A	I		N	A	D	E	R			
A	L	O	U	D		L	E	V	I	T	A	T	E	D
S	L	I	M		C	I	V	I	L		N	E	M	O
E	A	R	M	A	R	K	E	D		A	G	A	I	N
		I	C	I	E	R		A	L	E	R	T	S	
G	R	A	T	E	S		O	D	D					
R	U	N	T		P	E	A	K	D	E	M	A	N	D
U	L	N	A		I	L	S	A		N	I	M	O	Y
N	E	I	L		E	B	A	Y		T	R	I	T	E
T	R	E	K		R	A	P	S		E	A	S	E	D

PAGE 122

Knot or Not?
Knot: 1 and 2, Not: 3 and 4

BETWEENER
DOWN

PAGE 123

Find the Ships

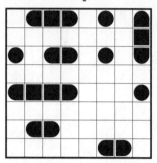

TWO-BY-FOUR
JEER, PURR

PAGE 124

Triad Split Decisions

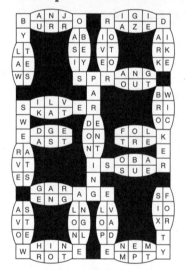

TRANSDELETION
FADE IN

PAGE 125

Rookies

P	O	S	H		S	H	O	D		S	P	A	R	S
A	L	T	A		M	A	D	E		C	O	R	A	L
I	G	O	R		I	D	O	L		A	L	I	V	E
R	A	W	M	A	T	E	R	I	A	L		S	E	E
			L	E	S		R	E	P	E	N	T		
T	O	T	A	L	S		A	R	E	S	O			
A	K	I	T	A		A	N	O	N		O	S	H	A
G	R	E	E	N	E	G	G	S	A	N	D	H	A	M
S	A	R	A		R	I	L	E		O	L	I	V	E
			S	C	O	N	E		A	P	E	M	E	N
S	P	R	E	A	D			T	B	A				
H	U	E		N	E	W	Y	E	A	R	S	E	V	E
A	T	B	A	T		R	A	N	T		A	R	I	D
R	O	U	T	E		E	L	S	E		N	I	C	E
E	N	T	E	R		N	E	E	D		K	E	E	N

PAGE 126

123

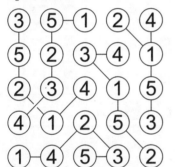

WRONG IS RIGHT
Manouver (should be *maneuver*)

PAGE 127

Square Routes

ADDITION SWITCH
1 9 7 + 3 2 6 = 5 2 3

PAGE 128

The Basics

PAGE 129

Find the Treasure

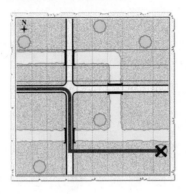

SAY IT AGAIN
LEFT

PAGE 131

Never the Same

WHO'S WHAT WHERE?
Züricher

PAGE 132

Hyper-Sudoku

6	2	3	8	9	1	4	7	5
7	5	1	3	2	4	6	9	8
4	8	9	7	6	5	3	2	1
9	4	2	6	5	8	7	1	3
1	7	6	9	4	3	5	8	2
5	3	8	1	7	2	9	4	6
3	6	4	2	8	7	1	5	9
2	9	7	5	1	6	8	3	4
8	1	5	4	3	9	2	6	7

MIXAGRAMS
S P O I L   O U T S
M I S E R   C E N T
S P L I T   E A S E
D E M U R   W O R M

PAGE 133

Let Us Illustrate

PAGE 134

One-Way Streets

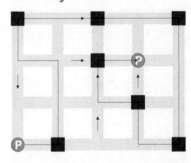

SOUND THINKING
EGGNOG

PAGE 135

Star Search

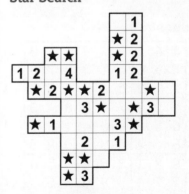

CHOICE WORDS
CACHET, ESTEEM, REGARD

PAGE 136
Conduct Yourself

A	A	H	S		E	R	A	S	E		S	P	R	Y
B	L	O	T		B	O	R	I	S		P	L	I	E
C	A	R	R		B	U	G	L	E	B	E	A	D	S
S	I	N	A	I		N	U	T		R	A	N	G	E
		I	N	C	O	D	E		V	E	R	S	E	S
Z	I	N	G	E	R			B	I	D	E			
E	D	G	E		G	A	R	B	O		D	D	A	Y
A	L	I			A	T	O	L	L			R	U	E
L	E	N	S		N	O	O	S	E		P	U	R	L
			C	H	I	P			N	O	R	M	A	L
C	O	U	R	I	C		S	I	T	C	O	M		
A	N	N	O	Y		I	N	K		T	W	E	R	P
C	E	L	L	O	P	H	A	N	E		E	D	I	E
H	A	I	L		B	O	R	O	N		S	U	P	S
E	M	T	S		S	P	E	W	S		S	P	A	T

PAGE 137
Dotty

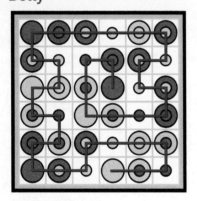

SMALL CHANGE
SHORT STORY

PAGE 138
Sudoku

4	3	2	8	7	9	5	1	6
5	9	6	4	1	3	2	7	8
7	1	8	6	2	5	4	3	9
1	2	9	7	5	6	8	4	3
6	5	3	9	8	4	1	2	7
8	4	7	2	3	1	6	9	5
9	8	1	3	6	2	7	5	4
2	7	4	5	9	8	3	6	1
3	6	5	1	4	7	9	8	2

CENTURY MARKS
10, 59, 19, 12

PAGE 139
Turkey Day

S	A	L	A	D		M	A	G	I		C	L	A	N
P	R	I	M	O		E	T	A	T		H	I	R	T
A	R	S	O	N		D	O	L	L		I	T	C	H
T	O	P	K	A	P	I	P	A	L	A	C	E		
E	Y	E		T	L	C			D	V	O	R	A	K
S	O	R	T	I	E		S	M	O	G		A	G	O
		H	O	A	G	I	E			S	T	A	B	
B	Y	Z	A	N	T	I	N	E	E	M	P	I	R	E
L	A	W	N			L	A	T	V	I	A			
A	L	I		B	A	L	I		I	N	S	I	S	T
B	E	E	F	U	P		N	A	N		N	E	A	
		B	I	C	O	N	T	I	N	E	N	T	A	L
S	C	A	N		L	O	O	N		L	E	A	V	E
K	I	C	K		L	O	I	N		L	I	K	E	N
Y	A	K	S		O	N	L	Y		I	N	E	R	T

PAGE 140
Split Decisions

TRANSDELETION
RECORD

PAGE 141
Number-Out

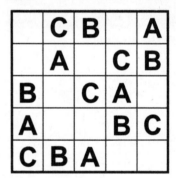

2	2	6	1	3	3
2	3	6	1	4	1
2	6	6	3	2	4
1	4	3	5	6	2
4	1	1	1	5	2
3	5	1	2	1	2

THINK ALIKE
FORM, SHAPE

PAGE 142
Pour It On

R	I	F	T		I	T	S	M	E		O	M	I	T
A	M	E	N		C	I	V	I	L		V	A	S	E
B	O	T	T	L	E	N	E	C	K		E	R	I	N
B	U	C		A	B	E	L			D	R	E	S	S
I	T	H	A	C	A		T	B	I	R	D	S		
			J	U	G	H	E	A	D	J	O	N	E	S
O	M	A	N		A	R	C	O			E	R	E	
I	N	E	X	A	C	T		A	L	T	O	S	A	X
M	E	A		H	A	U	L		E	A	T	S		
P	I	T	C	H	E	R	P	L	A	N	T			
		B	A	R	R	I	S		N	A	S	D	A	Q
W	R	A	P	S		C	O	N	N		I	C	U	
H	U	L	L		T	E	A	P	O	T	D	O	M	E
I	D	L	E		A	L	L	E	Y		I	D	E	S
Z	E	S	T		O	M	E	N	S		P	E	S	T

PAGE 143
ABC

	C	B	A		A
	A		C	B	
B		C	A		
A			B	C	
C	B	A			

CLUELESS CROSSWORD

F	I	D	G	E	T	Y
U		I		Q		A
R	E	S	C	U	E	R
R		P		A		D
I	N	E	R	T	I	A
E		L		O		R
R	O	S	T	R	U	M

PAGE 144
Bumper Crop

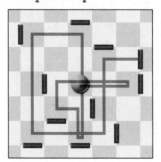

BETWEENER
YARD

PAGE 145
Line Drawing

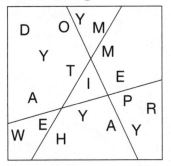

TODAY, MY, ME, I, WE, HAY, PRY

THREE OF A KIND
HE HAS <u>TO PAVE</u> HIS
GREEN <u>DRIVE</u>WAY WITH
BROWN ASP<u>HALT</u>.

PAGE 146
Table Talk

G	A	R	P		B	A	S	I	S		A	D	E	E
A	L	O	E		E	M	O	T	E		R	I	L	E
B	O	W	L	E	D	O	V	E	R		I	S	B	N
O	H	D	E	A	R			M	A	D	E	H	A	Y
N	A	Y		R	O	B	S		P	O	S	E		
		S	P	O	O	N	F	E	D		D	U	H	
C	A	F	E		M	O	I	L		G	O	O	S	E
A	C	O	R	N		I	D	E		E	L	U	D	E
S	T	R	A	Y		N	E	S	T		E	T	A	L
A	S	K		M	U	G	S	H	O	T	S			
		L	A	P	S		T	Y	P	E		P	O	D
S	K	I	S	H	O	P			P	A	N	I	N	I
O	A	F	S		P	L	A	T	E	M	A	K	E	R
A	N	T	E		E	I	D	E	R		S	E	A	T
P	E	S	T		N	E	E	D	S		A	R	M	Y

PAGE 147
Find the Ships

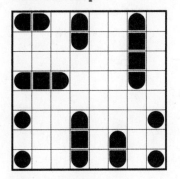

TWO-BY-FOUR
QUAY, BOLT (or BLOT)

PAGE 148
Hyper-Sudoku

8	1	7	3	2	9	6	4	5
6	4	3	7	8	5	1	2	9
5	2	9	6	1	4	7	8	3
2	8	5	1	4	6	9	3	7
4	9	6	2	3	7	8	5	1
3	7	1	9	5	8	4	6	2
1	6	4	5	7	3	2	9	8
9	3	2	8	6	1	5	7	4
7	5	8	4	9	2	3	1	6

MIXAGRAMS

```
C R U E T    L A S H
D E C O R    D U T Y
P S A L M    E G O S
I T C H Y    P I P E
```

PAGE 149
Watch Words

C	A	M	P		R	E	P	O		C	L	A	N	S
O	L	I	O		E	A	R	N		H	I	R	A	M
H	A	N	D	S	F	R	E	E	D	E	V	I	C	E
O	N	I	C	E		Z	I	O	N		E	R	A	
		A	C	D	C		D	R	I	L	L	E	R	
C	R	Y	S	T	A	L	G	A	Y	L	E			
H	O	O	T		D	O	H		L	O	U	P	E	
I	L	K		B	A	Y	O	N	N	E		T	O	W
C	L	E	A	R		S	O	O		S	A	M	E	
		B	A	N	D	T	O	G	E	T	H	E	R	
S	T	O	C	K	E	R		K	O	B	E			
O	R	S		E	V	E	S		A	W	A	S	H	
F	A	C	E	M	A	S	K	P	E	N	A	L	T	Y
I	M	A	G	E		S	E	A	T		R	O	A	M
A	P	R	O	N		Y	W	C	A		D	E	R	N

PAGE 150
Square Routes

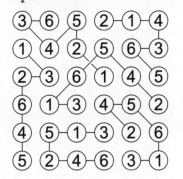

WRONG IS RIGHT
Charlatin (should be *charlatan*)

PAGE 151
Sitting Bull

SAY IT AGAIN
MEAN

PAGE 152
Number-Out

3	3	1	6	2	4
4	3	6	1	2	5
6	3	5	3	2	2
5	5	4	1	3	6
5	2	4	4	4	1
5	1	2	3	6	3

THINK ALIKE
SHOP, STORE

PAGE 153
In the Cards

H	A	U	L		A	L	S	O		F	A	C	T	S
E	D	N	A		S	E	A	R		A	L	O	H	A
L	O	W	B	R	I	D	G	E		R	A	T	E	S
P	R	E	S	E	N	T	S		W	R	I	T	E	S
S	E	T		B	I	O		S	E	E	N	O		
			N	U	N		I	T	L	L		N	B	A
D	E	B	A	T	E		V	I	L	L	A	G	E	S
E	R	I	N		A	I	R			W	I	S	H	
M	A	G	A	Z	I	N	E		P	L	E	N	T	Y
I	S	H		I	D	I	D		R	I	D			
		E	A	T	E	N		S	O	B		P	I	C
A	G	A	T	H	A		A	P	P	R	O	A	C	H
H	O	R	S	E		T	R	O	J	A	N	W	A	R
E	N	T	E	R		A	L	O	E		T	E	R	I
M	E	S	A	S		D	O	N	T		O	D	E	S

PAGE 154

123

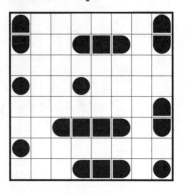

3	2	1	3	1	2	3	2	1
2	1	3	2	3	1	2	1	3
1	3	2	1	2	3	1	3	2
2	1	3	2	3	1	2	1	3
3	2	1	3	1	2	3	2	1
1	3	2	1	2	3	1	3	2
2	1	3	2	3	1	2	1	3
3	2	1	3	1	2	3	2	1
1	3	2	1	2	3	1	3	2

SUDOKU SUM

1	8	2
7	9	4
3	6	5

PAGE 155

Find the Ships

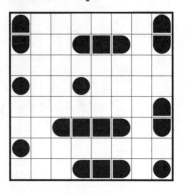

TWO-BY-FOUR
MAIN, TURN (or RUNT)

PAGE 156

Fetch

C	O	N	G	A		S	T	O	P		L	I	R	A
A	G	E	N	T		P	I	L	E		U	R	A	L
G	R	A	P	H	P	A	P	E	R		C	A	N	E
E	E	L		L	A	S	S		S	A	I	N	T	S
			H	E	L	M		S	I	L	L			
A	S	S	E	T	S		I	T	S	A	L	I	V	E
S	C	A	R	E		T	R	O	T		E	D	E	N
C	A	R	R		C	R	O	C	S		B	Y	R	D
A	L	A	I		O	I	N	K		C	A	L	V	E
P	E	N	N	A	N	T	S		F	E	L	L	E	D
			G	I	V	E		T	E	L	L			
E	D	I	B	L	E		T	A	L	E		P	A	S
Z	E	R	O		N	I	G	H	T	S	T	I	C	K
R	E	I	N		T	R	I	O		T	U	T	T	I
A	P	S	E		S	A	F	E		A	B	Y	S	S

PAGE 157

Serendipity

Missing word is HORSESHOE

IN OTHER WORDS
HANDKERCHIEF

PAGE 158

Alternating Tiles

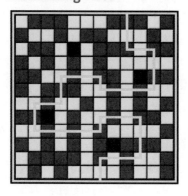

SMALL CHANGE
BEACH TOWEL

PAGE 159

Star Search

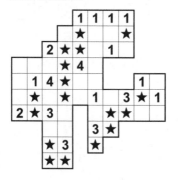

CHOICE WORDS
GOBLET, TEAPOT, TUREEN

PAGE 160

Cutting Class

F	A	K	I	R		F	L	A	P	S		W	E	T
T	B	O	N	E		E	I	L	A	T		A	W	E
S	C	I	S	S	O	R	K	I	C	K		R	E	V
	P	E	N	N	E		K	I	N	D	L	Y		
S	E	C	A	N	T	S		A	R	T	I	C	L	E
H	E	L	D	T	O		H	I	A	T	A	L		
A	R	I	E	S		W	A	R	T	S		E	S	T
D	I	P	S		G	A	Z	E	S		L	A	C	E
Y	E	P		T	O	N	E	D		N	E	V	E	R
	E	L	O	P	E	D		R	A	V	E	N	S	
S	P	R	A	W	L	S		R	E	T	I	R	E	E
N	O	S	T	R	A		D	E	B	U	T			
O	O	H		O	C	C	A	M	S	R	A	Z	O	R
U	R	I		P	E	T	R	I		A	T	A	R	I
T	S	P		E	S	S	E	X		L	E	G	U	P

PAGE 161

Sudoku

4	5	6	3	7	1	2	8	9
2	1	8	4	9	6	3	5	7
9	7	3	5	2	8	4	1	6
6	4	9	1	5	7	8	3	2
1	3	2	8	6	9	5	7	4
5	8	7	2	3	4	6	9	1
7	2	4	9	8	3	1	6	5
8	9	1	6	4	5	7	2	3
3	6	5	7	1	2	9	4	8

MIXAGRAMS

E M B E R	S I D E
T A K E N	H E F T
G L O R Y	O U C H
S T R U M	P E E L

PAGE 162

One-Way Streets

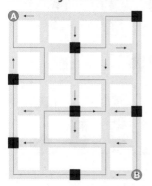

SOUND THINKING
HERALD

PAGE 163

ABC

B	A		C	
	C		B	A
A	B	C		
		B	A	C
C		A		B

NATIONAL TREASURE
TANGERINE

PAGE 164

Hard Sells

D	E	C	O	Y		T	O	A	D		Q	U	I	P
E	L	O	P	E		H	A	L	O		U	N	D	O
F	E	V	E	R	P	I	T	C	H		I	C	E	R
E	V	E	N		U	R	S	A		S	T	E	A	K
R	E	S	U	L	T	S		T	A	P	I	R		
		P	I	T	T	E	R	P	A	T	T	E	R	
M	O	N	T	E		V	A	I	N		A	G	O	
O	R	E	O		P	L	A	Z	A		F	I	G	S
O	A	R		W	E	A	N		P	A	N	S	Y	
G	L	O	C	K	E	N	S	P	I	E	L			
	W	O	R	L	D		A	N	T	L	E	R	S	
C	H	O	M	P		L	A	S	T		F	L	E	E
H	O	L	E		B	O	T	T	O	M	L	I	N	E
I	N	F	O		I	R	A	E		R	A	T	E	D
P	E	E	N		O	D	D	S		S	T	E	W	S

PAGE 165

Wheels and Cogs
Dollars

BETWEENER
WATCH

PAGE 166

Find the Ships

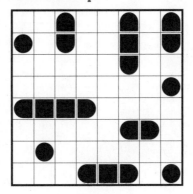

TWO-BY-FOUR
DATE, TOOT; TOAD, TOTE

PAGE 167

123

3	2	1	2	3	1	2	1	3
1	3	2	1	2	3	1	3	2
2	1	3	2	3	1	2	1	3
1	3	2	3	1	2	3	2	1
2	1	3	1	2	3	1	3	2
1	3	2	3	1	2	3	2	1
3	2	1	2	3	1	2	1	3
2	1	3	1	2	3	1	3	2
3	2	1	3	1	2	3	2	1

ADDITION SWITCH
$808 + 149 = 957$

PAGE 169

Letter Drops

N	U	T	S		S	T	R	A	P		S	P	O	T
A	T	O	P		T	E	A	S	E		W	A	D	E
R	A	G	A		E	R	N	I	E		A	I	D	E
C	H	A	R	L	E	S	D	A	R	W	I	N		
		E	I	D	E	R		O	N	T	V			
S	E	C	T	S			I	W	O		B	A	A	
U	G	L	I		B	O	B	B	Y	D	A	R	I	N
R	O	O	M		O	L	E	A	N		G	U	N	S
G	I	V	E	S	A	D	A	R	N		I	S	L	E
E	S	E		A	R	S			E	T	H	Y	L	
	T	R	E	K		M	A	N	I	A				
	L	I	E	U	T	E	N	A	N	T	D	A	N	
O	L	E	G		M	E	A	N	T		I	O	W	A
Y	E	A	H		P	A	D	U	A		O	D	E	S
L	O	F	T		S	M	E	L	L		N	O	S	H

PAGE 170

Square Routes

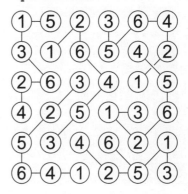

WRONG IS RIGHT
Spesious (should be *specious*)

PAGE 171

Number-Out

2	5	3	3	6	4
3	5	6	5	4	2
4	6	1	1	1	5
1	3	5	4	2	3
4	2	4	6	5	2
5	4	4	6	1	2

THINK ALIKE
REIGN, RULE

PAGE 172

All the Way

H	A	L	F		T	E	E	M		E	L	T	O	N
O	B	I	E		A	L	V	A		S	E	R	V	E
G	I	Z	A		B	O	E	R		S	N	E	E	R
S	T	A	R	T	L	I	N	G	L	E	G	E	N	D
			L	I	E		T	A	U	N	T			
M	O	M	E	N	T	S		R	I	C	H	T	E	R
A	Z	U	S	A		P	O	I	S	E		A	L	A
J	O	T	S		F	L	U	T	E		S	P	I	T
O	N	E		C	L	A	R	A		S	N	I	D	E
R	E	D	M	E	A	T		S	P	E	A	R	E	D
		U	N	I	T	S		U	M	P				
S	T	A	R	T	R	E	K	S	T	I	P	E	N	D
L	O	I	R	E		R	A	P	S		I	L	A	Y
A	R	D	O	R		E	T	A	T		S	K	I	N
G	N	A	W	S		D	E	M	O		H	O	L	E

PAGE 173
Pirate Ship

BETWEENER
TABLE

PAGE 174
Hyper-Sudoku

4	1	7	8	3	2	9	5	6
5	6	2	4	7	9	8	3	1
9	3	8	5	6	1	2	7	4
3	7	9	1	8	5	6	4	2
2	4	5	6	9	3	7	1	8
6	8	1	2	4	7	5	9	3
7	5	4	3	2	8	1	6	9
8	9	6	7	1	4	3	2	5
1	2	3	9	5	6	4	8	7

MIXAGRAMS

N A T A L   K I S S   S
T O U C H   I R O N   S
S E R U M   E M U S   S
M Y N A H   O U R S

PAGE 175
Speak Up

INITIAL REACTION
It Never Rains But It Pours

PAGE 176
Four-H Club

PAGE 177
Triad Split Decisions

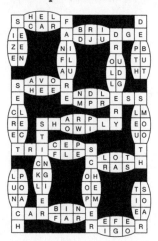

TRANSDELETION
FERTILE

PAGE 178
One-Way Streets

SOUND THINKING
JUDGE

PAGE 179
Off Your Chest

PAGE 180
Tile Maze

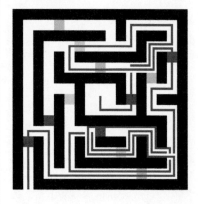

SAY IT AGAIN
COURT

PAGE 181
Star Search

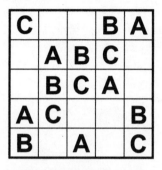

CHOICE WORDS
ENGAGE, RETAIN, SECURE

PAGE 182
Sudoku

8	1	9	3	7	5	4	6	2
4	7	2	8	9	6	3	5	1
3	5	6	2	1	4	9	8	7
9	4	5	1	2	8	6	7	3
7	6	1	5	4	3	8	2	9
2	3	8	9	6	7	5	1	4
5	9	7	6	3	1	2	4	8
1	8	3	4	5	2	7	9	6
6	2	4	7	8	9	1	3	5

CENTURY MARKS
19, 29, 27, 25

PAGE 183
Silver Bullets

B	I	A	S		E	L	S	E		M	C	J	O	B
E	T	C	H		M	O	L	L		G	O	U	D	A
E	C	H	O		P	A	I	L		M	O	L	E	S
T	H	E	W	O	L	F	M	A	N		R	I	T	E
		B	R	O	S		O	B	S	E	S	S		
T	H	E	O	R	Y		A	L	S	O				
A	U	R	A		C	R	A	I	G			T	U	G
K	N	O	T	T	S	B	E	R	R	Y	F	A	R	M
E	S	S		O	N	E	N	D			U	C	L	A
		T	A	R	A		A	T	M	O	S	T		
C	H	O	L	E	R		V	I	V	A				
H	A	R	I		L	O	N	E	R	A	N	G	E	R
E	L	E	G	Y		V	E	R	B		C	O	P	E
A	L	O	H	A		U	R	S	A		H	E	E	D
T	E	S	T	Y		M	O	O	G		U	S	E	S

PAGE 184
ABC

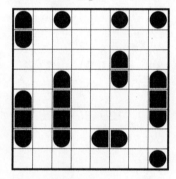

CLUELESS CROSSWORD

C	I	T	I	Z	E	N
O		H		O		O
U	N	I	F	O	R	M
P		A		L		I
L	A	M	P	O	O	N
E		I		G		E
T	I	N	T	Y	P	E

PAGE 185
Find the Ships

TWO-BY-FOUR
KNOB, RUNE; BORN, NUKE;
BURN, KENO

PAGE 186
Chief Cities

S	P	A		A	L	I	F	E		P	A	R	R	
O	O	P		M	O	D	U	S		O	N	E	A	M
P	R	E	S	I	D	E	N	T		I	G	I	V	E
H	E	R	O		I	A	G	O		R	O	G	E	R
		I	R	R		L	I	N	C	O	L	N	N	E
H	O	T	T	U	B	S		I	O	T	A			
A	R	I	O	S	O		D	A	N			T	A	C
J	E	F	F	E	R	S	O	N	C	I	T	Y	M	O
J	O	S		N	T	H		U	S	O	P	E	N	
		S	I	T	U		A	R	T	L	E	S	S	
J	A	C	K	S	O	N	M	S		H	E	F		
A	V	A	I	L		T	E	A	L		D	O	W	N
M	I	N	C	E		M	A	D	I	S	O	N	W	I
B	L	E	A	T		A	R	O	M	A		T	I	N
A	S	P	S		N	A	G	A	T		S	I	E	

PAGE 187
Dot to Dot

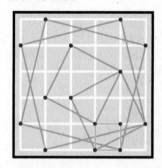

SMALL CHANGE
SLOW COOKER

PAGE 188
123

2	3	1	3	2	1	3	2	1
3	1	2	1	3	2	1	3	2
1	2	3	2	1	3	2	1	3
3	1	2	3	2	1	3	2	1
1	2	3	2	1	3	1	3	2
2	3	1	3	2	1	2	1	3
3	1	2	1	3	2	3	2	1
2	3	1	2	1	3	2	1	3
1	2	3	1	3	2	1	3	2

SUDOKU SUM

3	9	7
8	4	2
6	1	5

PAGE 189
Square Routes

5	1	2	4	6	3
2	4	6	1	3	5
6	3	1	5	2	4
3	5	4	6	1	2
4	6	3	2	5	1
1	2	5	3	4	6

WRONG IS RIGHT
Hominny (should be *hominy*)

PAGE 190
Mexican Menu

W	E	E	P			S	O	S	A			M	I	C	A	H
E	L	A	L			O	O	P	S			U	S	O	F	A
I	L	S	A			W	H	A	T			P	I	N	T	S
L	I	T	T	L	E	S	T	R	I	P	S					
	L	E	S	T	A	T			O	R	E			T	A	B
			I	O	N	A			I	T	H	A	C	A		
C	O	H	A	N			E	R	A	S			I	C	E	S
S	P	I	C	E	D	W	I	T	H	C	H	I	L	I		
P	E	L	T			I	T	E	M			I	O	T	A	S
A	R	L	I	S	S			L	S	A	T					
N	A	Y			O	C	T			N	E	S	T	O	R	
			A	V	O	C	A	D	O	S	A	U	C	E		
F	A	R	S	I			E	M	I	R			C	R	E	E
A	L	I	C	E			L	I	M	A			C	O	A	L
B	I	G	H	T			L	E	E	K			O	W	N	S

PAGE 191
Hyper-Sudoku

4	8	2	7	3	6	9	1	5
3	9	6	2	1	5	8	7	4
5	7	1	4	8	9	6	3	2
9	3	8	5	7	2	1	4	6
2	1	4	9	6	3	7	5	8
6	5	7	8	4	1	3	2	9
7	4	3	6	2	8	5	9	1
8	2	9	1	5	7	4	6	3
1	6	5	3	9	4	2	8	7

MIXAGRAMS

B	U	R	N	T	F	O	A	L
A	W	A	R	D	O	L	E	O
L	O	T	U	S	U	R	N	S
L	A	B	E	L	R	U	I	N

PAGE 192
Split Decisions

TRANSDELETION
LEOPARD

PAGE 193
Family Films

R	A	P	T		G	O	T	M	A	D		A	F	R
A	R	I	A		A	M	O	E	B	A		F	R	O
N	D	A	K		F	A	T	H	E	R	H	O	O	D
D	O	N	E		F	R	E	T		T	B	O	N	E
B	R	O	T	H	E	R	R	A	T		O	T	T	O
			W	A	S			I	S	M				
A	R	G	O	N		U	N	C	L	E	B	U	C	K
M	B	A		D	E	V	I	A	T	E		M	O	E
S	I	S	T	E	R	A	C	T		T	O	P	S	Y
			E	L	M			D	H	S				
F	A	L	A		A	U	N	T	I	E	M	A	M	E
E	X	E	C	S		N	O	I	R		O	B	I	S
M	O	T	H	E	R	L	O	D	E		N	O	D	S
U	N	A		G	U	I	S	E	S		D	U	D	E
R	S	T		A	T	T	E	S	T		S	T	Y	X

PAGE 194
Solitaire Poker

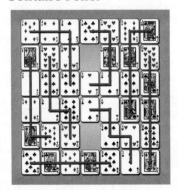

BETWEENER
AFTER

PAGE 195
Number-Out

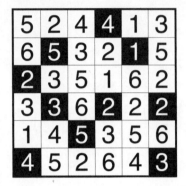

5	2	4	4	1	3
6	5	3	2	1	5
2	3	5	1	6	2
3	3	6	2	2	2
1	4	5	3	5	6
4	5	2	6	4	3

THINK ALIKE
OWN, POSSESS

PAGE 196
One-Way Streets

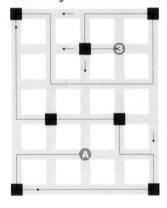

SOUND THINKING
CASSETTE

PAGE 197
Take the Plunge

D	I	O	N		H	O	A	R	D		E	P	I	C
A	N	N	E		E	R	R	O	R		L	O	C	I
B	L	E	W		R	A	I	S	E		I	K	E	A
B	E	A	S	B	O	L	D	A	S	T	H	E		
A	T	M	F	E	E	S		S	O	U	R	C	E	
			L	A	S		S	K	I	P		G	U	V
	P	D	A	S		R	U	N	E		G	A	B	E
F	I	R	S	T	M	A	N	O	R	W	O	M	A	N
U	T	A	H		A	I	N	T		E	D	E	N	
R	O	M		J	U	D	Y		S	A	D			
S	N	A	P	O	N			S	C	R	E	A	M	S
	T	O	E	A	T	A	N	O	Y	S	T	E	R	
D	R	I	B		K	A	Z	O	O		S	A	L	T
O	U	Z	O		E	X	U	R	B		E	L	B	A
O	B	E	Y		A	I	L	E	Y		S	E	A	S

PAGE 198

Sudoku

5	1	2	8	6	3	9	7	4
8	7	4	9	1	5	2	3	6
6	9	3	2	4	7	8	1	5
1	2	5	7	8	9	6	4	3
7	3	8	6	5	4	1	2	9
4	6	9	1	3	2	5	8	7
3	8	1	5	7	6	4	9	2
2	5	7	4	9	1	3	6	8
9	4	6	3	2	8	7	5	1

MIXAGRAMS

```
R O B I N    A R M Y
P H A S E    R O U T
T A C K Y    E O N S
B A K E R    S M U G
```

PAGE 199

Star Search

CHOICE WORDS

BUSHEL, FATHOM, MINUTE

PAGE 200

Flyday Puzzle

PAGE 201

Your Turn

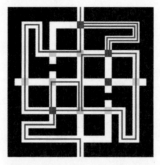

SAY IT AGAIN

MOUSE

PAGE 202

Greek Island Cruise

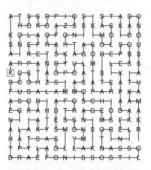

WHO'S WHAT WHERE?

Jarocho

PAGE 203

ABC

CLUELESS CROSSWORD

A	V	I	A	T	O	R
C		G		H		E
C	R	U	C	I	A	L
U		A		M		A
S	A	N	D	B	O	X
E		A		L		E
D	E	S	C	E	N	D

PAGE 204

Themeless Toughie

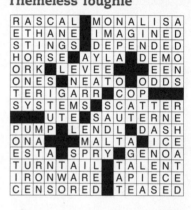

PAGE 206

Find the Ships

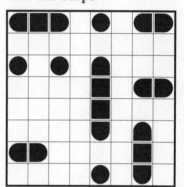

TWO-BY-FOUR

VIAL, TIDY; VITA, IDLY
(or IDYL)

PAGE 207

Hyper-Sudoku

4	3	7	2	5	8	9	6	1
6	5	9	7	4	1	3	8	2
1	8	2	3	9	6	7	4	5
8	1	4	6	7	2	5	9	3
2	9	5	4	8	3	1	7	6
3	7	6	9	1	5	8	2	4
5	4	8	1	2	9	6	3	7
9	2	3	5	6	7	4	1	8
7	6	1	8	3	4	2	5	9

BETWEENER

POCKET

PAGE 208
Themeless Toughie

```
S N A P B R I M █ S C H I S T
P O P U L A C E █ P R O N T O
U N T R A C E D █ L E A G U E
R O S E R E D █ Y E A R E N D
█ █ █ B E D █ L A N K Y █ █ █
P A A R █ S E N D █ █ R A M
A B L E T O T A K E A J O K E
T O L D I N O P E N C O U R T
C R Y S T A L D E T E C T O R
H T S █ D O A S █ K E N O
█ █ █ S T O N Y █ P I E █ █ █
T V S H O W S █ T O N Y D O W
R E T A I N █ G I U L I A N I
O R A C L E █ E N T E N T E S
T A N K E R █ L A S T G A S P
```

PAGE 209
Floor It
#6

SMALL CHANGE
GRAND TOTAL

PAGE 210
Square Routes

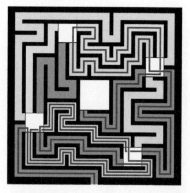

ADDITION SWITCH
2 4 3 + 6 1 7 = 8 6 0

PAGE 211
Themeless Toughie

```
A N C H O R A G E █ R A V E S
P O L O S H I R T █ A G E N T
T R I P L E S E C █ P L A T A
E S P █ O I L Y █ S T O L E N
R E S T █ M E H T A █ W O R D
█ █ I T S █ O R C A █ S T A
S P A D E █ S U E R S █ C A R
A L L E X P E N S E S P A I D
T A L █ T O D D S █ E A R N S
I C U █ S E A R █ S T Y █ █
R E D O █ S N A R E █ S O P S
I M E A S Y █ C A T V █ S A L
Z E S T A █ P I S T A C H I O
E N T E R █ O N E L I N E R S
S T O R K █ O G D E N N A S H
```

PAGE 212
123

```
2 1 3 1 2 3 1 2 3
1 3 1 2 3 1 2 3 2
2 1 2 3 1 2 3 1 3
3 2 3 1 2 3 1 2 1
1 3 1 2 3 2 3 1 2
2 1 2 3 1 3 2 3 1
3 2 3 1 2 1 3 1 2
1 3 2 1 3 2 1 2 3
3 2 1 2 3 1 2 3 1
```

WRONG IS RIGHT
Gondalier (should be *gondolier*)

PAGE 213
Number-Out

```
2 2 2 6 5 1
3 5 1 2 6 6
4 5 5 5 1 1
6 4 2 1 2 5
1 3 4 3 6 2
6 6 2 4 3 3
```

THINK ALIKE
HONE, SHARPEN

PAGE 214
Themeless Toughie

```
S T O P █ M A R A T █ C A S T
N A N A █ G L O B E █ A L P O
A B E L █ M O D E R A T I O N
R O S I N █ N E F E R T I T I
L O O S E Y G O O S E Y █ █ █
█ W A V E █ R A N █ S P A
C O N D E N A S T █ T E N A M
A H M E █ S U D A N █ P E P E
G N A S H █ S I S Y P H E A N
Y O N █ O F T █ P E E R █ █
█ █ █ H E A R T S D E S I R E
A F T E R C A R E █ L I N U S
H A I R S A L O N S █ A G T S
A M M O █ D I T S Y █ N A T E
B E E S █ E A S E D █ S T Y X
```

PAGE 215
Opera Jigsaw

```
B I L L A B O E U G E T H E M A G L U C R
B Y L F M E H N O E N T H R E C I A I Z E
U D L A E P E E G Y N N E P E F L B O R G
R D S T A S R N I O P E R A E T U P O A I
I G O F F E P H O T A L E S O P E G R S I
T E L M E R F E N I N T O H F E T Y A G E
T O E E I R A I R M R E F F M R G D N F R
A L N G L F O D I A M E Z N A I R B E E I
E B D N A P E R T H L O Z C I M E S S D B
R T H E P R I M U L U R E D N P A R S C O
N I R R E C N E R R Y E L L A F I S B C A
G N E B I G T N U O M W G R I A L D O C C
A H C U R O M A N Z Z O L E S O D I R I O
D N E C S E L N O E C K D A H A N D I S G
A Z Z A U T D O N E H T H G U N E A U D O
R I N N A V O I G D R O V E R E A S N O V
```

IN OTHER WORDS
PEKOE

PAGE 216
Color Paths

SAY IT AGAIN
STRAIN

PAGE 217
Themeless Toughie

```
A C C E S S E D   D U L L E R
C H U N K I E R   E M P I R E
T O R T I L L A   B A N T A M
S O L E     W I T S   E S O
U S E R S   L E D   S T R U T
P E R T H   I R A N   R A R E
      A I D E S   O R A T E S
A S P I R I N   S O O N E S T
L O A N E R   M I N U S
L U T E   T A R T   G L A D S
A V E R S   I D S   H A B I T
Y E N   H E R E     T R E E
I N T R O S   E M A C I A T E
N I E C E S   D O G O O D E R
G R E A S E   S C A N N E R S
```

PAGE 218
ABCD

C		A	D	B
B	A	D	C	
	A	D	B	C
A	D		B	C
	B	C		A	D
D	C	B		A

NATIONAL TREASURE
UKRAINIAN

PAGE 219
Sudoku

6	8	5	2	4	7	9	1	3
9	1	3	5	6	8	7	2	4
4	2	7	1	3	9	8	5	6
7	5	9	3	8	6	2	4	1
1	6	2	7	5	4	3	9	8
8	3	4	9	2	1	6	7	5
2	7	8	6	1	5	4	3	9
3	4	1	8	9	2	5	6	7
5	9	6	4	7	3	1	8	2

MIXAGRAMS
```
G R A Z E   H O S T
B I S O N   F E U D
A L L O Y   V E I L
C H U T E   U N T O
```

PAGE 220
Themeless Toughie

```
A S P S   O N C E   S A B O T
S Q U A D R O O M   Q U I R E
H U R R I E D U P   U N D U E
E A S E R S   P L A I T S
S T E E N   S L A W S   A W L
      D O D E C A H E D R A
L A C K L U S T E R   R I I S
O B O I S T     D R I E S T
E E O C   F O R P E A N U T S
W A L K A L L O V E R
E M S   D O E S T   I M P E L
D R O W S E   S T E R N A
A R O A R   T O O K A R E S T
N O W I N   R I D I N G O U T
T E N D S   A L E S   E P E E
```

PAGE 221
One-Way Streets

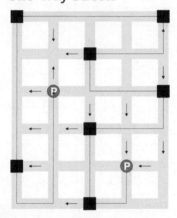

SOUND THINKING
ELEGANT

PAGE 222
Split Decisions

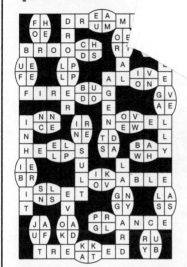

TRANSDELETION
PAR THREE

PAGE 223
Themeless Toughie

```
S P A R E D   A I R L A N E S
A R C A N E   C R E A T U R E
F E T I S H   C I N N A M O N
A C I D   U N U S E D   E D S
R E V S   M U S E   S C R E E
I D A   W I D E S T   L O S S
S E T   I D E S   O F A
  D E B R I S   S L I N K S
    R E F   U T E S   I T S
T O N I   Y O G U R T   T E L
E R E C T   U L N A   A T E E
N I B   A S S I S T   L Y R E
S O U L M A T E   I C E C A P
E L L I P S E S   O U T A G E
R E A S S E R T   N E A T E R
```

PAGE 224

Pig Races

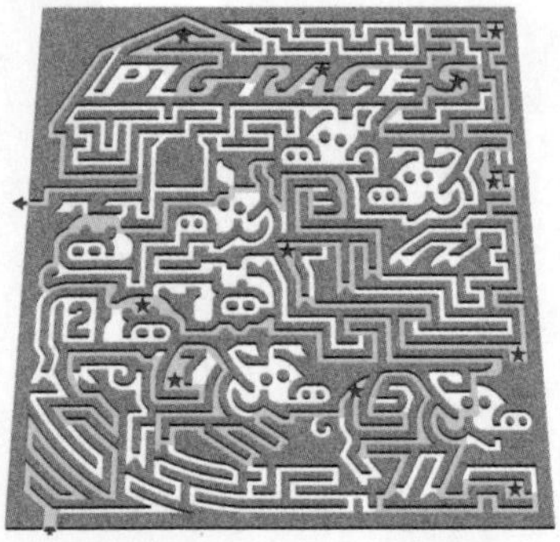

SAY IT AGAIN

OUTLAW

PAGE 225

Star Search

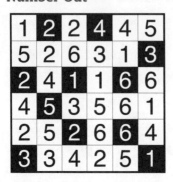

	1			2	2		1		
	★	2		★	★	2		★	
2		★	4	★		3	★	3	
★		★		2	2		★		
★		1			★	4		2	★
1		1		3	★	★	3		2
		2	★	4	5	★	3	★	
	1	★		★	★				

CHOICE WORDS

GRUMPY, SLEEPY, SNEEZY

PAGE 226

Themeless Toughie

M	N	E	M	O	N	I	C		U	P	L	I	F	T
V	I	G	O	R	I	S	H		M	E	A	N	I	E
I	N	A	S	E	N	S	E		P	A	R	E	R	S
I	O	N	S		T	U	R	F		C	U	B	E	S
				T	H	E	R	E	T	H	E	R	E	
A	R	C	H	E	S		I	M	A	Y		I	A	N
R	E	A	I	R		D	E	M	I		S	A	T	O
U	P	P	E	R	C	A	S	E	L	E	T	T	E	R
B	A	A	S		A	D	J	S		A	L	E	R	T
A	C	C		U	R	D	U		C	R	O	S	S	E
	K	I	D	N	E	Y	B	E	A	N				
M	A	T	R	I		O	I	N	K		A	J	A	R
E	G	O	I	S	M		L	O	I	S	L	A	N	E
S	E	R	V	O	S		E	L	E	C	T	I	N	G
A	S	S	E	N	T		E	A	R	H	O	L	E	S

PAGE 227

Number-Out

1	2	2	4	4	5
5	2	6	3	1	3
2	4	1	1	6	6
4	5	3	5	6	1
2	5	2	6	6	4
3	3	4	2	5	1

THINK ALIKE

FACTUAL, TRUE

PAGE 228

Line Drawing

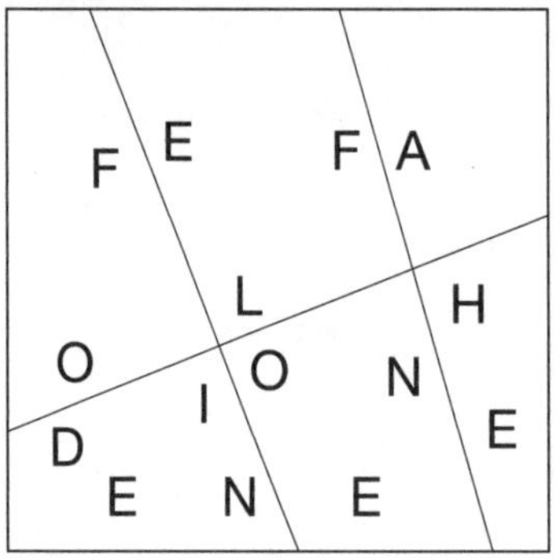

OF, ELF, A, DINE, ONE, HE; then add an X to each region for FOX, FLEX, AX, INDEX, OXEN, HEX

TWO-BY-FOUR

CAKE, GREW; CRAG, WEEK; CRAW, GEEK

PAGE 229

Themeless Toughie

L	E	S	S	E	R	A	P	E		Y	I	E	L	D
O	N	H	O	L	I	D	A	Y		A	S	N	E	R
U	S	E	B	Y	D	A	T	E		M	A	T	T	E
N	L	R	B		E	M	T	S		S	Y	R	I	A
G	A	M	E	R		S	E	R	F			A	T	M
E	V	A	D	E	S		D	I	A	T	R	I	B	E
S	E	N		M	C	I		G	R	O	A	N	E	R
			B	A	R	N		H	O	O	F			
N	A	B	O	K	O	V		T	U	T		B	I	N
I	S	R	A	E	L	I	S		T	H	R	O	N	E
C	A	Y			L	O	W	E		Y	E	L	P	S
E	R	N	S	T		L	A	V	A		C	O	L	T
D	U	N	C	E		A	N	E	C	D	O	T	A	L
O	L	E	A	N		C	E	N	T	E	R	I	C	E
G	E	R	M	S		Y	E	S	I	N	D	E	E	D

PAGE 230

Triad Split Decisions

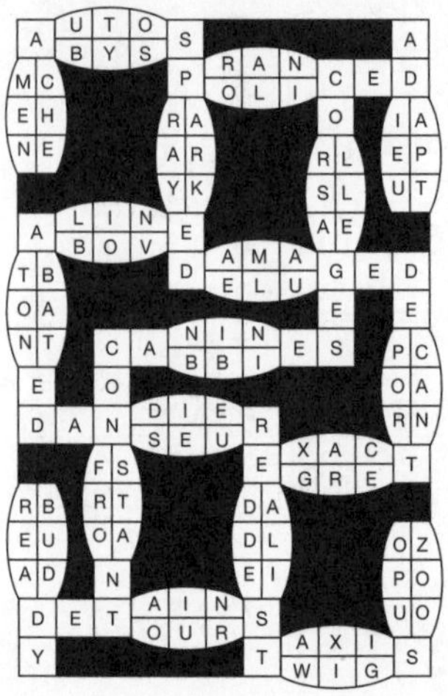

TRANSDELETION

SPECULATE

PAGE 231

Piece It Together

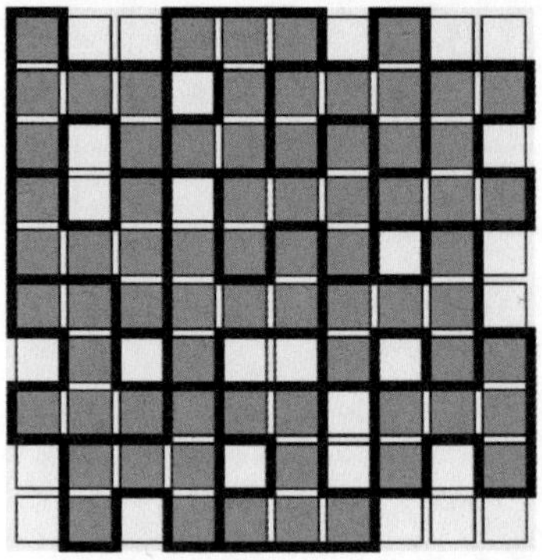

SMALL CHANGE

FLEA MARKET

PAGE 232

Themeless Toughie

A	L	I	B	I	S		S	H	A	D	I	E	S	T
R	E	S	E	N	T		T	O	M	O	R	R	O	W
A	M	O	E	B	A		E	M	I	N	E	N	C	E
P	O	L	T	E	R	G	E	I	S	T		E	I	N
A	N	A		D	R	A	P	E	S		L	S	A	T
H	A	T				P	E	R		H	O	T	L	Y
O	D	E		E	Y	E	D		M	A	O			
	E	D	U	C	E	D		N	O	R	M	A	L	
			R	O	W		T	I	C	K		L	O	T
E	M	A	I	L		W	A	N				T	I	E
L	A	G	S		M	O	T	T	O	S		I	T	A
O	R	E		T	O	O	T	H	P	A	S	T	E	S
P	I	N	N	A	C	L	E		A	L	L	U	R	E
E	N	C	I	P	H	E	R		L	O	U	D	E	R
S	O	Y	B	E	A	N	S		S	N	E	E	R	S